Early Praise for *Your Code as a Crime Scene, Second Edition*

Adam presents tools, techniques, and insight that will change the way you develop software. You can't unread this information, and you will see software differently.

➤ **Michael Feathers**
Author, *Working Effectively with Legacy Code*

Adam Tornhill presents code as it exists in the real world—tightly coupled, unwieldy, and full of danger zones even when past developers had the best of intentions. His forensic techniques for analyzing and improving both the technical and the social aspects of a code base are a godsend for developers working with legacy systems. I found this book extremely useful to my own work and highly recommend it!

➤ **Nell Shamrell-Harrington**
Lead developer, PhishMe

As a manager overseeing multiple teams with both individual and shared code bases, it's difficult for me to have an in-depth understanding of all the code. However, the strategies and techniques outlined in this book have enabled me to identify significant problems and provide guidance on how to resolve them.

➤ **Thomas Manthey**
Director of engineering at Flaschenpost SE

Adam presents techniques to improve the technical and social characteristics of your code. We know that writing maintainable code is crucial, it can be challenging to convey this to our managers. Here we get those arguments, and they are all backed up by science. This is the book our industry desperately needs!

➤ **Markus Westergren**
Staff consultant, Umecon

This book casts a surprising light on an unexpected place—my own code. I feel like I've found a secret treasure chest of completely unexpected methods. Useful for programmers, the book provides a powerful tool to smart testers, too.

➤ **James Bach**
   Author, *Lessons Learned in Software Testing*

If you are a software architect, DevOps leader or leader of any type in software-intensive services, then this book can help you grasp some essential concepts and ideas on how to understand and lead with the help of data.

➤ **Heimo Laukkanen**
   Software systems professional

An excellent introduction to data-driven analysis of software systems with many additional gems from behavioral psychology! The second edition blends in the latest research results and adds even more experiences from practice.

➤ **Markus Harrer**
   Software Development Analyst

You think you know your code. After all, you and your fellow programmers have been sweating over it for years now. Adam Tornhill uses thinking in psychology together with hands-on tools to show you the bad parts. This book is a red pill. Are you ready?

➤ **Björn Granvik**
   Competence manager

By enlisting simple heuristics and data from everyday tools, Adam shows you how to fight bad code and its cohorts—all interleaved with intriguing anecdotes from forensic psychology. Highly recommended!

➤ **Jonas Lundberg**
   Senior programmer and team leader

After reading this book, you will never look at code in the same way again!

➤ **Patrik Falk**
   Agile developer and coach

Do you have a large pile of code, and mysterious and unpleasant bugs seem to appear out of nothing? This book lets you profile and find out the weak areas in your code and how to fight them. This is the essence of combining business with pleasure!

➤ **Jimmy Rosenskog**
   Senior consultant, software developer

Adam manages to marry source code analysis with forensic psychology in a unique and structured way. The book presents tools and techniques to apply this concept to your own projects to predict the future of your code-base. Brilliant!

➤ **Mattias Larsson**
   Senior software consultant

Your Code as a Crime Scene, Second Edition

Use Forensic Techniques to Arrest Defects,
Bottlenecks, and Bad Design in Your Programs

Adam Tornhill

The Pragmatic Bookshelf

Dallas, Texas

When we are aware that a term used in this book is claimed as a trademark, the designation is printed with an initial capital letter or in all capitals.

The Pragmatic Starter Kit, The Pragmatic Programmer, Pragmatic Programming, Pragmatic Bookshelf, PragProg and the linking *g* device are trademarks of The Pragmatic Programmers, LLC.

Every precaution was taken in the preparation of this book. However, the publisher assumes no responsibility for errors or omissions, or for damages that may result from the use of information (including program listings) contained herein.

For our complete catalog of hands-on, practical, and Pragmatic content for software developers, please visit *https://pragprog.com*.

The team that produced this book includes:

Publisher:	Dave Thomas
COO:	Janet Furlow
Managing Editor:	Tammy Coron
Development Editor:	Kelly Talbot
Copy Editor:	Karen Galle
Indexing:	Potomac Indexing, LLC
Layout:	Gilson Graphics

For sales, volume licensing, and support, please contact *support@pragprog.com*.

For international rights, please contact *rights@pragprog.com*.

ISBN-13: 979-8-88865-032-5
Book version: P1.0—February 2024

Contents

Part II — Build Supportive Software Architectures

Part III — Meet the Social Side of Your Code

Foreword

Your codebase is overflowing with stories.

There are, of course, the narratives of control and data that flow through each function, threading blocks and objects together to build an application's behavior, which itself reflects the user stories that shape the development timeline.

There are the personal stories that accompany each individual connected to the software, whether developer or manager, architect or customer. These are the successes, frustrations, weddings, children, delights, losses, fashions, ups and downs of well-being, and all those things we call life that make up the backdrop against which code is written, heads are scratched, whiteboard discussions are had, bugs are fixed, and logs are puzzled over. For those involved in the creation of software, the stories of the code and the stories outside the code are woven together. Software development is made of people.

From the perspective of a compiler, code is a technical construct, one formal notation to be translated into another so that it can run. The compiler's view is simple and certain: just as with ones and zeroes, code compiles or it doesn't. From the perspective of an organization, however, code's complexity is drawn in shades of gray. Software is a socio-technical construct, where team dynamics, deadlines, personal preferences, skills, and organizational values leave their mark on a codebase and its history.

And this is the perspective Adam takes in this book. The new edition of *Your Code as a Crime Scene* retains the soul and wisdom of the first edition, while updating its examples and extending its reach. Adam shows us that to truly understand a codebase, we cannot simply view it through the keyhole of our editor in the moment of editing. We need a larger and more holistic view, one that invites novel ways of thinking about and visualizing code. This is the journey Adam takes us on. But this is not code tourism: Adam offers us the context, details, and insights that will grant us local knowledge.

Our source code has a spatial structure—top to bottom, left to right, indented and aligned—but we can invent and use spatial metaphors to further enrich our mental models and reveal the shape of our system—cities, graphs, maps, enclosures, fractals, and more. And where there is space, there is also time. To gain a deeper understanding of our code and its development, we need to learn to see it as temporal, not just spatial. There is a story that led to the code we see today; there are stories that may flow from it in future. A system is no more a static snapshot of its code than a film is a single frame. Adam shows that, buried within your version-control system, you have more than a repository: you have a history. Buried in the commits and the diffs is a story of what changed and when, who made changes and why. This is where you will find the system.

Among the hotspots and dead spots, trends and coupling, you can find connections to requirements, to technical debt, to team structure, to project practices, to defects, to technology evolution, to programming paradigms, to organizational change, and more. With the forensic tools and mindset Adam presents, you can see what's happened and what's happening and, therefore, what might happen and how you and others can change that.

The story of a system is not just yours to discover; it is also yours to tell.

Kevlin Henney

Acknowledgments

Writing a second edition is very much like stepping into legacy code. Some things are outdated, your style has evolved, and many things can be simplified, improved, and expressed with greater clarity. At the same time, you don't want to break what works. As such, modernizing *Your Code as a Crime Scene* turned out to be a challenging task. In the end, it was worth all the effort, and I'm super proud of the book you're reading right now. I owe that to all the amazing people who helped me out.

My editor, Kelly Talbot, supported me in making this a much better book than what I could've written on my own. Another big thank you to all technical reviewers: Aslam Khan, Markus Harrer, Markus Westergren, Thomas Manthey, Heimo Laukkanen, Jeff Miller, Einar W. Høst, Vladimir Kovalenko, Simon Verhoeven, and Arty Starr. I could also count on my amazing colleagues to help with their technical expertise and encouragement: Joseph Fahey, Juraj Martinka, and Markus Borg.

Twenty years ago, Kevlin Henney's work inspired me to start writing about software. I remain a big fan of Kevlin, and that's why I'm extra proud to include his foreword.

The case studies in this book were possible due to skilled programmers who have made their code open source. Thanks—I have a lot of respect for your work.

My parents, Eva and Thorbjörn, have always supported me. You're the best.

Finally, I'd like to thank my family for their endless support: Jenny, Morten, and Ebbe—thanks. I love you.

@AdamTornhill
Malmö, Sweden, February 2024

Welcome to the Crime Scene

The central idea of *Your Code as a Crime Scene* is that we'll never be able to understand complex, large-scale systems just by looking at a single snapshot of the code. As you'll see, when we limit ourselves to what's visible in the code, we miss a lot of valuable information. Instead, we need to understand both how the system came to be and how the people working on it interact with each other and the code. In this book, you'll learn to mine that information from the evolution of your codebase.

Once you have worked through this book, you will be able to examine any system and immediately get a view of its health—both from a technical perspective and from the development practices that led to the code you see today. You'll also be able to track the improvements made to the code and gather objective data on them.

Why You Should Read This Book

There are plenty of good books on software design and programming. So why read another one? Well, unlike other books, *Your Code as a Crime Scene* focuses on *your* codebase. This immediately helps you identify potential problems, find ways to fix them, and remove productivity bottlenecks one by one.

Your Code as a Crime Scene blends forensics and psychology with software evolution. Yes, it is a technical book, but programming isn't just about lines of code. We also need to focus on the psychological aspects of software development.

But *forensics*—isn't that about finding criminals? It sure is, but you'll also see that criminal investigators ask many of the same open-ended questions programmers ask while working through a codebase. By applying forensic concepts to software development, we gain valuable insights. And in our case, the offender is problematic code that we need to improve.

As you progress through the book, you'll

- predict which sections of code have the most defects and the steepest learning curves;

- use behavioral code analysis to identify, prioritize, and remediate technical debt and maintenance issues;

- understand how multiple developers and teams influence code quality;

- learn how to track organizational problems in your code and get tips on how to fix them; and

- get a psychological perspective on your programs and learn how to make them easier to understand.

Who Should Read This Book?

To get the most out of this book, you're probably a programmer, software architect, or technical leader. Perhaps you're looking for effective ways to uncover the secrets of an existing codebase. Or, you might be embarking on a legacy migration project and looking for guidance. You might also strive to reduce defects, helping both yourself and your team to succeed. Maybe you're under pressure to deliver more code faster and want to figure out how to strike a balance between adding new features vs. improving existing code. No matter the scenario, you care about good code. Great—you're reading the right book.

It doesn't matter what language you program in. Our case studies mix Java, Go, JavaScript, Python, C++, Clojure, C#, and several other languages. However, the big advantage of crime-scene techniques is that you don't have to know any of these languages to follow along. All techniques are language-independent and will work no matter what technology you use. We also make sure to focus the discussions on principles rather than specifics.

The hands-on examples interact with version-control systems. To get the most out of the book, you should know the basics of Git, Subversion, Mercurial, or a similar tool.

Why Read This Book Now?

Never before has there been a larger shortage of software developers. Sure, the occasional economic downturn might slow things down, but at a macro level, this gap in supply and demand will continue to widen as society becomes more digitalized. Superficially, this might sound like good news for us: being in demand does wonders for salaries. However, combine this shortage with an ever-increasing pressure to deliver on shorter cycles, and we can easily find ourselves mired in stress, unsustainable workloads, and software death marches.

A significant part of the problem is technical debt. The average software company wastes a large portion of developers' time dealing with the consequences of technical debt, bad code, and inadequate software architectures. It doesn't have to be that way.

Yet, technical debt is only part of the equation. A high staff turnover—which we've always had in the IT industry—means that companies continuously lose collective knowledge of their codebases. Unless we take measures to prevent it, our codebases end up as *terra nullius*—land belonging to nobody. This means it's more important than ever to pay attention to bad code so we can mitigate any offboarding impact. We also must be able to quickly orient ourselves in an unfamiliar codebase. Statistically, chances are we'll encounter this situation frequently.

Ultimately, it's all about freeing our time for more rewarding work to innovate interesting features and cool product ideas. Burning the midnight oil the day before a release, looking for that multithreaded bug in a file with 15,000 lines of opaque C++ code written by someone who quit last month after shunning documentation for years, is a miserable experience. Programming is supposed to be fun, and this book is here to help you reclaim that ideal.

How to Read This Book

This book is meant to be read from start to finish. Later parts build on techniques that you'll learn gradually over the course of several chapters. Let's look at the big picture so you know what lies ahead.

Part I: You'll Learn to Detect Problematic Code

You'll start by learning techniques for identifying complex code that you must work with often. No matter how much we enjoy our work, when it comes to commercial products, time and money always matter. That's why you'll explore methods for prioritizing refactoring candidates that give you the most value.

You'll build techniques based on forensic methods used to track down serial offenders. You'll see that each crime forms part of a larger pattern. Similarly, each change you make to your software leaves a trace. Analyzing those traces offers deep clues for understanding the system you're building. Analyzing the history of your code also empowers you to predict the code's future. This helps you start making fixes ahead of time.

Part II: You'll Learn to Improve Software Architectures

Once you know how to identify offending code in your system, you'll want to look at the bigger picture. That way, you can ensure that the high-level design of your system supports the features you implement and the way the codebase evolves.

Here, you'll take inspiration from eyewitness testimony to see how memory biases can frame both innocent bystanders and code. You'll use similar techniques to reduce memory biases and even interview your own codebase. The reward is information that you cannot deduce from the code alone.

After you've finished Part II, you'll know how to evaluate your software architecture against the modifications done to the code, looking for signs of structural decay and expensive duplication of knowledge. In addition, you'll understand how the same techniques provide you with refactoring directions and potential new modular boundaries, which support important use cases such as breaking up monoliths or surviving legacy modernization projects.

Part III: You'll Learn How Your Organization Affects the Code

The majority of today's software systems are developed by multiple teams. That intersection between people and code is an often-overlooked aspect of software development. When there's a misalignment between how you're organized vs. the work style your software architecture supports, code quality and communication suffer. As a result, you wind up with tricky workarounds and compromises to the design.

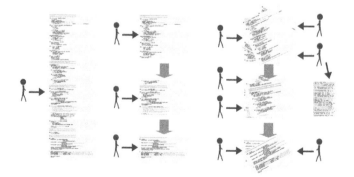

In Part III, you'll get to identify organizational problems in your code. You'll see how to predict bugs from the way you work, understand how social biases influence software development, and uncover the distribution of knowledge among developers. As a bonus, you'll learn about group decisions, communication, false serial killers, and how they all relate to software development.

What's New in the Second Edition?

The core techniques in *Your Code as a Crime Scene* have stood the test of time because they focus on human behavior—people are a fairly stable construct, after all.

If you've read the first edition, you'll recognize most sections in the book. However, you'll still want to read those chapters because the case studies have been modernized and the text expanded with new insights, research findings, and actionable advice. This second edition brings extensive new content, reflecting all the lessons from applying crime-scene techniques at scale for a decade.

In addition, there are several new chapters which expand on the original work:

- Chapter 6, Remediate Complicated Code, on page 63 explores a cognitive perspective on code complexity, which lets you focus on the code smells that actually matter.

- Chapter 7, Communicate the Business Impact of Technical Debt, on page 83 makes the business case for paying down technical debt and refactoring in general. That way, you get all the data you need, so you can have conversations with non-technical stakeholders around something as deeply technical as code quality.

- Chapter 14, See How Technical Problems Cause Organizational Issues, on page 215 flips the software organization on its head. Getting the "people side" of software development wrong will wreck any project, but here you learn why the reverse is true as well: how your code is written impacts the people and the organization.

Code as a Crime Scene Is a Metaphor

The crime scene metaphor helps to remind you that software design has social implications. Good code directs human behavior: in any well-designed system, there's one obvious place to touch when modifying code. The book's crime scene name is also an homage to the forensic techniques that inspired the analyses. At some point, however, it's useful to leave the metaphor and dive deeper into our core domain—programming. Hence, you'll examine knowledge drawn from many other sources, such as cognitive psychology, group theory, and software research.

Toward a New Approach

In recent decades, there's been some fascinating research on software evolution. Like most ideas and studies from academia, these findings have failed to cross over into the industry. This book bridges that gap by translating academic research into examples for the practicing programmer. That way, you know that the recommendations have a solid basis and actually work, instead of being mere opinions or personal preferences.

But, even if we stand on the shoulders of academia, this book isn't an academic text. *Your Code as a Crime Scene* is very much a book for the industry practitioner. As such, you may be wondering how the new strategies in this book relate to other software development practices. Let's sort that out:

- *Test automation*—The techniques you are about to learn let you identify the parts of your code most likely to contain defects. But they won't find the errors themselves. You still need to be testing the code. If you invest in automated tests, this book will give you tools to decide what to automate first and to monitor the maintainability of the resulting tests.

- *Static analysis*—Static analysis is a powerful technique for finding errors and dangerous coding constructs. Static analysis focuses on the impact your code has on the machine. In this book, you'll focus on the other audience: how humans deduce meaning and intent from code. Hence, the techniques in this book complement static analysis by providing information you cannot get from code alone.

- *Code metrics*—Code complexity metrics have been around since the 1970s, but they're pretty bad at, well, spotting complexity. Metrics are language-specific, which means they cannot analyze a polyglot codebase. Another limitation of metrics is that they erase social information about how the code was developed. Instead of erasing that information, you'll learn to derive value from it. Only then can you take on the big problems like technical debt remediation or making sure your software architecture supports the way your organization works as a team.

- *Code reviews*—Being a manual process that is expensive to replicate, code reviews still have their place. Done right, they're useful for both bug hunting and knowledge sharing. The techniques you'll learn in this book help you prioritize the code you need to review.

To sum it up, *Your Code as a Crime Scene* is here to improve and enhance existing practices rather than replace them.

Software Development Is More Than a Technical Problem

In a surprisingly short time, we've moved from lighting fires in our caves to reasoning about multicores and CPU caches in cubicles. Yet, we handle modern technology with the same biological tools our prehistoric ancestors used for basic survival. That's why taming complexity in software must start with how we think. Programming needs to be aligned with the way our brain works.

Real-World Case Studies

Throughout the book, you will apply the crime-scene techniques to real-world codebases: prioritize technical debt in React, visualize growing code complexity in Kubernetes, get cognitive exercise when refactoring a cohesion problem in Hibernate, discover troublesome dependencies in Spring Boot, and determine the truck factor in a popular codebase from Facebook. And that's only part of it.

The case studies have been selected because they represent both popular applications and some of the best work we—as a software developer community—produce. This means that if the techniques you're about to learn can identify improvement opportunities in these codebases, chances are you'll be able to do the same in your own work.

Since these codebases are moving targets under constant development, we're going to use stable forks for this book. See the footnote[1] for all the relevant Git repositories.

Get Your Investigative Tools

To perform the behavioral code analyses, you obviously need to get your hands on behavioral data. That is, you need to trace how you and your team interact with the code. Fortunately, you're likely to already have all the data you need—although you might not be used to thinking about it as a data source. I'm referring to version control, which is a gold mine covering most of your needs.

To analyze version control, you need some tools to automate the mining and processing. When I wrote the first edition of this book, there weren't any tools available that could do the kind of analysis I wanted to share with you. So, I

---

1. https://github.com/code-as-a-crime-scene

had to write my own tools. The tool suite has evolved over the years and is capable of performing all the analyses in the book:

- *Code Maat*—Code Maat is a command-line tool used to mine and analyze data from version-control systems. It's completely free and open source, which means you can always dig in and inspect the details of various algorithms.

- *Git*—We focus our analysis on Git. However, you can still apply the techniques even if you use another version-control system, such as Perforce or Subversion. In that case, you'll need to perform a temporary migration to a read-only Git repository for the purpose of the analysis. The conversion is fully automated, as described in the excellent Pro Git book.[2]

- *Python*—The techniques don't depend on you knowing Python. We just include it here because Python is a convenient language for automating the occasional repetitive tasks. As such, the book will link to a Python script from time to time.

In addition, the case studies are available as interactive visualizations in the free community edition of *CodeScene*.[3] CodeScene is a SaaS tool, so you don't have to install it. Instead, we'll use it as an interactive gallery for our analyses. This saves you time as you can jump directly to the results instead of focusing on the mechanics of the analyses (unless you want to). And full disclosure: I work for CodeScene. I founded the company as a way of exploring the fascinating intersection of people and code. Hopefully, you'll find it useful, too.

Forget the Tools

Before you get to the installation of the tools, I want to mention that this book isn't about a particular tool, nor is it about version control. The tools are merely there for your convenience, allowing you to put the theories into practice. Instead, the crucial factor is you—when it comes to software design, there's no tool that replaces human expertise. What you'll learn goes beyond any tool.

Instead, the focus is on applying the techniques and interpreting and acting on the resulting data. That's the important part, and that's what we'll build on in the book.

---

2. https://git-scm.com/book/en/v2/Git-and-Other-Systems-Migrating-to-Git
3. https://codescene.com/

Install Your Tools

Code Maat comes packaged as an executable JAR file. You download the latest version from its release page on GitHub.[4] The GitHub README[5] contains detailed instructions. We'll cover the relevant options as we go along, but it's always good to have this information collected in one place.

You need a JVM such as OpenJDK to execute the Code Maat JAR. After installing that Java environment, make sure it functions properly by invoking it:

```
prompt> java -version
openjdk version "18.0.2"
```

After that, you're ready to launch Code Maat from the command line:

```
prompt> java -jar code-maat-1.0.4-standalone.jar
```

If everything was successfully installed, then the previous command will print out its usage description. Note that the version of Code Maat is likely to be different now—just grab the latest version.

To avoid excess typing, I recommend creating an alias for the command. Here's how it looks in a Bash shell:

```
prompt> alias maat='java -jar /adam/tools/code-maat-1.0.4-standalone.jar'
prompt> maat # now a valid shortcut for the full command
```

Use Git BASH on Windows

You can run Git in a DOS prompt on Windows. But, some of our commands will use special characters, such as backticks. Those characters have a different meaning in DOS. The simplest solution is to interact with Git through its *Git BASH shell* that emulates a Linux environment. The Git BASH shell is distributed together with Git itself.

This book also has its own web page.[6] Check it out—you'll find the book forum, where you can talk with other readers and with me. If you find any mistakes, please report them on the errata page.

---

4. https://github.com/adamtornhill/code-maat/releases
5. https://github.com/adamtornhill/code-maat
6. https://pragprog.com/titles/atcrime/your-code-as-a-crime-scene/

Know What's Expected

The strategies and tooling work on Mac-, Windows-, and Linux-based operating systems. As long as you use a version-control system sensibly, you'll find value in what you're about to learn.

You'll run the tools and scripts from a command prompt. That way, you'll truly understand the techniques and be able to extend and adapt them for your unique environment. Don't worry—I'll walk you through the commands.

As a convention, we'll use prompt> to indicate an operating system-independent, generic prompt. Whenever you see prompt>, mentally replace it with the prompt for the command line you're using. We'll also use the maat alias introduced in the previous section as a shorthand for the full command. So, now is a good time to add that alias. Optionally, whenever you see maat on a prompt, you'll need to type the actual command, for example, java -jar code-maat-1.0.4-standalone.jar.

Tools will come and go; details will change. The intent here is to go deeper and focus on timeless aspects of large-scale software development. (Yes, timeless sounds pretentious. It's because the techniques are about people and how we function—we humans change at a much more leisurely rate than the technology surrounding us.)

With that said, let's get started on the challenges of building software at scale.

Part I

Identify Code That's Hard to Understand

Let's start with the evolution of software systems. We'll discuss the consequences of scale and the challenges of legacy code. In this part, you'll learn novel techniques to assess and analyze your codebase.

By looking into the history of your system, you'll learn how to predict its future. This will allow you to act on time, should there be any signs of trouble.

CHAPTER 1

Optimize for Understanding

Building software at scale might be the most challenging task humanity ever attempted. *Accidental complexity*—code that is more complicated than the problem calls for—adds to the challenge. Such code becomes expensive to maintain, bug-ridden, and hard to change.

To remain productive over time, we need to keep our programs' accidental complexity in check. Our main tool for that purpose is the human brain. As amazing as the brain is, it never evolved to deal with walls of conditional logic nested in deep loops, nor does it come equipped with a brain center dedicated to parsing asynchronous CQS events with implicit dependencies. If it had, our programming life would undoubtedly have been easier, but our evolution isn't there yet.

We can always write more tests, try to refactor, or even fire up a debugger to help us understand complex code constructs. As the system scales up, everything gets harder. Dealing with over-complicated architectures, inconsistent solutions, and changes that break seemingly unrelated features can kill both our productivity and joy in programming. As W. Edwards Deming said, "A bad system will beat a good person every time."[1]

In this chapter, we explore the challenges inherent to software development at scale. Once we have laid the core issues bare, you'll be prepared for the upcoming crime-scene techniques that offer a radically different view of code. Let's start by taking a look at what we programmers actually do.

---

1. https://deming.org/a-bad-system-will-beat-a-good-person-every-time/

Know the Difference Between Essential and Accidental Complexity

Problem and solution complexities are disparate, which is well explained in Fred Brooks' influential *No Silver Bullet [Bro86]* essay. Brooks categorizes complexity into essential and accidental complexity. Essential complexity reflects the problem domain itself, the very reason we write a program in the first place, while accidental complexity is a consequence of *how* we solve the problem.

As programmers, we control the accidental side, the solution complexity. Limiting the essential complexity means solving a different problem, for example, by cutting the scope or decommissioning a feature.

Understand That Typing Isn't the Bottleneck in Programming

We programmers don't write code. Sure, we do that, too, but coding is not where we spend most of our time. Instead, our most common task is to make improvements in existing code, and the majority of that time is spent trying to understand the current solution. Consequently, our primary work as programmers isn't to write code but to understand what's already there.

The code we need to decipher may have been written by our teammates, a long-gone contractor, or—often—our younger and less-informed selves. Once we know what to change, the modification may be trivial. But the road to that enlightenment can be painful.

This is particularly important during *software maintenance*. In *Facts and Fallacies of Software Engineering [Gla92]*, Robert Glass argues that maintenance is the most important phase of any software product. Depending on the product, maintenance accounts for 40 to 80 percent of the total life-cycle cost. So what do we get for all this money? Glass estimates that 60 percent of our maintenance work is genuine enhancements, not just bug fixes.

These enhancements reflect a growing understanding of our product. Our users might request new features, and the business could strive to expand its capabilities and market coverage. Software development is a learning activity, and maintenance reflects what we've learned thus far: a successful product is never done.

So, even if maintenance is time-consuming, it isn't a problem in itself but rather a good sign: only useful applications get maintained. The trick is to make maintenance effective by reducing potential waste. Given that we developers spend most of our time on understanding existing code, we have one clear candidate. If we want to optimize any aspect of software development, then we should optimize for understanding. That's the big win.

> **Joe asks:**
> ## What if My Code Is Complex Because I Solve Complicated Problems?
>
> It's tempting to think that hard problems require complex code. I'd like to argue that the opposite is true: the harder the business problem, the more we should invest in making the solution as easy as possible to understand.

Understand Maintenance in an Agile World

Before we continue, I have to make a confession. Those maintenance numbers that we just discussed are showing their age. They are based on projects from the 1990s, and the software world has been radically transformed since then.

One of the main transformations is that we are now—or, at least claim to be—*agile*. Agile development is fundamentally iterative and originated as a reaction to the traditional software development phases front-loaded with big up-front designs. At this point, you might ask how any of this maintenance stuff is relevant in an agile context: where's "maintenance" in an agile product team?

Well, let's go beyond the maintenance term by looking at its essence: when do we start making changes and enhancements to our codebase? Iteration two, at the latest. This means that in today's agile environments, we enter maintenance mode immediately. It also implies that we now spend most of our time on the most expensive coding activity there is: understanding existing code.

But it doesn't stop there. As evident in the figure on page 6, these numbers have increased dramatically, and maintenance now accounts for over 90 percent of a typical product's life-cycle costs. Glass was an optimist, after all. (See *Which factors affect software projects maintenance cost more?* [DH13] for a summary of maintenance costs.)

Good code was always important. These software trends indicate that it's even more so now.

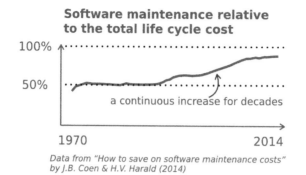

Data from "How to save on software maintenance costs"
by J.B. Coen & H.V. Harald (2014)

The Passage of Time Makes Code Worse

Software doesn't get worn down or rusty like physical products, yet the mere passage of time drives code complexity. What used to be idiomatic code a decade ago might be today's antipattern; for example, consider how the introduction of generics into Java transformed our coding style. Working in pre-generics Java code means losing valuable compile-time checks that you have grown accustomed to.

Personal development has a similar impact on maintainability. Did you ever look at code you wrote a couple of years ago only to blush in shame? It happens to me regularly, and it's a good sign. Embarrassment reflects learning. We notice opportunities that our younger selves were ignorant about. Yesterday's pride is today's problem.

Meet the Challenges of Scale

Optimizing for understanding is a hard problem. Consider the last large codebase you worked on. If you could make any improvement to that codebase, what would it be? Since you spent a lot of time with the code, you can probably think of several problematic parts. But do you know which of those changes would impact your productivity most and make maintenance easier for the whole team?

Your choice has to balance several factors. Obviously, you want to simplify any tricky elements in the design. You may also want to address defect-prone modules. To get the most out of the redesign, you'd also consider which parts of the code you and your teammates—future and current—are most likely to continue to work on so you can make those parts as simple as possible.

Striving for simplicity is, ironically, a hard task. The mere scale of today's codebases makes it virtually impossible to identify and prioritize those areas of improvement. This is unfortunate, as redesigning complex code can be risky, and even if you get it right, the actual payoff is uncertain.

Find the Needle in the Digital Haystack

Take a look at the next figure. Like many modern systems, this codebase has a rich set of back-end services, a couple of databases that might be both relational and object-based, and multiple clients such as mobile devices, web users, and REST. It's complex.

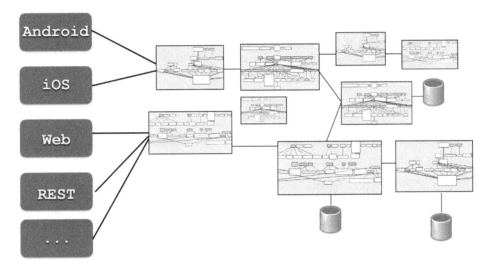

This general system complexity obscures the lower-level parts in need of attention. No matter how experienced we are, the human brain is not equipped to effectively step through a hundred thousand lines of code, sorting out the good from the bad while assessing the relative importance of each piece.

The problem increases with the size of your development team, as shown in the figure on page 8. At scale, nobody has a holistic picture of the code, and you risk making biased decisions since long-lived codebases have code that no one knows well or feels responsible for. Each person will have their own view of what the system looks like.

Finally, a system under active development is a moving target. Combining these factors, we see that in a large codebase, everyone only gets a limited view of the system. Decisions made on incomplete information are troublesome. Such decisions may optimize one part of the code but push inconsistencies to areas maintained by other developers. Or, we might improve some

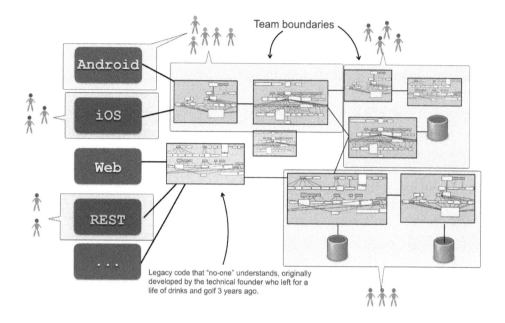

Legacy code that "no-one" understands, originally developed by the technical founder who left for a life of drinks and golf 3 years ago.

code, only to find that it didn't have any effect whatsoever on our overall ability to maintain the system.

You can address a part of this problem by rotating team members and sharing experiences. But, you still need a way to aggregate the team's collective knowledge. We'll get there soon, but let's first discuss one of the traditional approaches—complexity metrics—and why they don't work on their own.

> **Joe asks:**
> ## Can't I Avoid Complexity by Getting It Right the First Time?
>
> No, a certain level of accidental solution complexity is inevitable. Let's say we insist on every single line of code being perfect, simple, and correct. As we will see in Design for Human Problem-Solving, on page 173, even this noble approach isn't enough. The nature of software development and human problem-solving, in general, is inherently iterative. We learn by doing and by observing the outcome.

Beware the Lure of Complexity Metrics

Complexity metrics focus on specific coding constructs. The best known metric is *cyclomatic complexity*, invented by Thomas McCabe back in 1976 (*A Complexity Measure [McC76]*). Cyclomatic complexity works by counting the number of logical paths through a function. That is, each if-statement and each control structure, like a for or while loop, adds complexity. As shown in the following figure, we can count them and sum them up to get a complexity value. Simple enough.

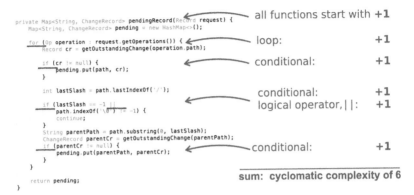

At the surface level, this sounds like what we're looking for: we point a tool to our codebase and get a nice summary of the most complex parts of our code. Problem solved, right? Unfortunately, code metrics on their own are inadequate because they fail to capture the most important aspect of complexity: impact. Let's see why.

Approach Code from the Behavioral Perspective

Complex code is only a problem if we need to deal with it. Maybe our most complex piece of code has been stable for years, works wonderfully in production, and no one needs to modify it. Does it really make a difference whether it's complex? Well, you may have a potential time bomb waiting to go off, and it's a long-term risk you need to be aware of. But large-scale codebases are full of unwarranted complexity. It's unreasonable to address them all at once. Each improvement to a system is also a risk for introducing new bugs, particularly when working on complex code we might not fully understand.

This limitation isn't specific to cyclomatic complexity but is a fundamental property of code metrics in general. No matter how accurate our metrics are—and there are better options than cyclomatic complexity out there—if we limit ourselves to a static view of the code, then we will never be able to prioritize the parts that really matter.

Instead, we need strategies that consider the people side of code and help us understand how we work with the system. Where do you find such strategies, if not within the field of offender profiling? Turn to the next chapter, and we'll explore those techniques together.

CHAPTER 2

Treat Your Code as a Crime Scene

You've seen how today's codebases are getting increasingly more complicated, making it impossible for any individual to maintain a holistic overview of the system. Further, you've also learned how traditional complexity metrics are inadequate on their own, lacking context and priorities.

Now, imagine for a moment that you had a map of your codebase. A map that would not only point out the strong and weak parts of the code but also highlight the main productivity bottlenecks where accidental complexity impacts your team the most. Having this information would let you prioritize improvements to the most urgent problems, guided by data.

In this chapter, we turn the thought experiment into reality. We do so by taking inspiration from the exciting field of forensic psychology. Let's get you started with a crash course in offender profiling.

Take a Crash Course in Offender Profiling

You probably know a little bit about offender profiling already. Movies such as the 1990s hit *The Silence of the Lambs* popularized the profession, and that popularity still exists decades after the movie's theatrical release.

In *The Silence of the Lambs*, Dr. Hannibal Lecter, portrayed by Anthony Hopkins, is an imprisoned convicted killer. Throughout the movie, he is presented with a few cryptic details from crime scenes. Based on that information alone, Dr. Lecter can deduce not only the personality but also the offender's motive. This information leads to the capture of the offender, the serial killer Buffalo Bill. (Sorry for the spoiler!)

The first time I watched *The Silence of the Lambs*, I was massively impressed. I wanted to learn Lecter's tools of the trade (for forensics—not the other stuff, mind you). Years later, as I studied criminal psychology, I was terribly disappointed. It turns out that Dr. Lecter's stunning forensics skills have a serious limitation: they only work in Hollywood movies.

Fortunately, we have scientifically valid profiling alternatives that extend to the real world. Read along, and I'll show you how the techniques psychologists use to attack these open-ended problems are useful for software developers, too.

Learn Geographical Profiling of Crimes

Geographical profiling is a technique for capturing serial offenders. It calculates a probability surface, which lets investigators pinpoint the most likely location of the offender. Geographical offender profiling is a complex subject with its fair share of controversies (just like programming!), but the basic principles are simple enough to cover in a couple of minutes.

The fundamental fact underlying geographical profiling is that criminals aren't that different from us. Most of the time, they aren't committing crimes. Instead, they spend time going to work, visiting restaurants or shops, and keeping in touch with friends. As they move around in an area, they build mental maps of the places they go. This is not specific to criminals—we all build mental maps of our surroundings. But, an offender might use their mental map to decide where to commit a crime.

This implies that the locations of the crime scenes are never random: the geographical locations contain information about the offender. Think about it for a moment. For a crime to occur, there must be an overlap in space and time between the offender and victim, right?

Find Patterns in Crimes

For serial offenders, their crimes form patterns over time. Geographical profiling is about uncovering those patterns in the spatial distribution of crimes. This works because even if an offender's deeds are bizarre, the rationale on *where* to commit a crime is often logical. (See *Principles of Geographical Offender Profiling [CY08a]* for an in-depth discussion.) Like people in general, criminals tend to be risk-averse. And—again, like people in general—criminals are often opportunistic. These traits work to the advantage of an offender profiler, so look at the figure on page 13 to see how the spatial movement serves to determine the location of the criminal.

Once a crime is committed, the offender realizes it would be too dangerous to return to that area. Typically, the location of the next crime is in the opposite direction from the first scene. Over time, the crime scenes tend to become distributed in a circular form on a map. Based on this information,

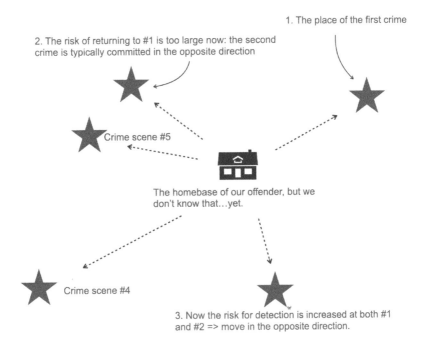

1. The place of the first crime

2. The risk of returning to #1 is too large now: the second crime is typically committed in the opposite direction

Crime scene #5

The homebase of our offender, but we don't know that…yet.

Crime scene #4

3. Now the risk for detection is increased at both #1 and #2 => move in the opposite direction.

we can apply statistical analyses to discover the most likely home base of the offender. Let's look at a real-world case by tracking down the most notorious serial killer in history, Jack the Ripper.

Profile the Ripper

Back in 1888, Jack the Ripper haunted the poverty-stricken streets of Whitechapel, London. The Ripper was never identified, but there were strong similarities in his gruesome crimes. Those similarities made it possible to connect him to five victims.

You have already seen the geographical pattern behind his crimes. The preceding figure used as an example depicts the movement of the Ripper. Let's turn this information into a profile. See the figure on page 14.

The profile in the preceding figure was generated by Professor David Canter[1] using Dragnet, a software developed by The Center for Investigative Psychology. Dragnet considers each crime location a center of gravity. It then combines the individual centers mathematically, using one important twist: psychologically, all distances aren't equal. Thus, the crime locations are weighted depending on their relative distances. That weighted result points to the

1.   https://en.wikipedia.org/wiki/David_Canter

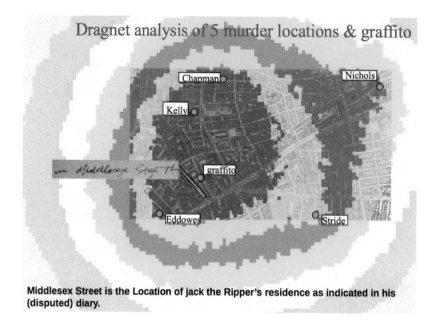

Middlesex Street is the Location of jack the Ripper's residence as indicated in his (disputed) diary.

geographical area most likely to contain the home base of the offender, also known as a *hotspot*. The central red area on the map indicates the hotspot.

The resulting hotspot is gold for investigators, allowing them to focus time and effort on the smaller area instead of patrolling an entire city.

Apply Geographical Offender Profiling to Code

As I learned about geographical offender profiling in criminal psychology, I was struck by its possible applications to software. What if we could devise techniques to identify hotspots in large software systems? A hotspot analysis that could narrow down a large system to a few critical modules would be a big win in our profession.

Instead of speculating about potential design problems among a million lines of code, geographical profiling would give us a prioritized list of areas needing refactoring. It would also be dynamic information, reflecting shifts in development focus over time.

Explore the Geography of Code

Before we can reason about hotspots, we need a geography of our code. Despite its lack of physics, software is easy to visualize. My favorite tool is Code City.[2]

2. https://wettel.github.io/codecity.html

Joe asks:
Who Was Jack?

Since Jack the Ripper was never caught, how do we know if the geographical offender profile is any good? One way is to evaluate the known suspects by seeing how they fit the profile; the Ripper case never lacked potential suspects, so a profile would help the investigating officers to zoom in on the most likely individuals. Let's look at one of them, Mr. James Maybrick. In the early 1990s, a diary supposedly written by Liverpool cotton merchant James Maybrick surfaced. In this diary, Maybrick claimed to be the Ripper. Since its publication in *The Diary of Jack the Ripper [Har10]*, thousands of Ripperologists around the world have tried to expose the diary as a forgery using techniques such as handwriting analysis and chemical ink tests. No one has yet proven the diary is fake, and its legitimacy is still disputed.

The diary reveals that Maybrick used to rent a room on Middlesex Street whenever he visited London. Now, pick up a map of London, and you will see that Middlesex Street is right inside our hotspot. This should make Maybrick a prime suspect.

It's fun to work with and matches the offender-profiling metaphor well. The following figure shows a sample city generated by the tool.

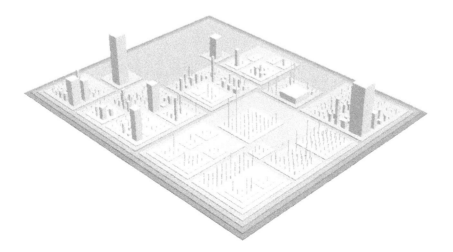

In Code City, the blocks represent packages, and each class is a building. The number of methods in each class defines the height, and the number of attributes specifies the base of the building.

When looking at the city visualization, the large buildings pop out and draw our attention. If that information is all we have, the corresponding classes would be our prime suspects. Despite a cool visualization, we haven't really advanced: this is just another static view of code complexity, with all the limitations we discussed in Beware the Lure of Complexity Metrics, on page 8. Perhaps those large classes have been stable for years, are well-tested, and have little developer activity. It doesn't make sense to start there when other parts of the code may require immediate attention.

To turn our code cities into actionable geographical profiles, we need to add the missing piece: the dynamic movement and actions. This time, though, it won't be about criminals but programmers.

Limit the Search Area: Spatial Patterns in Code

When we profiled the Ripper, we used his spatial information to limit the search area. We pull off the same feat with code by focusing on areas with high developer activity.

Your organization probably already applies tools that track your movements in code, as shown in the following figure. Oh, no need to feel paranoid! It's not that bad—it's just that we rarely think about these tools this way. Their traditional purpose is something completely different: they primarily serve as backup systems for code and, occasionally, as collaboration tools, too. Yes, I'm talking about version-control systems.

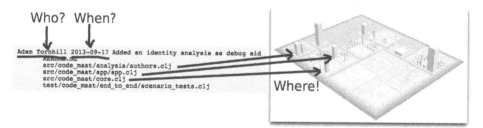

The data in our version-control system is an informational gold mine. Every modification to the system and the related steps you took are recorded. It's also more detailed than the crime scene patterns investigators use, meaning we should be able to make even more precise predictions. Let's start with a high-level initial example, and we'll cover the details in the next chapter.

The following figure presents the most basic version-control data via a tree-map algorithm.[3]

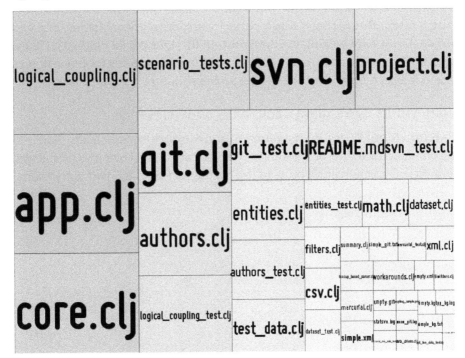

The size and color of each tile are weighted based on how frequently the corresponding code changes. The more recorded changes the module has, the larger its rectangle in the visualization. Volatile modules stand out and are easy to spot.

Measuring change frequencies is based on the idea that code that has changed in the past is likely to change again. Code always changes for a reason. Perhaps the module has too many responsibilities, the problem is poorly understood, or maybe the feature area is undergoing heavy expansion. In any case, version-control data lets us identify the modules where the team has spent the most effort.

Use Change Frequency as a Pointer for Inspection

In the preceding tree-map visualization, we saw that most changes were in a module named logical_coupling.clj, followed by app.clj. If those two modules turn out to be a mess of complicated code, redesigning them will significantly impact future work. After all, that's where we currently spend most of our time.

---

3.   https://github.com/adamtornhill/MetricsTreeMap

While looking at effort is a step in the right direction, we need to also reconsider code complexity. The temporal information is incomplete on its own because we don't know anything about the nature of the code. Sure, logical_coupling.clj changes often. But perhaps it is a perfectly structured, consistent, and clear solution. Or, it may be a plain configuration file with trivial changes. Change frequency on its own can only tell us about the relevance of a piece of code. Without information about the code itself, we cannot tell if it's a problem or not.

Find Hotspots by Merging Complexity and Relevance

Let's return to our Code City visualization and combine its complexity dimension with our new measure of relevance. We indicate it by color in the following illustration. The interesting bit is in the overlap between the two dimensions.

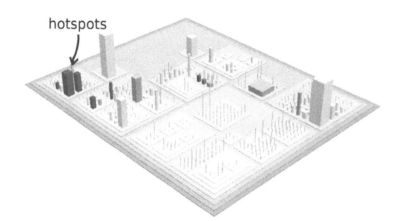

When put together, the overlap between complexity and effort signals a hotspot, an offender in code. Hotspots are complicated code that you have to work with often.

Throughout the book, we'll use hotspots to guide to impactful improvements and refactorings. But there's more—hotspots are intimately tied to quality, too. So, before we move on, let's dig into the research on the topic.

Know That Hotspots Predict Defects

Research has shown that frequent changes to complex code predict declining quality:

- After studying a long-lived system, a research team found that the number of times code changes is a better predictor of defects than pure size. (See *Predicting fault incidence using software change historyPredicting fault incidence using software change history [GKMS00 GKMS00a].*)

- In a study on code duplication, modules that change frequently are linked to maintenance problems and low-quality code. (See *An Empirical Study on the Impact of Duplicate Code [HSSH12]*.) We'll investigate code duplication in Chapter 9, Architectural Reviews: Support Redesigns with Data, on page 117.

- Several studies report a high overlap between these simple metrics and more complex measures. The importance of change to a module is so high that more elaborate metrics rarely provide any further predictive value. (See, for example, *Does Measuring Code Change Improve Fault Prediction? [BOW11]*.)

- This message was reinforced in a study that tested different predictor models for detecting quality issues in code. The number of lines of code and the modification status of modules turned out to be the two strongest individual predictors. (See *Where the bugs are [BOW04]*.)

- Finally, a 2021 study looking at security vulnerabilities identified a strong positive correlation between security error density (errors per 1K SLOC) and the presence of hotspots. (See *The Presence, Trends, and Causes of Security Vulnerabilities [AWE21]*.)

All of this predictive power is there for us once we embrace the behavioral perspective of how we—as an organization—interact with the code.

Be Aware That Hotspots Reflect Probabilities

Geographical offender profiling is based on probabilities, but there's no guarantee that the hotspot points investigators to the offender. Hotspots in code share this property. Code that changes frequently doesn't have to be a problem, but—again—it's likely. This is why it's important to complement the probability surface given by our hotspots with code-level insights, a topic we'll expand on throughout Part I.

The main value of a hotspot analysis is that it shines a light on how any complex code impacts an organization. This is information that's invisible in the code itself. You use this information to refactor the most expensive technical debt first, making your code easier to understand. Hotspots are a lightweight technique that helps us use our time wisely.

Now that you know how hotspots work and their important connection to software quality, you're ready to apply the technique in your code. So, let's turn the page and walk through your first offender profile together.

CHAPTER 3

Discover Hotspots:
Create an Offender Profile of Code

Now that you know how offender profiling works, it's time to turn theory into practice. Together, we'll analyze real-world codebases by applying hotspot analysis to identify and remediate accidental complexity.

We'll start by pointing our forensic techniques to React, a popular JavaScript library from Facebook. Once you've worked through this analysis, you will have an offender profile similar to the figure on page 22.

Before we get to the visualizations, we need to cover the mechanical steps of fetching the necessary evidence. Our tool chains can automate these steps, yet it's good to know where the data comes from. Understanding the core algorithm builds understanding, even if you never perform the steps manually. Hence, this first pass through the intersection of people and code is more detailed than in later chapters.

Mine the Evolution of Code

A hotspot analysis consists of multiple steps. You might want to keep the completed profile from the online gallery by your side.[1] That way, you know what we're building up to.

To understand how the profile is made, we start at the command line. Follow along by cloning the React repository[2] so that you have the complete source tree on your computer:

---

1. https://tiny.one/react-hotspots-full
2. https://github.com/code-as-a-crime-scene/react

```
prompt> git clone git@github.com:code-as-a-crime-scene/react.git
Cloning into 'react'...
Updating files: 100% (2460/2460), done.
prompt>
```

You should now have a local react folder with the source code. Move into that directory:

```
prompt>cd react
```

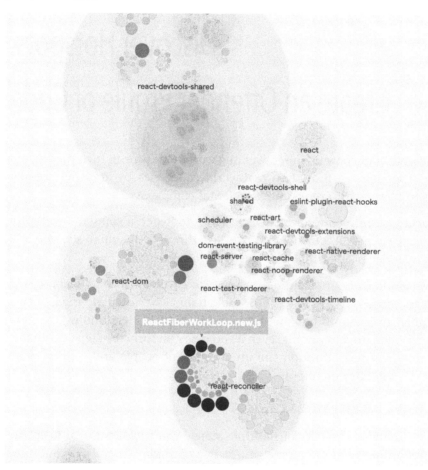

Become Familiar with Git Logs

With the repository cloned, we're ready to look at the developer activity. This is done via Git's log command, which lets us inspect historical commits. To get the level of detail we need, we add the --numstat flag:

```
prompt> git log --numstat
```

This command outputs a detailed log of all commits, as shown in the next figure.

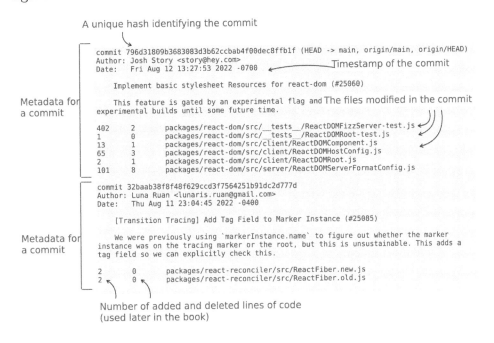

To calculate hotspots, we only need to count how frequently each file name occurs in the Git log. Of course, a codebase under active development might have tens or hundreds of commits each day. Manually inspecting commit data is error-prone and, more importantly, takes time away from all the fun programming. This calls for automation.

Create a Git Log for Code Maat

You met Code Maat in the introduction, and now we will use it to analyze change frequencies. If you haven't done so already, flip back to Get Your Investigative Tools, on page xxi and install Code Maat.

To run the tool, we first need to adapt the input data. Git's defaults for the --numstat output are fine for human consumption but too verbose for a tool like Code Maat. Fortunately, the log command allows us to simplify:

```
prompt> git log --all --numstat --date=short \
            --pretty=format:'--%h--%ad--%aN' --no-renames
```

The previous command introduces the --pretty=format option for controlling output. The option instructs Git to include only the hash, date, and author of each commit header. Try it out on your React repository. The output should look like this:

```
--796d31809--2022-08-12--Josh Story
402     2          packages/react-dom/src/__tests__/ReactDOMFizzServer-test.js
1       0          packages/react-dom/src/__tests__/ReactDOMRoot-test.js
13      1          packages/react-dom/src/client/ReactDOMComponent.js
...

--32baab38f--2022-08-11--Luna Ruan
2       0          packages/react-reconciler/src/ReactFiber.new.js
2       0          packages/react-reconciler/src/ReactFiber.old.js
2       0          packages/react-reconciler/src/ReactFiberBeginWork.new.js
...
```

With these options, our output is more structured. This is a log format that we can feed to Code Maat. To do so, we redirect the Git output to a local file that will serve as input to the tooling:

```
prompt> git log --all --numstat --date=short  \
                --pretty=format:'--%h--%ad--%aN' --no-renames  \
                --after=2021-08-01 > git_log.txt
```

The added flag, --after, determines how far back in time we go to collect evolutionary data. We'll cover the timespan in more depth once we get to Determine How Hot a Hotspot Is, on page 41, but for now, we settle on one year as a sensible default.

Inspect Commit Activity

Now that you have a persisted Git log, you're ready to launch the tooling. Fire up Code Maat by entering the following command—we'll discuss the options in just a minute:

```
# remember to replace `maat` with the actual command,
# e.g. java -jar code-maat-1.0.4-standalone.jar
prompt> maat -l git_log.txt -c git2 -a summary
statistic,         value
number-of-commits, 773
number-of-entities, 1651
number-of-authors, 107
```

The -a flag specifies the analysis we want. In this case, we're interested in a summary for inspecting the input data. In addition, we need to tell Code Maat where to find the logfile (-l git_log.txt) and which version-control system we're using (-c git2). That's it. These three options should cover most use cases.

The summary statistics displayed above are generated as comma-separated values (.CSV). We note that there have been 773 commits by 107 authors over the past year. Let's see whether we can find any patterns in those commits.

Pure Text Is the Universal Interface

By generating results as .CSV, a well-supported text format, other programs can read the output. You can import the .CSV into a spreadsheet or, with a little scripting, populate a database with the data. This minimalistic model allows you to build more elaborate visualizations and analyses on top of Code Maat. Pure text is the universal interface, allowing us to decouple the calculations from their presentation.

Analyze Impact: Calculating Change Frequencies of Code

The next step is to analyze the distribution of changes across the files in the React codebase. You do that by specifying the revisions analysis:

```
prompt> maat -l git_log.txt -c git2 -a revisions
entity,n-revs
packages/react-reconciler/src/ReactFiberCommitWork.old.js, 72
packages/react-reconciler/src/ReactFiberCommitWork.new.js, 71
packages/react-reconciler/src/ReactFiberWorkLoop.new.js,   65
packages/react-reconciler/src/ReactFiberWorkLoop.old.js,   64
packages/react-reconciler/src/ReactFiberBeginWork.old.js,  60
...
```

The output is sorted on the number of revisions. That means our most frequently modified candidate is ReactFiberCommitWork.old.js with 72 commits, closely followed by 71 changes to the fuzzily named ReactFiberCommitWork.new.js. Great—you have your first hotspots. Now, persist the results to a local file, which you will re-use in the next section. Here's how to persist it:

```
prompt> maat -l git_log.txt -c git2 -a revisions > react_revisions.csv
prompt>
```

Explore the Complexity Dimension

The data collected so far reveals the spatial movements of programmers within the codebase. This is the behavioral perspective, and as we discussed in Chapter 2, Treat Your Code as a Crime Scene, on page 11, we now have to combine it with a complexity dimension. Adding a complexity view lets you quickly separate problematic code from areas that often change but are in good shape. Perhaps React's ReactFiberCommitWork module—the most frequently changed file—is a marvel of clean code whose expressiveness puts James

Joyce's *Ulysses* to shame. Or perhaps you're about to meet a mean-looking legacy code monster. Let's see where the complexity is hiding in React.

Get Complexity by Lines of Code

There are several code complexity metrics to choose from. You met cyclomatic complexity in *Beware the Lure of Complexity Metrics*. Another classic is *Halstead's complexity measures.*[3] Both of these metrics are fairly old, yet they remain in widespread use and have influenced many derived metrics. One such approach is *Cognitive Complexity*, which aims to address modern programming language structures by considering the control flow of the code. (See *Cognitive Complexity: A New Way of Measuring Understandability [Cam18].*)

At first glance, the multitude of options might seem hard to choose from. Don't worry. The good news is that you can pick any complexity metric you want. The bad news is the rationale behind that advice: basically, what most code complexity metrics have in common is they are poor predictors of, well, *complexity.* (See *Program Comprehension and Code Complexity Metrics [PAPB21]*, which investigated 41 metrics, including the ones mentioned above, using fMRI brain imaging, finding weak to medium correlations between metrics and programmers' response time.)

Given that existing metrics fare equally well (or badly, depending on how generous we feel), we can aim for true simplicity: let's use lines of code as a proxy for code complexity. It's a rough metric, but it gives some real advantages:

- *It's simple and intuitive*—Cyclomatic complexity might be a popular metric, but it's not widely understood. As someone who analyses code for a living, I find myself explaining the metric at a rate that outpaces even the zombie-slaying frequency of my eight-year-old's Minecraft sessions. That time is better spent communicating your findings (or even hunting pixelated zombies). Lines of code don't require any description.

- *It performs as well as more elaborate metrics*—Multiple studies have shown that lines of code perform at the level of more complicated code-level metrics. (We'll visit that research in Chapter 5, Detect Deteriorating Structures, on page 49.)

- *It's language-neutral*—Because lines of code are meaningful across programming languages, it gives us a holistic picture of all parts. That's useful in today's polyglot codebases.

---

3.   https://en.wikipedia.org/wiki/Halstead_complexity_measures

Later in the book, we'll turn to language-specific techniques for more sophisticated insights. For now, let's stick with lines of code as a reasonable proxy for complexity.

Count Lines with cloc

My favorite tool for counting lines of code is cloc. It's free and easy to use. You can get a copy of cloc on GitHub.[4]

With cloc installed, let's put it to work inside the React repository:

```
prompt> cloc ./ --unix --by-file --csv --quiet \
        --report-file=react_complexity.csv
```

Here, we instructed cloc to count statistics --by-file (the alternative is a summary) and --csv output. Since we're already inside the React repository, we specify the current directory, ./, as the target. Finally, we ask cloc to output the report to a file, react_complexity.csv. As you can see in the following output, cloc does a good job of detecting the programming language the code is written in.

```
language,filename,blank,comment,code,

Markdown,AttributeTableSnapshot.md,547,0,13128
JSON,package-lock.json,0,0,12684
JavaScript,__tests__/ESLintRuleExhaustiveDeps-test.js,147,234,7840
JavaScript,pe-class-components/benchmark.js,185,0,5400
JavaScript,pe-functional-components/benchmark.js,185,0,4917
...
```

Based on language, cloc separates lines containing comments from real code. We don't want blank lines or comments in the analysis.

Working with Non-Normalized Data

Many statistical models require we scale and normalize our data. For example, complexity and change frequencies have different ranges, and if we wanted to put them into a machine learning model based on Euclidean distance, then we'd have to translate the values into a common scale, often [0, 1]. You will come across such scaling techniques later in the book as we start to compare data from different samples.

However, not all data should be normalized. The natural units of code complexity are more intuitive to reason about. Reporting the file size as 2,500 lines of code communicates more clearly than, say, a scaled 0.07 value. When possible, present non-normalized values to humans and save the scaled values for the algorithms requiring them.

---

4. https://github.com/AlDanial/cloc

Intersect Complexity and Effort

At this point, you have two different views of the codebase: one that reveals the code complexity and one that shows change frequencies. We find potential hotspots where the two views intersect, as shown in the following figure.

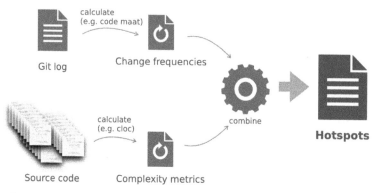

Merging the two views is straightforward: iterate through the .CSV file containing change frequencies, and look up the corresponding code field from cloc's data. I have prepared a Python script that relieves you of writing that tedious code yourself. Grab a copy of merge_comp_freqs.py from GitHub,[5] and run the script with the previously persisted result files as input. This gives you a prioritized list of suspects:

```
prompt> python merge_comp_freqs.py react_revisions.csv react_complexity.csv
module,revisions,code
packages/react-reconciler/src/ReactFiberCommitWork.old.js,   72, 3302
packages/react-reconciler/src/ReactFiberCommitWork.new.js,   71, 3302
packages/react-reconciler/src/ReactFiberWorkLoop.new.js,     65, 2408
packages/react-reconciler/src/ReactFiberWorkLoop.old.js,     64, 2408
packages/react-reconciler/src/ReactFiberBeginWork.old.js,    60, 3220
packages/react-dom/src/__tests__/ReactDOMFizzServer-test.js, 43, 4369
packages/shared/ReactFeatureFlags.js,                        42,   56
...
```

When inspecting that list, remember how we restricted the Git log to the past year. Our top hotspot ReactFiberCommitWork.old.js has 72 commits during that period. This implies that a couple of times during a typical week, a developer needs to understand its details. With 3302 lines of code, it's fair to conclude that it's a challenging task: the code is complex. You've found your first hotspot!

---

5. https://tinyurl.com/merge-complexity-script

\]//   **Joe asks:**
ǯ   **Why Are the Files in React Duplicated?**

Good catch! Indeed, most hotspots in React seem to come in pairs where the name contains either .old or .new as the suffix. This pattern isn't related to the analysis. Instead, it represents a design choice by the React team where a codebase fork is maintained on the same branch. It's an unorthodox option, meaning that the team might have to apply the same code changes twice to non-trivial modules.[a]

---

a.   https://twitter.com/acdlite/status/1402982845874909186

Drive Refactoring via a Probability Surface

The change frequency component of the hotspots is a relative metric. All codebases will have some code that's more volatile than other parts. When you combine change with complexity, you can start to draw conclusions.

When analyzing your own code, you might find that all hotspots have low complexity. In that case, you are in a great position: the code you work on the most is also the best. You and the team simply need to keep up the good work and remain on a positive trajectory.

Building quality systems is the foundation for successful and sustainable software development. We can never know what our product's future might hold, but we know there's a high probability it will involve the hotspots. The simpler your code, the better.

However, more often than not, hotspots point to real problems. Let's dig deeper by viewing hotspots through the lens of technical debt.

Know Why You Don't Have to Fix All Technical Debt

Our React case study revealed several hotspots containing complex code. When that happens, we need to act. Back in Know That Hotspots Predict Defects, on page 18, we learned that complex hotspots expose the product to quality issues. Mitigating defects is a good driver for improvements on its own, but as we will see in Chapter 7, Communicate the Business Impact of Technical Debt, on page 83, the actual impact is deeper, affecting throughput and developer happiness alike.

Should you come across similar issues in your code, keep in mind that hotspots send a positive message. Let's clarify that by looking at the next figure.[6]

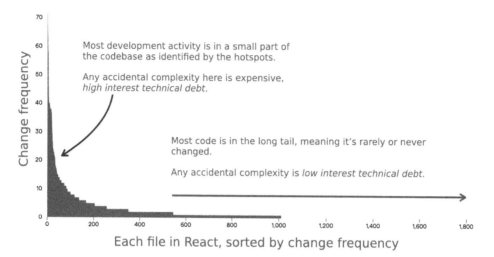

Each file in React, sorted by change frequency

This preceding figure might be the most important data point in this book. As you can see, the development activity in React isn't evenly distributed across the codebase. Instead, the development activity forms a power law distribution where a few files dominate, and most files end up as part of the curve's long tail. This pattern isn't unique to React. Over the past decade, I have analyzed over 300 codebases of all sizes, scales, and domains. Every single one of them exhibited a power law distribution. It seems to be how software evolves, which spells good news for us. (To read more on the subject, check out Michael Feathers's pioneering article on "The Active Set of Classes," which offers an additional perspective.[7])

A power law evolution means that we don't have to fix all technical debt, nor should we. Looking back at the hotspot list on page 28, you see that the change frequency levels off after the first six hotspots. Ignoring the forked copies, we see that the React hotspots make up 9,000 lines of code. Those hotspots illuminate the parts of the codebase where improvements in ease of understanding are likely to give us the largest effects.

Admittedly, 9,000 lines of code is still a respectable number. But 9,000 is much less than 400,000 lines of code, which is the total size of the React codebase. More importantly, if this was your code, you would now be able to

6.   https://tiny.one/react-change-distro
7.   https://tinyurl.com/feathers-active-set-of-classes

drive refactoring based on data from how you—as a development organization—interact with the code. How good is that?

Right now, we are at the book's central idea, and you know how to identify hotspots yourself. The next chapter digs deeper into the concept by investigating ways of visualizing hotspots and code. We also make sure to cover the core use cases. But try the exercise below so that you get the chance to become comfortable with the analysis.

Exercises

The following exercise allows you to explore a special case of the hotspot analysis. Should you get stuck, flip ahead to Appendix 1, Solutions to the Exercises, on page 267, and I'll be happy to offer my guidance.

Restrict the Hotspot Analysis to Parts of a Codebase

- Repository: https://github.com/code-as-a-crime-scene/react
- Language: JavaScript
- Domain: React is a UI library.
- Analysis snapshot: https://tiny.one/react-hotspots-map

In most situations, you want to include the complete codebase in your hotspot map. However, occasionally, it's interesting to focus on a smaller part of the overall codebase such as a specific subsystem or service. A typical use case includes a large system where you're only responsible for a part of the solution. Having a dedicated view of just that piece is useful.

There are multiple ways of restricting the analysis scope to parts of a codebase. You could, of course, analyze the full codebase and filter the resulting CSV. Another more direct option is to let your tooling do the filtering for you. Both Git and cloc let you limit their output by specifying a path of interest. With Git, you just append a directory path to the log command. For example, git log --numstat packages/react-reconciler restricts the log to the react-reconciler package. With cloc it's even simpler since you just give the folder of interest as the first argument.

Try it out on the React project by restricting the hotspot analysis to packages/react-dom. What are the main hotspots in react-dom?

CHAPTER 4

Hotspots Applied:
Visualize Code from the People Side

You now have your first offender profile. That's great. Starting from simple techniques, we pieced together a list of the main suspects in React. In this chapter, we'll continue to build upon hotspots so that you are prepared to apply the analysis at scale. Once we have filled in the blanks, you'll also see how to integrate the hotspot information into your daily work.

We start by exploring different approaches for visualizing multidimensional evolutionary data. Code itself is an abstract concept, which we tend to view in a textual format. That representation makes it difficult to spot patterns; as the old saying goes, we cannot see the forest for all the code.

Instead, we need to present the hotspots together with our code. Just as the following offender profile shows crime patterns (see the figure on page 34), we need a map that visualizes commits in code.

Visualizing source code within the context of developer behavior offers a much-needed higher-level view. You will be able to spot problematic modules within seconds, even in large-scale systems. It's a true superpower that you'll get to try for yourself by profiling *Kubernetes*, a massive application with three million lines of code. Let's start our journey in familiar territory: Code City.

Visualize Source Code

Back in Apply Geographical Offender Profiling to Code, on page 14, we used Code City to visualize the spatial movement of developers. The city metaphor is a powerful visualization idea.

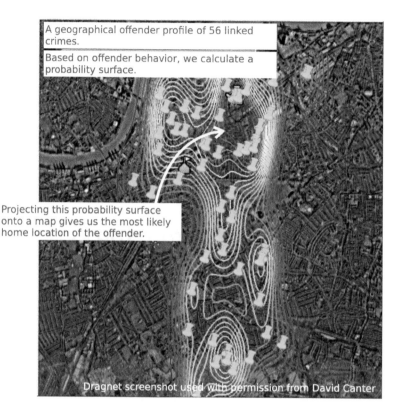

A geographical offender profile of 56 linked crimes.

Based on offender behavior, we calculate a probability surface.

Projecting this probability surface onto a map gives us the most likely home location of the offender.

Dragnet screenshot used with permission from David Canter

Code City was my starting point in 2010 as I formalized the concept of behavioral code analysis. Visualizations were key since they enabled a shift in perspective. Most code looks innocent enough in the constrained view of a code editor. Not so in Code City: you'll notice patterns you didn't spot before. This works because visual images tap into the most powerful pattern detector in the known universe—the human brain.

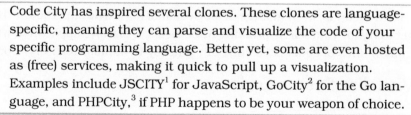

Language-Specific Code City Clones

Code City has inspired several clones. These clones are language-specific, meaning they can parse and visualize the code of your specific programming language. Better yet, some are even hosted as (free) services, making it quick to pull up a visualization. Examples include JSCITY[1] for JavaScript, GoCity[2] for the Go language, and PHPCity,[3] if PHP happens to be your weapon of choice.

---

1. https://github.com/ASERG-UFMG/JSCity/wiki/JSCITY
2. https://github.com/rodrigo-brito/gocity
3. https://github.com/adrianhuna/PHPCity

Compare Visualizations

The natural connection to geographical profiling from forensics made cityscapes an obvious starting point. However, as much as I came to love Code City, I soon found that the style isn't optimal for hotspots. Let's look at the following React visualization from JSCITY to see what I mean:

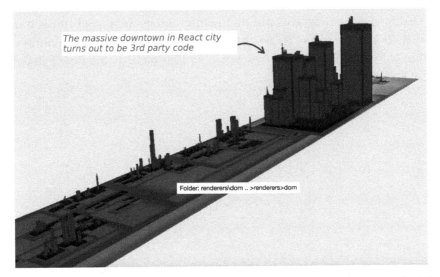

The massive downtown in React city turns out to be 3rd party code

Folder: renderers\dom .. >renderers>dom

The 3D visualizations don't scale well to large systems. And I mean that from multiple perspectives: the city visualizations take time to render. This is a solvable problem, but existing tools aren't optimized for scale.

The second scaling issue is more fundamental since it applies to your wetware: a rich 3D view takes up screen real estate, meaning you cannot get a holistic overview of the system at a glance. This takes away the key power behind visualizing data. Further, it puts an additional load on your working memory, meaning you need to keep pieces of information in your head while scrolling to other parts of the system. When reasoning about code, we cannot afford to waste any brain cycles.

Finally, the city visualizations lead with the complexity dimension. Looking back at the preceding React city figure, your attention is most likely drawn to the downtown with its imposing skyscrapers. Those are all false positives, representing third-party code that's checked in and not part of the team's responsibilities.

As we discussed in Beware the Lure of Complexity Metrics, on page 8, complexity is the least interesting dimension in a behavioral code analysis. What if we could instead draw attention to the dynamics of how you and your team interact with the code? That would immediately filter out both stable code and any third-party code while retaining the relevant pieces of information. Let's dig into a visualization with this quality.

Build a Mental Model of Your Codebase

Enclosure diagrams present an alternative visualization that cognitively scales well. Our enclosure diagrams are highly interactive, an aspect that's hard to illustrate in a static book. To get the full experience, turn to the online visualization of React.[4] You should now see a familiar picture: the React visualization we saw earlier on page 22.

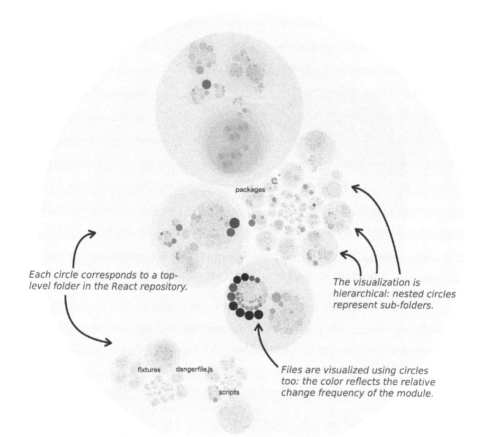

Each circle corresponds to a top-level folder in the React repository.

The visualization is hierarchical: nested circles represent sub-folders.

Files are visualized using circles too: the color reflects the relative change frequency of the module.

Visualizing the hotspot profile of React

The resulting patterns do look cool—who said large-scale software isn't beautiful? But we're not here to marvel at its beauty. Instead, click on one of

---

4.   https://tiny.one/react-hotspots-full

the circles. You'll notice first that the visualization is interactive, as shown in the following figure.

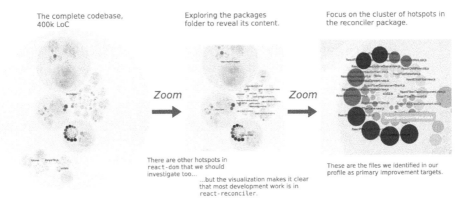

The complete codebase, 400k LoC

Exploring the packages folder to reveal its content.

Focus on the cluster of hotspots in the reconciler package.

Zoom

Zoom

There are other hotspots in react-dom that we should investigate too... ...but the visualization makes it clear that most development work is in react-reconciler.

These are the files we identified in our profile as primary improvement targets.

An interactive visualization lets you choose your level of detail. If you see a hot area, zoom in to explore it further. Enclosure diagrams make it easy to toggle between analysis findings and the actual code they represent. Another win is that you get a quick overview of both volatile clusters and the stable parts of the system. Look at the preceding figure again for an example. See how the hotspots pop out? The reason is that the entire codebase is visualized, not just the code we have recorded changes for. We get that for free since cloc includes size metrics for all modules.

Enclosure diagrams are based on a geometric layout algorithm called *circle packing*. Each circle represents a part of the system. The more complex a module, as measured by lines of code, the larger the circle. We then use color to serve as an attention magnet for the most critical property: change. See the following image.

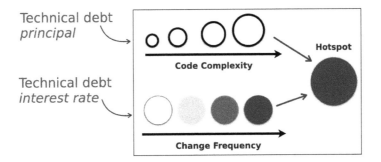

Technical debt *principal*

Code Complexity

Hotspot

Technical debt *interest rate*

Change Frequency

Even if you don't know anything about React, the visualization gives you an entry point into understanding the system. You see both good and fragile parts at a glance. This simplifies communication: presenting a hotspot map to your team helps everyone build a mental model of what the code looks like.

And that's even before you actually look at the code. Can you think of a better starting point for demystifying a large-scale codebase?

Intuition Doesn't Scale

Expert intuition can lead to high-quality decisions, and Malcolm Gladwell even wrote a whole book to its praise. (See *Blink [Gla06]*.) So why even bother with a hotspot analysis? Asking your local expert—who might be yourself—would be even quicker. Well, intuition is an automatic, unconscious process. Like all automated brain processes, intuition is sensitive to cognitive and social biases. Even factors in your specific situation—like the weather or your mood—will influence your judgment. Most of the time, you aren't aware of that influence. (You'll see some examples in Chapter 12, Meet Norms, Groups, and False Serial Killers, on page 183.) This means we cannot rely on the quality of snap judgments alone.

Verifying your intuition with supporting data lets you keep the biases in check. Further, intuition just doesn't scale, especially not to systems with a million lines of code undergoing constant change by multiple development teams in parallel.

Create Your Own Visualizations

Before we move on, let's see how to visualize your code with a set of simple tools. This chapter's code offender profile visualizations are based on an algorithm from D3.js,[5] a JavaScript library for data-driven documents. More specifically, the enclosure diagrams use the Zoomable Circle Packing algorithm.

The data-driven characteristic of D3.js helps since you can ignore most details and treat the visualization as a black box. You'll find that the linked D3.js examples[6] are surprisingly easy to experiment with, so let's focus on generating their input data.

The D3.js circle-packing algorithm expects a JSON document. In our case, this means converting from the .CSV results you created in Chapter 3, Discover Hotspots: Create an Offender Profile of Code, on page 21 to a tree structure that can be fed into D3.js. The figure on page 39 illustrates this process.

To maintain an intuitive visualization, you want the JSON tree to follow the structure of the codebase. For highlighting hotspots, you add the change

---

5. http://d3js.org/
6. https://observablehq.com/@d3/zoomable-circle-packing

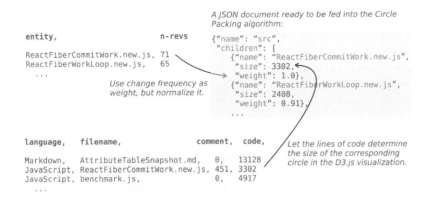

frequency of each file as a weight but normalized to the value range 0.0 (no commits) to 1.0 (the hottest hotspot in the codebase).

To help you get started, I have prepared a Python script for the transformation.[7] Run the script with the -h flag as python csv_as_enclosure_json.py -h to get the usage description.

And should you prefer an all-batteries-included package, there's always Appendix 2, Get Started with Enclosure Visualizations, on page 281 waiting for you. That appendix is a step-by-step guide using examples combining HTML and JavaScript code.

Try it out. Visualizing data is fun!

Explore the Visualization Space

At this point, I want to remind you that the strategies in this book don't depend on D3.js. It's just one of many ways to visualize the code. Other options include:

- *Spreadsheets*—Since we're using .CSV as the output format, any spreadsheet application lets you visualize the hotspot results. Spreadsheet applications are a great low-tech approach for processing analysis results (for example, sorting and filtering the resulting data).

- *Jupyter notebooks*[8]—Jupyter has become the go-to tool for data scientists, and it's a great web-based and interactive development environment that works well for exploring hotspots too. Jupyter gives you access to Python's rich set of libraries for statistical computations and data visualizations.

---

7. https://tinyurl.com/visualize-enclosure-json
8. https://jupyter.org/

- *R programming language*[9]—If Python isn't your thing, then I'd recommend you take a look at the R language, which offers capabilities comparable to Jupyter. It has a slightly steeper learning curve, but it pays off if you want to dive deep into data analysis. Besides, R is a fun programming language.

Break Barriers via Language Agnostic Analyses

So far, we have only analyzed code written in one programming language, Java-Script. However, there's nothing language-specific in our analysis: the beauty of mining version control is that all data is language agnostic. It's just content. This means we can analyze codebases implemented in any programming language. Let's look at an example from *Zulip*, a powerful chat solution for distributed teams. The following figure illustrates how hotspots transcend language barriers. This is important, as today's systems tend to be polyglot codebases.

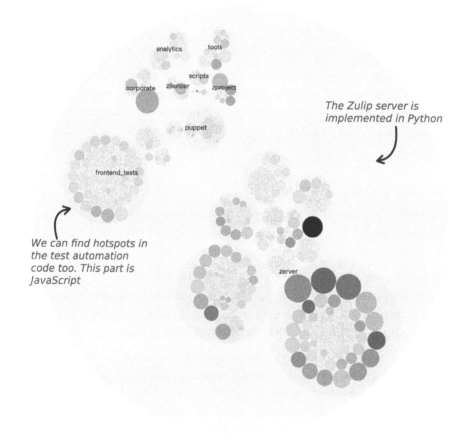

The Zulip server is implemented in Python

We can find hotspots in the test automation code too. This part is JavaScript

Modern software development, like all knowledge work, trends toward increased specialization. This is by necessity; there are fewer and fewer Renaissance persons in our increasingly complex world. How do you find time to expand into back-end development when there's a constant inflow of new front-end frameworks to keep up with?

Even if our specialization is inevitable or desired, it can still pose a communication obstacle within engineering teams. Pretend that you're part of a platform like Zulip. You sit down with your peers to discuss a much-needed feature. Perhaps the back-end people find the proposed feature simple, whereas the proposed UI changes send shivers down the spines of your front-end friends. Visualizing the whole system is an invaluable communication tool, allowing everyone to speak the same language and share a common understanding of the design. Hotspots are the Babel fish in a polyglot sphere.[10]

Commuting Offenders Give Rise to Multiple Hotspot Clusters

Geographical offender profiling makes one assumption: an offender's home location must be within an area defined by the locations of the crimes. This assumption holds true in the majority of all cases, but some offenders exhibit a different behavior: they travel out from their base to commit serial offenses and only later return home. (Pulling a consultancy joke here would be easy, but let's avoid that.) This is a type of traveling offender, a commuter. A classic case is the shoplifter who might have to travel to a commercial area to find targets. (See *Mapping Murder: The Secrets of Geographical Profiling [CY04]* for a deeper discussion.)

In code, we could become commuters, too, when working on multirepository codebases, where separate hotspot clusters might appear in different repositories. This is a pattern that we'll investigate in Part II.

Determine How Hot a Hotspot Is

So far, we've used the relative rank within a codebase to identify hotspots. We based that rank on whatever happened to be the maximum number of revisions over the past year. What if that number was 3? Or 845? As you can see in the figure on page 42, without any context, they're just numbers. Let's see how we decide the scope of the analysis.

---

10. https://en.wikipedia.org/wiki/The_Hitchhiker%27s_Guide_to_the_Galaxy_(TV_series)

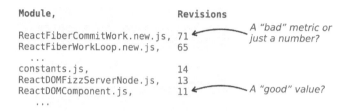

Choose an Analysis Period

Hotspots have a temporal component to them. Over time, your development focus shifts, and the hotspots shift correspondingly. Similarly, as design issues get resolved, prior hotspots cool down. If they don't, that means the problem still exists.

So, how much data should you include when mining version control? Well, this is the place in the book where I would very much like to point you toward a definitive, authoritative source that delivers a simple and universally applicable answer. Yet, there is no such thing as a hard and fast rule. Like so much else in software design, the correct answer is an equivocal "it depends." That said, there are some strong heuristics covering all practical purposes:

- *Focus on recent development*—If you include too much historical data, you risk skewing the results by obscuring important recent trends. You could flag old hotspots that cooled down years ago.

- *One year is a good default*—I always start my hotspot analyses by including one year of historical data. It's a nice balance since you get enough history to explore the system and its long-term trends. If you find that the project has a high development activity (think thousands of commits per day), then select a shorter initial period, perhaps as little as one month.

- *Use major events as the starting point*—Finally, you could define the temporal period around significant events, such as reorganizations of code or personnel. When you make large redesigns or change how you work, it will reflect in the code. With this analysis method, you can investigate both impact and outcome.

Unify Commit Styles

Individual commit styles vary; many developers commit frequently using small, isolated changes, while others prefer a big-bang commit that changes half the world. Could this cause a bias in our hotspot analysis?

In practice, I've never experienced those variations as a problem. First of all, individual differences even out at scale. Second, the number of revisions isn't intended to be viewed in isolation. As long as you're complementing the metric with a complexity dimension, as we did in this chapter, false positives will be sorted out, and the actual hotspots will be revealed.

That said, even if your hotspot analysis works fine with variations in style, you have a lot to gain by getting your team to adopt a shared convention for all commits. Tools like Git even let you verify those conventions via automated pre-commit hooks.[11] Consistency simplifies all workflows.

Understand That Bugs Breed Bugs

Another important property of hotspots is that they make good predictors of defects. In a much-cited study, a research team built a set of machine-learning algorithms to compare the defect prediction power of complexity metrics vs. change metrics from version control. They found that the change-based model outperformed code complexity, correctly predicting greater than 75 percent of all defects. (See *A comparative analysis of the efficiency of change metrics and static code attributes for defect prediction [MPS08]* for the full study.) Changing code, it seems, is a risky activity.

> **Joe asks:**
> ## Really? Wouldn't It Be a Higher Risk to Change Complex Code?
>
> Great question! Thanks for asking. Indeed, the keyword is "change." As reported in *How, and why, process metrics are better [RD13]*, code-level metrics tend to stabilize; they don't change much from release to release. Let's illustrate with an example.
>
> Consider a hypothetical module that is overly complicated. The mere thought of having to understand it makes you reconsider your career choice; developing functional fusion power looks comparatively easy. Even such code can still be functionally correct after being debugged into correctness. If that module represents a stable part of your domain, then there won't be any reason to modify the code. Restricting ourselves to complexity means that this module would repeatedly pop up as a false positive. Again, code alone doesn't tell the full story.

---

11. https://git-scm.com/book/en/v2/Customizing-Git-Git-Hooks

Explore the Relationship Between Hotspots and Defects

These days, most development teams use an issue tracker such as Jira, GitHub, or Azure DevOps. If you also do *smart commits* where each commit message references the corresponding issue, then it's possible to map fixed defects to specific modules in the code. The following figure shows an example of how it typically looks.

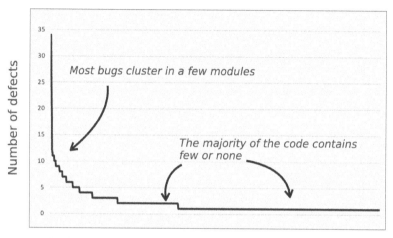

Each file in the codebase, sorted by number of defects

As you see in the preceding diagram, defects tend to cluster. Bugs attract each other. Similarly, most modules have few or even no bugs. In this particular system, the hotspots comprised only 4 percent of the code, yet that code contained 72 percent of all defects.

This ratio represents a typical pattern, although at the higher end of the scale. In general, hotspots stretch across only 1 to 5 percent of the total codebase, yet that code is responsible for 25 to 75 percent of all bugs. You see, power laws are everywhere in software.

We touched upon this topic back in Know That Hotspots Predict Defects, on page 18. Now that we have more data, you can use these research findings to your advantage by improving the code that needs it the most. Guided by hotspots, you encircle buggy areas with high precision.

Know That Information Is Only Good When Acted Upon

The best part of a hotspot analysis is that you get all that information faster than a CSI agent can hack together a Visual Basic GUI to track an IP address in real time. This enables you to focus attention and actions on the parts of the code that need it the most:

- *Prioritize technical debt remediation*—Over the years, I've seen organizations spend months on rewrites that don't have a clear business outcome or aren't urgent. In addition to being wasteful, it's also a missed opportunity to improve the parts that *do* make a difference. Hotspots allow you to dodge that bullet.

- *Drive legacy code modernization*—The need to plan and prioritize improvements in a legacy system drove my first applications of forensics to code. The suggested improvements were all redesigns that would each cost weeks of intense work. I had to ensure we chose improvements that actually benefited future development efforts: complex code that changes frequently identifies great candidates.

- *Perform code reviews*—Research consistently finds that code reviews have high defect-removal rates. But, a code review done right is also time-consuming. Given what we know about the relationship between hotspots and buggy code, use the analysis to identify the modules where deeper reviews are a good investment of time.

- *Guide end-to-end test automation*—When building a new system, it's natural and advisable to grow the tests in parallel to the code. However, many companies are also adding test coverage to existing systems. Just like with code improvements, we should start covering the most critical areas first. Again, hotspots are an excellent impact guide.

- *Get onboarding superpowers*—Let's pretend you join the React project. You're faced with 400,000 lines of unfamiliar code. Talking to the 700-plus developers who've contributed to the project is impractical at best, particularly since some of them may have left. Onboarding is a long game, taking three to six months in the average company. A hotspot analysis kickstarts the process by revealing the most critical parts of the codebase, allowing you to zoom in and focus your learning. Besides, hotspots are a great conversation starter.

Now that we know how to apply hotspots, we are ready to dive into codebases of any size. However, to make better use of our time, we should add one more investigative tool. You see, not all hotspots are equal. This means we cannot tell if our hotspots are a growing problem or, perhaps, represent an issue that the team is already aware of and working to improve. In the next chapter, you'll see how complexity trends highlight this temporal aspect of code. But first, try the following exercises to apply what you've learned in this chapter.

Exercises

The following exercises will help you become more familiar with the techniques and use cases. You'll also get to test my initial claim that hotspot visualizations let us spot problematic code within seconds, even in massive codebases.

Try the Language-Agnostic Analysis on Your Own

- Repository: https://github.com/code-as-a-crime-scene/zulip
- Language: Python, TypeScript, JavaScript
- Domain: Chat application.
- Analysis snapshot: https://tinyurl.com/zulip-hotspots-map

The multilanguage dive into Zulip earlier in this chapter didn't require any special handling. It followed the offender profiling steps we covered before. So, now is a good time to try the hotspot analysis yourself so you are comfortable with the process.

To analyze Zulip, follow the hotspot receipt on page 23. The only difference is that you need to drive from the Zulip repository. That is, clone the repository as shown below:

```
prompt> git clone git@github.com:code-as-a-crime-scene/zulip.git
Cloning into 'zulip'...
Updating files: 100% (2460/2460), done.
prompt>
```

From here, the remaining instructions are identical. To verify your results, check them against the completed hotspot analysis.

Meet Vue.js—the Other Kid in Town

- Repository: https://github.com/code-as-a-crime-scene/vue
- Language: TypeScript
- Domain: Vue is a framework for building user interfaces.
- Analysis snapshot: https://tinyurl.com/vue-js-hotspots-map

React is, of course, not the only option for building a UI for the web. Another popular option is Vue.js. When selecting an open-source library, its feature space and style have to fit into your context. That's an important criterion. However, now that you know how to identify complex code, it's straightforward to also consider the maintenance angle: you don't want to build your new product on a library that is hard to evolve.

Navigate to the analysis snapshot, and investigate the top hotspots in Vue. Compare them to the corresponding size/complexity numbers in React. Which codebase has the lowest risk in terms of future maintenance?

Spot Technical Debt in Kubernetes

- Repository: https://github.com/code-as-a-crime-scene/kubernetes

- Language: Go

- Domain: Kubernetes is a popular solution for managing containerized applications.

- Analysis snapshot: https://tinyurl.com/k8-hotspots-map

If you want to deploy a new service into production, chances are you have come across Kubernetes, or *K8s* as it is also known. K8s has become the dominant platform (no judgment). It's always interesting to peek under the hood and see what a mission-critical codebase looks like. In the case of K8s, we're met with nearly three million lines of code. Given that amount of code, how quickly can you spot the technical debt with the highest interest?

Go to the analysis snapshot and zoom in on the kubernetes/pkg package. Look at the size of the hotspots. Without diving into the code, can you tell if those modules will likely be problematic?

CHAPTER 5

Detect Deteriorating Structures

A healthy codebase allows you to add new features with successively less effort. It's a powerful advantage, enabling you to iterate progressively faster. Unfortunately, the reverse is more common: new features add complexity to an already tricky design, and eventually, the system breaks down with development slowing to a crawl.

The phenomenon was identified and formalized by Manny Lehman[1] in a set of observations on how software evolves. In his *law of increasing complexity*, Lehman states that "as an evolving program is continually changed, its complexity, reflecting deteriorating structure, increases unless work is done to maintain or reduce it." (See *On Understanding Laws, Evolution, and Conservation in the Large-Program Life Cycle [Leh80]*.)

You already know about hotspot analyses, which you can use to identify these "deteriorating structures" so that you can act and reduce complexity. But how do you know if you are improving the code over time or just contributing to the grand decline? Let's see how to uncover complexity trends in your programs.

Calculate Complexity Trends from Your Code's Shape

A few years ago, I used to commute to work by train. I went to the station at about the same time each day and soon recognized my fellow commuters. One man used to code on his laptop during the ride. I don't know whether he wrote Java, C++, or C#, but even with a hurried glance, I knew his software was overly complicated.

---

1. http://en.wikipedia.org/wiki/Manny_Lehman_%28computer_scientist%29

You've probably encountered similar situations. Isn't it fascinating that we can form an impression of something as intricate as code with a quick look?

Humans are visual creatures. Our brain processes a tremendous amount of visual information in a single glance. As programmers, when we glimpse code, we automatically compare the code's visual shape against our experience. Even if we aren't consciously aware of it, after years of coding, we know what good code looks like. This is a skill we can use more deliberately.

Determine Complexity at a Glance

Have a quick look at the following image depicting two modules, A and B. I intentionally blurred the code to obscure any details, but the overall structure will offer enough information to answer the question: Which one would you rather maintain and extend?

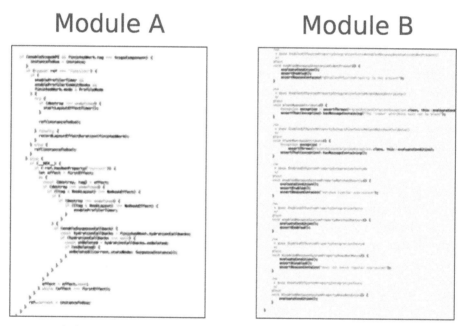

Independent of the programming language used, the differences in complexity are striking. Module B looks straightforward, while module A winds down a complex, conditional slope. My guess is that you chose module B and did so quickly. What's fascinating is that you made this judgment without seeing the actual code. Do you see how the shape of the code reveals its complexity?

Get Insights from the Shape of the Code

I started to investigate the idea of using the shape of code while teaching test-driven development (TDD). TDD is a powerful design technique and a high-discipline methodology littered with pitfalls. (See http://www.adamtornhill.com/articles/codepatterns/codepatterns.htm for the original writeup.) By inspecting compact overviews of the resulting code's shape, the programming team was able to:

- Compare differences in complexity across unit tests.

- Identify inconsistent parts of the design that diverge from the rest of the structure.

- Let the visual contrast serve as a tool to highlight basic design principles. For example, a solution using polymorphism looks quite different from one based on conditional logic.

Inspect Negative Space in Code

The visual inspection you just did is fine for analyzing individual units. However, it's clear that manually comparing code visualizations won't scale up to a large hotspot.

These days, image comparison is a solved problem within computer science, even though it requires throwing a deep neural network at the challenge. A machine must use complex algorithms to achieve what your brain does with the flick of some neurons, consuming serious computing power. So, let's stick to the textual representation of the code but simplify the process by shifting our perspective: let's focus on the negative space.

Negative space is a key concept in visual art. The concept refers to the empty space around or even within an image, for example, the unpainted parts of a canvas. When properly used, negative space can become the subject of an image itself. See Rubin's vase in the image on page 52 for a well-known example.[2]

---

2.   https://en.wikipedia.org/wiki/Rubin_vase

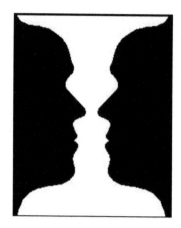

Rubin's vase: a famous illustration on how a single image can have two separate interpretations.

Note that the core image is entirely based on negative space.

The power of negative space is also useful in programming as a tool for measuring code complexity. Look at the next figure to see how it works.

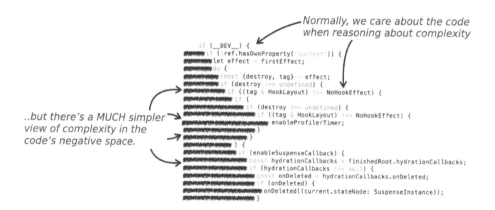

Normally, we care about the code when reasoning about complexity

..but there's a MUCH simpler view of complexity in the code's negative space.

The reason this works is because we never indent at random. (If we do, we have bigger problems.) Virtually all programming languages use whitespace indentation to improve readability. (Even Brainf***[3] programs seem to use it, despite the goal implied by the language's name.) So, instead of focusing on the code itself, we look at what's not there, the negative space. We'll use indentation as a proxy for complexity.

The idea can sound over-simplistic at first. Surely, an intricate property of code cannot be operationalized as easily as this. Complex problems require complex solutions, don't they? You'd be relieved to hear that research backs

3.   http://en.wikipedia.org/wiki/Brainfuck

the idea of indentation as a proxy for complexity. (See the paper, *Reading Beside the Lines: Indentation as a Proxy for Complexity Metric [HGH08]*.) It's a simple metric, yet it correlates with more elaborate methods, such as McCabe cyclomatic complexity and Halstead complexity measures.

The main advantage of a whitespace analysis is that it's easy to automate. It's also fast and language-independent. Even though different languages result in different shapes, the concept works just as well on Java as it does on Clojure or C.

However, there is a cost: some constructs are non-trivial despite looking flat. (List comprehensions[4] come to mind.) But again, measuring software complexity from a static snapshot of the code is not supposed to produce absolute truths. We are looking for hints. Let's move ahead and see how useful these can be.

> **Joe asks:**
> ## Does It Really Work for All Languages?
>
> Good question. Assembly languages and machine code, in general, have flat structures. They *could* be indented, but I've never seen that happen in practice. Perhaps because they pre-date the structured programming movement? I should have known myself, given that I started my career hacking away on the glorious Commodore 64 back in the 8-bit days. Thanks for pointing that out!

Conduct a Whitespace Analysis of Complexity

Back in Chapter 3, Discover Hotspots: Create an Offender Profile of Code, on page 21, we identified the ReactFiberCommitWork module in React as a likely maintenance problem. A whitespace complexity measure offers further evidence.

Calculating indentation is trivial: just read a file line by line and count the number of leading spaces and tabs. Let's use the Python script, complexity_analysis.py, in the miner folder of the code you downloaded from the GitHub repo.[5]

The complexity_analysis.py script calculates logical indentation. All leading spaces are converted into tabs. Four spaces or one tab counts as one logical indentation, and any empty or blank lines are ignored.

Open a command prompt in the React repository root and fire off the following command. Just remember to provide the real path to your own scripts directory:

---

4. http://en.wikipedia.org/wiki/List_comprehension
5. https://github.com/adamtornhill/maat-scripts/tree/python3

```
prompt> python scripts/miner/complexity_analysis.py \
 packages/react-reconciler/src/ReactFiberCommitWork.old.js
n,    total,   mean, sd,    max
3753, 6072.25, 1.62, 1.07, 5.5
```

Like an X-ray, these statistics give us a peek into a module's inner structure. The total column is the accumulated complexity. It's useful to compare different revisions or modules against each other. (We'll build on that soon.) The rest of the statistics tell us how that complexity is distributed:

- The mean column reveals that there's plenty of complexity, on average, 1.62 logical indentations per line. It's high but not too bad.

- The standard deviation, sd, specifies the variance of the complexity within the module. A low number like we got indicates that most lines have a complexity close to the mean. Again, not too bad and also not a number I put too much emphasis on.

- But the max complexity is arguably the most important, and it shows signs of trouble. A maximum logical indentation level of 5.5 is high. Very high.

A large maximum indentation implies there's a lot of indenting, meaning you can expect islands of nested complexity in the code. This insight alone is useful when diagnosing accidental complexity, yet we can do more. Let's apply the whitespace analysis to historical data to track hotspot trends.

Analyze Code Fragments

One promising application of the whitespace technique is to analyze differences between code revisions. An indentation measure doesn't require a valid program—it works fine on partial programs, too. That means we can analyze the complexity delta in each changed line of code. If we do that for each revision in our analysis period, we can detect trends in our modifications. This usage is a way to measure modification effort. A progressively lower effort is the essence of good design.

Prefer Trends over Absolute Values

So far, all evidence in our React investigation points to real issues: the hotspots are complex, and the indentation analysis pointed out further concerns. But what if the team is already aware of those issues and working to fix them? Extensive refactoring efforts could even be the reason why the file showed up as a hotspot in the first place. If that's the case, you'd expect the code to improve over time, being in better shape today than a week ago.

A snapshot alone doesn't reveal this essential evolutionary trail. Fortunately, we have already seen how version-control data lets us step back into history. If we combined this capability with our new whitespace analysis, then you could plot a *complexity trend* over time.

Looking back, there will be a lot of code to process. Remember that ReactFiber-CommitWork alone has 3,000-plus lines of code, which we need to analyze over its 72 commits to reveal the trend. Luckily, an indentation analysis is blazingly fast. It scales to a range of revisions without eating up your precious time, while still keeping power consumption low.

Focus on a Range of Revisions

You've already seen how to analyze a single revision. Now, we want to

1. take a range of revisions for a specific module;

2. calculate the indentation complexity of the module as it occurred in each revision; and

3. output the results, revision by revision, for further analysis.

The recipe for a trend analysis is pretty straightforward, although it requires some interactions with the version-control system. For Git, you fetch the range of revisions via git log. You then retrieve the historical version of the code via git show, providing a revision and file name as arguments.

Since this book isn't about git, we're going to skip over the implementation details and just use the script already in your scripts directory. Feel free to explore the code if you want all Git details. Let's keep it high-level for now and walk through the main steps.

Discover the Trend

In your cloned React Git repository, type the following into the command prompt (and remember to reference your own scripts path) to run git_complexity_trend.py:

```
prompt> python scripts/miner/git_complexity_trend.py \
  --start fc3b6a411 --end 32baab38f \
  --file packages/react-reconciler/src/ReactFiber.old.js
rev,       n,    total,  mean, sd
a724a3b57, 761, 652.25, 0.86, 0.77
a6987bee7, 780, 667.25, 0.86, 0.77
57799b912, 784, 674.75, 0.86, 0.78
72a933d28, 788, 681.25, 0.86, 0.78
...
```

At first, this looks cryptic, but the output is the same format as our earlier whitespace analysis on the latest ReactFiberCommitWork revision. The difference here is that we get the complexity statistics for each historical revision of the code. The first column specifies the commit hash from each revision, the oldest version first.

The range of revisions is determined by the --start and --end flags. Their arguments represent our analysis period by referencing the corresponding commit hashes. As seen in the following image, you will find those hashes in the Git log that we already mined during the hotspot analysis.

The --end revision determines the last commit to our hotspot of interest.

```
commit 32baab38f
Author: Luna Ruan <lunaris.ruan@gmail.com>
Date:   Thu Aug 11 23:04:45 2022 -0400

        [Transition Tracing] Add Tag Field to Marker Instance (#25085)

    2         0         packages/react-reconciler/src/ReactFiber.new.js
    2         0         packages/react-reconciler/src/ReactFiber.old.js
    2         0         packages/react-reconciler/src/ReactFiberBeginWork.new.js
    2         0         packages/react-reconciler/src/ReactFiberBeginWork.old.js
```

The --start revision represents the code a year ago (tip: we could also include the full history, giving us long-term trends).

```
commit fc3b6a411
Author: Bowen <bowen31337@users.noreply.github.com>
Date:   Mon Aug 23 04:11:35 2021 +1000

        Fix a few typos (#22154)

    2         2         packages/react-reconciler/src/ReactFiberBeginWork.new.js
    2         2         packages/react-reconciler/src/ReactFiberBeginWork.old.js
    1         1         packages/react-reconciler/src/ReactFiberCommitWork.new.js
    1         1         packages/react-reconciler/src/ReactFiberCommitWork.old.js
    7         7         packages/react-reconciler/src/ReactFiberCompleteWork.new.js
    7         7         packages/react-reconciler/src/ReactFiberCompleteWork.old.js
```

We could restrict the trend to the hotspot window of one year, as in the preceding figure. However, by instead specifying the first revision of the file, we uncover the long-term trends of a hotspot. Let's visualize the result to discover those patterns.

Visualize the Complexity Trend

Spreadsheets are excellent for visualizing complexity trends. Just save the .CSV output into a file and import it into Excel, OpenOffice, or a similar application of your choice. You can also follow along in the online gallery, where a dedicated view contains the complete complexity trend.[6] First, let's look at the total complexity growth in the figure on page 57.

As you can see, ReactFiberCommitWork is on a steep upward trajectory, with no sign of slowing down. This growth can occur in two basic ways:

1. New code is added to the module.
2. Existing code is replaced by more complex code.

---

6. https://tiny.one/react-fiber-complex

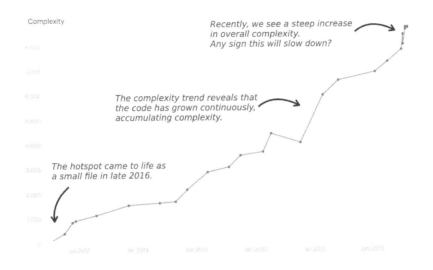

At some point, even a pure growth in terms of lines of code becomes problematic. (We'll discuss this soon in Design for Cohesion, on page 65). But case 2 is particularly worrisome—that's the "deteriorating structure" Lehman's law warned us about.

Differentiating between the two cases is a complex problem with a trivial solution: plot a second data vector representing the historical lines of code over time. A glance at the curves in the following figure will immediately tell us *how* the hotspot grows.

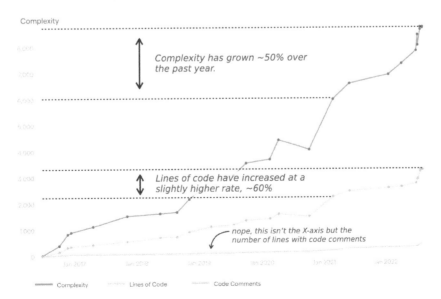

By including lines of code, we see that while the React hotspot increases its total complexity, the increase is via additions, not existing lines becoming more complex. Overall, that's better than seeing the complexity line taking off on its own.

To experience the latter, have a look at the following trend from another prominent codebase that I analyzed a couple of years ago: BitCoin.[7]

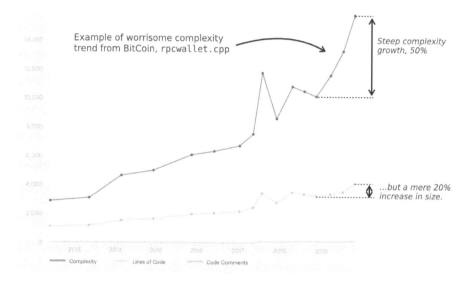

Evaluate the Growth Patterns

The BitCoin hotspot data brings us to an important point: when investigating complexity trends, the interesting thing isn't the numbers themselves but the shape of the evolutionary curve. The following figure summarizes the patterns you're most likely to find in your code.

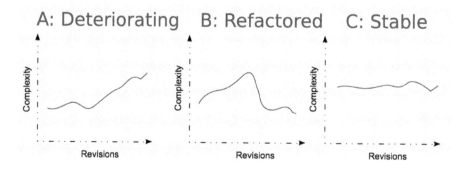

7.   https://bitcoin.org/

- *Deteriorating*—You have already experienced Case A, which is a warning sign. As the file gets more complex, it becomes harder to understand. This pattern is a call for refactoring.

- *Refactored*—The dip in the curve for Case B is a positive sign reflecting a refactoring. Keep monitoring future trends to ensure the code doesn't deteriorate again.

- *Stable*—Case C is common when there's little change to a module's structure and responsibilities. It represents an overall stable module where we make small tweaks and changes.

Learn from Complex Code

A project's success depends on the coding skills of the people involved. As humans, we vary in capabilities, training, and experience. Those differences give variations in code quality across programmers, even on the same team. If the same person designs all the modules within one area, the results will be similar. Occasionally, this results in clusters of hotspots with skyrocketing complexity trends attributable to the same individual.

However, remember that when looking at the current hotspots, we lack the original context. All mistakes look obvious in hindsight, but there could be multiple reasons why the code is as it is. Perhaps it was a strategic decision to build on top of a fragile base—a deliberate technical debt. Or, your former project manager made the hasty decision to deploy what was intended as a throw-away prototype into production. Now it's your problem. (True story.)

Of course, hotspots could reveal a skill gap, too. When that happens, use the opportunity to educate your team with better methods or rearrange the teams to shift skills around. A strong culture of collaboration, peer reviews, and continuous learning goes a long way. We'll devote Part III of this book to those areas.

Watch for Changes in Style

When relying on a technique as simple as whitespace analysis, you may wonder if different indentation styles could affect the results. Let's look into that.

This chapter has its theoretical foundations in the study on *Reading Beside the Lines. [HGH08]* that we discussed earlier. Their research evaluated indentation-based complexity on 278 projects. They found that indentation is relatively uniform and regular, and—importantly—they concluded that deviating indentations don't affect the results significantly.

The lack of variation is also why the technique works in the first place: indentation improves readability and, hence, aligns closely with underlying coding constructs. We don't just indent random chunks of code (unless we're competing in the International Obfuscated C Code Contest).[8]

That said, there is an edge case where the analysis can cause surprises. A change in indentation style midway through a project could disturb your results. For example, running an auto-indent program on your codebase would wreck its history and show an incorrect complexity trend. If you are in that situation, you can't compare revisions made before and after the change in indentation practices.

Understand Complexity

With style covered, we've taken the concept of hotspot analyses full circle. We learned how to analyze code in mid-sized systems, such as React, and how to scale to large codebases by visualizing our offender profiles. We also drilled into individual modules to reveal their internal complexity. A natural next step is to act upon all this information. What do we do once we confirm a problematic and deteriorating hotspot? In the next chapter, you'll investigate the coding patterns that make or break a software design. But first, try the following exercises to apply what you've learned in this chapter.

Exercises

Working through the following exercises lets you evaluate complexity trends on real-world codebases. You also get a chance to experience the examples and use cases firsthand.

Investigate the Main Suspect in Kubernetes

- Repository: https://github.com/code-as-a-crime-scene/kubernetes

- Language: Go

- Domain: Kubernetes is a popular solution for managing containerized applications.

- Analysis snapshot: https://tiny.one/kubernetes-complexity

The exercises in the previous chapter had you create a hotspot profile of Kubernetes. One of the main suspects is pkg/apis/core/validation/validation.go, a hotspot with more than 5,000 lines of code.

---

8.   https://www.ioccc.org/

Create a visual complexity trend of validation.go using the script and steps in Discover the Trend, on page 55. Which growth pattern do you see, and how does it contrast with the evolution of the React hotspot?

Use Trends as Canaries for Code Complexity

- Repository: https://github.com/code-as-a-crime-scene/folly
- Language: C++
- Domain: Folly is a C++ component library used at Facebook.
- Analysis snapshot: https://tiny.one/folly-complexity

There's an old mining tradition of using canaries as a biological warning system for carbon monoxide. Complexity trends can serve a similar purpose in code by alerting us to rapidly increasing levels of complexity.

Click on the analysis snapshot above and inspect the trend for the module AsyncSocketTest2.cpp in Folly. What does it reveal, and, more importantly, should we worry if this was our code? When would it have been a good time to act?

As a bonus question, considering that this is test code, does it matter, and in which way?

CHAPTER 6

Remediate Complicated Code

At this stage, you know how to detect hotspots in codebases of any scale, visualize the issues, and prioritize code that deteriorates over time. You've come a long way already, and now it's all about making the findings actionable. In this chapter, we'll highlight common code smells that you'll likely come across when inspecting hotspots.

We'll start from the perspective of the human brain with its cognitive limitations. The cognitive perspective clarifies the impact of complexity-inducing coding constructs such as nested logic, the bumpy roads code smell, and low cohesion. Once we know what to look for, we'll be ready to dig into the code and simplify. Let's get started.

Meet Your Brain on Code

For a programmer, one of the most interesting cognitive concepts is *working memory*. Working memory is the mental workbench of the mind, enabling you to perceive, interpret, and manipulate information in your head. You engage working memory when doing crosswords, solving a sudoku puzzle, or—what we're focusing on—trying to understand a piece of code. Working memory is vital to us programmers.

Unfortunately, working memory is also a strictly limited cognitive resource, and there's only so much information we can actively hold in our heads at one time. Any attempts at pushing beyond this biological limit are mentally taxing and increase the risk of mistakes as we operate at the edge of our cognitive capabilities.

Try Overloading Your Working Memory

Take a moment and try the *N-Back task* to experience what a working memory filled to the brim feels like. The N-Back task was developed for cognitive research, and it's an efficient way of exhausting working memory. (This is almost as effective as trying to understand the rules for C++ template argument deduction.[1]) There are several interactive N-Back versions on the web, for example the one from Brainturk.[2]

Now, imagine that you found a magic brain hack that upgrades both working- and long-term memory. How would that impact the way you code? Picking up the latest Perl syntax or the intricacies of Kubernetes would be effortless. Passing any AWS certification just requires a lazy look through the relevant documentation.

Interestingly enough, there are people with these capabilities. In a classic case study, renowned psychologist A. R. Luria shares the tale of S., a synesthetic man with limitless memory. On average, we can keep three to four items in our heads, but without active rehearsal, the memory traces soon vanish. This is in remarkable contrast to S., who effortlessly memorized 70 items and, more impressive, could still recall the information in any given order when retested on the same information weeks, months, or even years later. Despite elaborate laboratory studies, Luria's team couldn't find any apparent limits to S's memory capacity.

Would S. be a great programmer? Unfortunately, we will never know for sure, since Luria met S. in the 1920s, way before the computing age. But my bet is that S.—perhaps surprisingly, given his cognitive gifts—would struggle as a developer. Let's look at the purpose of software design to figure out why.

Tune Code to Fit Your Brain

Given a perfect memory, the only one interpreting your code would be the compiler. At first, it's an attractive proposition because programming would be immensely simplified if we no longer needed to cater to a demanding audience of forgetful humans. Care about giving your functions and variables proper names? Stop that. There wouldn't be any need, effectively ending all entertaining programming style wars instantly. Is encapsulation, then, the pinnacle of good design? Well, if we can remember every single business rule

---

1.   https://en.cppreference.com/w/cpp/language/template_argument_deduction
2.   https://www.brainturk.com/dual-n-back

and where they are located, then there's no point in encapsulating anything. Suddenly, typing would be the bottleneck in coding.

Hopefully, this kind of coding style comes across as the stuff programming nightmares are made of. There's a reason we care about software design. Most of us don't have S's capabilities, yet we need to find a way of tuning our code into a form fitting the brain's cognitive bottlenecks—a form that plays to our brain's strengths rather than fighting with its weaknesses. Let's look at something fundamental for brain-friendly code: cohesion.

\\//
ʒ̆ɾ
Joe asks:
What Is Synesthesia?

Synesthesia is a condition where a sensory stimulus activates another sensory modality so that the sensations blend together. For example, hearing a specific word triggers "seeing" a picture representing the specific word. Another example of synesthesia is when numbers get associated with certain shapes, colors, or even tastes. S's synesthesia served as strong memory cues for organizing and retrieving information. Nevertheless, visual strategies quickly break down when it comes to abstract concepts. Consider the concept of "nothing" or "eternity." How would you visualize them? S. couldn't, and consequently struggled with both remembering and understanding abstract terms. There's no such thing as a free lunch in the world of cognition.

Design for Cohesion

Looking back at our case studies, you might have noticed that most hotspots were large files. You already know how lines of code correlate with complexity and defects, so when is a module too large?

As is often the case with software design, general rules regarding numbers aren't that interesting: having 100, 1000, or even 2000 lines of code in a module isn't, by itself, what makes or breaks a design. Instead, the determining factor is what led to the current size: is the module cohesive?

Cohesion is a design principle describing how well the parts of a module fit together. (See *Structured Design, 1979 [YC79]* for the classic source.) Modern research highlights cohesion as one of the most impactful properties of maintainable software, so let's explore how you uncover the cohesion of your own hotspots. (See *Ranking of Measures for the Assessment of Maintainability of Object-Oriented Software [YS22]* for a comparison of OO measures.)

Code with low cohesion implements multiple responsibilities within the same class. Low cohesion is problematic from a cognitive perspective since we now need to keep multiple concepts in our heads when reading the code. Further, there's always the risk of introducing bugs due to unexpected feature interactions: we want to modify the salary calculation but inadvertently impact the email notifications contained in the same module, spamming our three million users in the process. As such, large files are frequently, but not always, the symptom of a deeper problem with cohesion.

We can determine the cohesion of our designs using two separate techniques: a formal one and a heuristic based on function names. We'll cover both, but let's start with the heuristic since it's more straightforward—and fun.

Refactor Hotspots Guided by Function Names

As you identify a hotspot, look at the names of its methods and functions. They hold the key to the future. Let's look at an example from Hibernate, a widely used Object/Relational Mapper (ORM).[3]

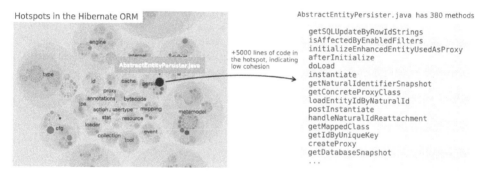

The preceding example presents a selection of the methods within AbstractEntityPersister.java, a hotspot in Hibernate. Given that the hotspot has 5000 lines of code and is closing in on 400 methods, we can suspect the Abstract prefix is an oxymoron—we're likely to find complex logic here. A true crime scene.

Starting from the functions' names, group them by task to identify the responsibilities of the hotspot. When refactoring, make those responsibilities explicit by extracting them into separate modules using *Extract Class* refactoring, as shown in the image on page 67. (See *Refactoring: Improving the Design of Existing Code, 2nd Edition [Fow18]*.)

Measure Cohesion Using Formal Analysis

The function name technique is my default approach when refactoring toward cohesive designs, but, as mentioned earlier, there are formal metrics, too.

---

3. https://github.com/code-as-a-crime-scene/hibernate-orm

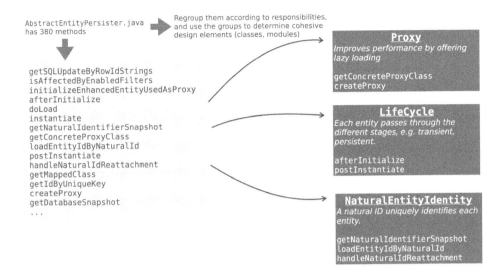

These metrics come in handy when our hotspots are too complex to reason about, or their function names are too non-descript. The most commonly supported cohesion measure is *Lack of Cohesion in Methods*, or LCOM4 for short.[4]

The "4" postfix in LCOM4 indicates there have been three prior attempts at the measure, reinforcing how cohesion is a non-trivial problem. The following figure illustrates the basic principles behind LCOM4.

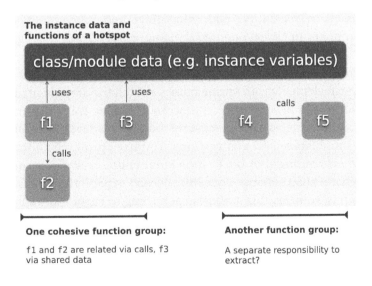

LCOM4 captures connected graphs of function dependencies via shared data and call chains. Two functions belong to the same graph if a) they access the same data or b) one function invokes the other. Of course, two functions—say f1 and f3—can be indirectly related via a call chain like f1 -> f2 -> f3. Applying the measure across a module reveals the groups of related functions. A perfectly cohesive unit has exactly one group, meaning all functions are connected. The more function graphs, the lower the cohesion.

Several code analysis tools implement LCOM4, but the main advantage is not necessarily in applying the metric but in how the algorithm helps explain cohesion. The underlying rules serve as a recipe for determining what belongs together vs. which responsibilities are better off when encapsulated in a separate module. That way, analyzing cohesion lets you transform a problematic hotspot into a sustainable design. Let's look into it.

Cohesion Can Be Understood via Team Interactions

 While this chapter focuses on the cognitive effects of cohesion, its impact goes far beyond coding. As you'll see in Visualize Organizational Friction, on page 222, cohesion also influences teamwork and coordination between staff members. Cohesion is a fundamental property for scaling the people side of code.

Design to Isolate Change

Cohesive modules are a prerequisite for high-quality software due to their proven impact on reliability, maintainability, and extendibility. (See the research summary in *Object oriented dynamic coupling and cohesion metrics: a review [KNS19]*.) Cohesion is important because it facilitates ease of understanding. Remember our working memory with its limited capacity? Cohesive design elements with strong names stretch the amount of information you can hold in your head at once, a process known as *chunking*. In cognitive psychology, chunking is the process of taking low-level information and grouping it into higher-level abstractions. You use chunking all the time, for example, when reading this book: individual characters are organized into words, which are abstractions. Chunking doesn't expand the number of items you can keep in your head but allows each thing to carry more information.

In programming, chunking is the key to readable code, improving our ability to change the code as a response to another task. Compare the resulting context after extracting cohesive modules from the Hibernate hotspot on page 67. The design to the right will be much easier to reason about: each responsibility has an obvious place, making it quicker to mentally navigate existing code while, as a bonus, minimizing the risk of unexpected feature interactions.

Cohesive designs have the added benefit of stabilizing code in terms of development. In your domain, different areas evolve at different rates, and cohesion lets you reflect this in your design. You see an example of the rates of change in the following figure where engine represents a stable package, a property that should apply to most of your code. Contrast the stable package with the subsystems dialect and query, which both contain multiple hotspots evolving together.

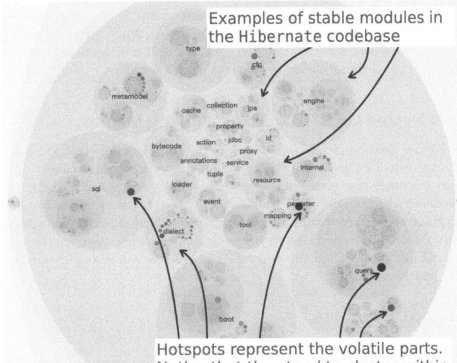

Examples of stable modules in the Hibernate codebase

Hotspots represent the volatile parts. Notice that they tend to cluster within the same packages.

A failure to stabilize code often stems from low cohesion; subsystems and modules keep changing because they have many reasons to do so. Cohesion lets you isolate change, and the more code you can stabilize, the less you need to keep in your head. Stable code that works is a much-underestimated design property. It's cognitive economy, enabling you to maintain long-term mental models of how the system works.

Ask if It's Needed. Twice.

I was only a year into my career as a software developer when I experienced my first death-march project. The project was late, and a main feature still wasn't working correctly, leading to crashes, late hours, and a burnt-out development team. A heroic rewrite saved not only the day but the project, too. Only later did someone ask the critical question: "Why do we need that feature?" Turns out it had sneaked into the requirements as a relic from an older system with very different hardware characteristics. The whole feature could safely be dropped.

The takeaway is that it doesn't matter how simple and clean our code is if we implement the wrong system. When investigating hotspots, always question the feature set. Could parts of the code be removed? Great. Less code is always better.

Spot Nested Logic That Taxes Working Memory

In Explore the Complexity Dimension, on page 25 you saw that the most popular code-level metrics are poor at capturing accidental complexity. The main reason is that cyclomatic complexity doesn't reveal much about the relative effort required to understand a piece of code. The metric cannot differentiate between code with repeatable patterns that are straightforward to reason about vs. truly messy implementations requiring cognitive effort to understand. Let's look at the next figure to see how misleading cyclomatic complexity can be.

Example A:
Code that can be read and understood without effort

```
switch choice {
    case 1:                              +1
        subscription = "small";
        break;

    case 2:                              +1
        subscription = "medium";
        break;

    case 3:                              +1
        subscription = "large";
        break;

    default:                             +1
        subscription = "unknown";
}
```

cyclomatic complexity 4

Example B:
Perhaps not rocket science, but still quite tricky and requires effort to understand.

```
if ( properties != null ) {                              +1
    boolean[] updateability = getPropertyUpdateability();
    int[] tableNumbers = getPropertyTableNumbers();

    for ( int property : properties ) {                  +1
        int table = tableNumbers[property];

        if ( getColumnSpan( property ) == 0 ) {          +1
            final Versioning v = getVersion(table);

            if ( v.supported(property) ) {               +1
                saveProperties(v, table);
            }
        }
    }
}
```

cyclomatic complexity 4

The two samples have the same measured complexity, yet there's a striking difference in perceived simplicity.

Instead, when on the hunt for complexity, consider the shape of the code, as you learned in Calculate Complexity Trends from Your Code's Shape, on page 49. Code with deep, nested logic heavily taxes your working memory.

To experience the problem, look at case B in the preceding figure and pretend you need to change the saveProperties() call. When making this change, all preceding if statements represent the program state you need to keep in your head. There are four branches in the code, meaning you're operating at the edge of your cognitive capacity while reasoning about this code, and you still need to find some mental room for the logic of the actual change. It's no wonder that things go wrong in nested code.

The cognitive costs of nested logic were confirmed in a comprehensive survey of software engineers at seven leading Swedish companies (such as Volvo, Ericsson, Axis). This survey reveals that nesting depth and a general lack of structure are the two issues that introduce the most perceived complexity when reading code, significantly more than the number of conditionals by itself. (See *A Pragmatic View on Code Complexity Management [ASS19]* for the full treatment.)

Fortunately, nested logic is straightforward to refactor by encapsulating each nested block within a well-named function, as shown in the next figure.

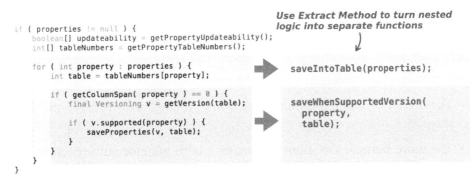

Stay Clear of Bumpy Roads

Nested logic might be problematic, but, as always, there are different levels in complexity hell. A more serious issue is the *bumpy road* code smell, nested logic's sinister cousin.

The bumpy road smell is a function with multiple chunks of nested conditional logic. Just like a bumpy road slows down your driving speed and comfort, a bumpy road in code presents an obstacle to comprehension. Worse, in imperative languages, there's also the increased risk of feature entanglement, leading to complex state management with bugs in its wake.

Bumpy roads are prevalent in code (it's what you get if you cut down on maintenance), and you'll find the issue in many hotspots independent of programming language. An illustrative example is the JavaScript function commitMutationEffectsOnFiber in React's ReactFiberCommitWork.old.js hotspot.[5] The next figure shows a small slice of the code.

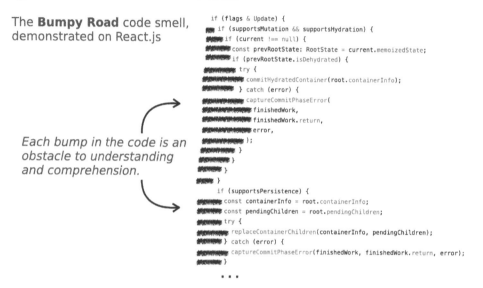

The **Bumpy Road** code smell, demonstrated on React.js

Each bump in the code is an obstacle to understanding and comprehension.

When inspecting bumpy roads, there's a set of heuristics for classifying the severity of the code smell:

- The deeper the nested logic in each bump, the higher the tax on working memory.

- The more bumps, the more expensive it is to refactor since each bump represents a missing abstraction.

- The larger the bumps—that is, the more lines of code they span—the harder it is to build up a mental model of the function.

Fundamentally, a bumpy code road represents a lack of encapsulation. Each bump tends to represent a responsibility or action. Hence, the initial remediation is the same as for deep nested logic: extract functions corresponding to the identified responsibilities to even out the road.

5. https://tinyurl.com/react-fiber-code2202

Before we continue our tour of code smells, let's take a step back and discuss method extraction. It's such a critical refactoring in laying the foundation for better designs to come.

Refactor Complex Code via Simple Steps

The code smells seen so far all stem from overly long classes and functions. Take ReactFiberCommitWork as a prominent example: its three central functions span 200 to 400 lines of code each. This raises the question: should we prefer many small methods—the logical outcome of the recommended refactorings—or is it better to keep related code in one large chunk?

The main advantage of modularizing a piece of code isn't that we get shorter functions. Rather, it's about transforming the context, as discussed in design to isolate change on page 68. By extracting cohesive, well-named functions, we introduce chunks into our design, as shown in the following figure. These chunks let us reason more effectively about the problem we're trying to solve, often suggesting more radical refactoring in the process.

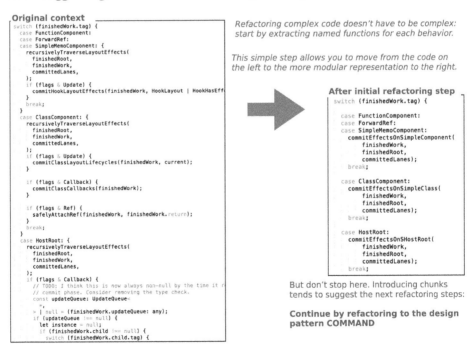

The preceding figure shows how introducing chunks in a complex hotspot reveals the overall intent of the code. The original implementation is high in complexity, with deep, nested logic paving an uncomfortably bumpy road. The mere act of extracting relevant methods delivers multiple benefits:

- *Isolate change*—The entanglement of the original code is like an open invitation to bugs and coding mistakes; we change one behavior, only to discover that we broke another seemingly unrelated feature. Modularizing the code serves to protect different features from each other. As a bonus, increased modularity clarifies the data dependencies.

- *Guide code reading*—Cohesive functions guide code reading since there's one obvious place to go for details on how a specific business rule is realized.

- *Reveal intent*—Extracting functions brings out the overall algorithm, which in turn suggests the deeper design changes that make the real difference. In the preceding example, the code starts to look like a match for the *command pattern* (See *Design Patterns: Elements of Reusable Object-Oriented Software [GHJV95].*) Replacing each case statement with an object would increase the cohesion and make the bulk of the function go away. There's nothing sweeter than deleting accidental complexity.

These refactoring steps and benefits can come across as overly simplistic at first. It's like we expect complex problems to always require complicated solutions. Yet, the simplicity of a refactoring like the Extract Method is deceiving since modeling the *right* behaviors and chunks is far from trivial. Refactoring requires domain expertise for finding the right abstractions and properly naming them.

Recognize Bad Names

Back in Understand That Typing Isn't the Bottleneck in Programming, on page 4, you learned that we spend most of our time trying to understand existing code. How we name our chunks of code is vital in that program comprehension process. As research shows, we try to infer the purpose of unfamiliar code by building up mental representations largely driven by reading the names of classes or functions. (See *Software Design: Cognitive Aspects [DB13]* for the empirical findings.)

This implies that a good name is descriptive and expresses intent. A good name also suggests a cohesive concept; remember, fewer responsibilities means fewer reasons to change. Bad names, on the other hand, are recognized by the following characteristics:

- Bad names carry little information and convey no hints to the purpose of the module, for example, StateManager (isn't state management what programming is about?) and Helper (a helper for what and whom?).

- A bad name is built with conjunctions, such as and, or, and so on. These are sure signs of low cohesion. Examples include ConnectionAndSessionPool (do connections and sessions express the same concept?) and FrameAndToolbarController (do the same rules really apply to both frames and toolbars?).

Bad names attract suffixes like lemonade draws wasps on a hot summer day. The immediate suspects are everything that ends with Manager, Util, or the dreaded Impl. Modules baptized like that are typically placeholders, but they end up housing core logic elements over time. You know they will hurt once you look inside.

Naming Object-Oriented Inheritance Hierarchies

Good interfaces express intent and suggest usage. Their implementations specify both what's specific and what's different about the concrete instances. Say we create an intention-revealing interface: ChatConnection. (Yes, I did it—I dropped the cognitive distractor, the I prefix.) Let each implementation of this interface specify what makes it unique: SynchronousTcpChatConnection, AsynchronousTcpChatConnection, and so on.

Optimize for Your Brain, Not a Metric

Code smells, like large functions, complex logic, fuzzy names, and bumpy roads, are mere symptoms of an underlying problem: lack of encapsulation. Refactoring complex code is very much an iterative process. Start simple and reduce error-prone constructs step-by-step to align the code with how your brain prefers it. And remember that modularization is a start, not the end.

Never base the decision to split a method on length but on behavior and meaningful abstractions. Splitting functions based on thresholds alone makes the code worse, not better; code that belongs together should stay together. Always.

That said, a general heuristic like "max 30 lines of code per function," as recommended by David Farley in *Modern Software Engineering [Far22]*, still serves well as an alert system: the longer the method, the more likely it's lacking in abstraction. Just remember to treat the limit as the heuristic it is, and optimize for your brain, not a measure.

Evade Object Disorientation

As you investigate hotspots, you'll likely encounter several violations of the principles of information hiding and encapsulation, often more subtle than the code smells seen so far. Two common offenses are *primitive obsession* and breaking the *Law of Demeter*. Let's discuss them in detail since both problems serve as an open invitation for letting more complexity into our code.

Avoid Primitive Obsession

Quick, how many times have you come across code similar to the next listing?

```
boolean changePassword(
  String userName,
  String existingPassword,
  String newPassword) {
  ...
}
```

The preceding code uses a String for representing two separate domain concepts, which is a poor choice in any API and just reflects a wider problem. Overuse of built-in types like strings and integers leads to primitive obsession, a code smell with several drawbacks:

- *Poor communication*—A String doesn't reveal anything about its intent or purpose. Except for user names, a generic String could carry anything from Latin flower names to the secret codes for launching nukes. We'd better not get them mixed up, yet there's nothing in the code that guides a maintenance programmer toward either the proper use or its purpose.

- *Breaks encapsulation*—Primitive types in method signatures drive accidental complexity since any validation has to be performed in application code. Consequently, should the business rules change, we have to do shotgun surgery when hunting down all impacted usages across the codebase.

- *Short-circuits the type system*—One selling point of statically typed languages is that the compiler can catch mistakes early. This advantage is lost the moment we express separate domain concepts using the same general data type.

- *Security vulnerabilities*—Primitive types fail to restrict the value range—String, Integer, or Double can contain virtually anything. This makes it impractical to run dynamic tests, which could otherwise detect critical issues early in your build pipeline. Further, primitive types make it too easy to inadvertently dump sensitive data into logs and diagnostics.

Let's look at one more example from a news feed implementation to highlight how primitive obsession hampers readability:

```
public ActionResult ListRss(int languageId) {
  ...
}

public ActionResult NewsItem(int newsItemId) {
  ...
}
```

"Language" and "News" are clearly different domain concepts with separate business rules and user behavior, yet the code fails to capture these distinctions.

Primitive obsession is remediated by introducing domain types expressing code in the language of your domain. Not only do you raise the level of abstraction, but when used in function signatures, domain types liberate the variable name so that it can be used to communicate context. It's an important advantage, so let's see what the preceding code would look like with proper types:

```
// Look, now that our types capture the domain, we're free to use
// the argument name to communicate context which guides the code
// readers coming after us.
public ActionResult ListRss(Language preferredRssFeedLanguage) {
  ...
}

// We do the same thing with the NewsItem, and can now also
// rest assured that nobody accidentally mixes the different
// IDs; these are mere implementation details, encapsulated
// within our domain types.
public ActionResult NewsItem(NewsItem clickedHeader) {
  ...
}
```

The combination of increased readability and added type safety makes a strong argument for domain types. Use them in all public function signatures.

Follow the Law of Demeter

The Law of Demeter (LoD) is a design principle for object-oriented code, summed up beautifully in the maxim of "Don't talk to strangers." (See *Assuring good style for object-oriented programs [LH89]*.) Within this context, you talk to a stranger each time you invoke a method on objects returned by another method or access data properties contained in other objects.

Adopting the LoD principle helps ensure loosely coupled designs by limiting the assumptions on your code's dependencies. Let's clarify via a real-world example from ASP.NET Core, a framework for building web applications:[6]

```
if (!viewContext.ViewData.ModelState.ContainsKey(fullName) &&
    formContext == null) {
    return null;
}
var tryGetModelStateResult =
    viewContext.ViewData.ModelState.TryGetValue(
                                        fullName,
                                        out var entry);
...
```

The preceding code queries deep into a ViewData object, first accessing a ModelState to invoke a ContainsKey method. Should the query succeed, the code traverses the same chain again, but this time fetching the value associated with the fullName key. By doing so, we have coupled the code to three attributes of separate objects and leaked the implementation detail that ModelState contains a dictionary. Not only does it breach the principle of information hiding, but it also puts the code at risk for cascading changes. Violating the Law of Demeter creates a coding style reminiscent of Jack the Ripper: reach for the interiors and dig them out. (Disclaimer: no objects were harmed in this case study.)

You address this code smell by moving and encapsulating the relevant behavior to the object owning the data. In the preceding example, querying the model state should probably not be done at all. Rather, a design pattern like *State* or even *Strategy* would let you delegate any stateful operations to another object. By aligning the code with the LoD principle, you no longer need to know the implementation details of how model states are stored or if retrieving them involves interactions with further objects. Following the Law of Demeter is a path to modular and well-encapsulated code. Use it to your advantage.

Code Smells Combine

 When left unmitigated, code smells in hotspots tend to worsen and eventually become more serious concerns. Methods with Bumpy Road logic frequently accumulate more responsibilities, making them dependent on an increasing amount of instance variables. In time, such methods become a *Brain Method* aka a *God Function*.

---

6.   https://github.com/code-as-a-crime-scene/aspnetcore

Code Smells Combine

Brain Methods are large and complicated functions that centralize the behavior of the enclosing module, making them painful time sinks for the development team. While the remedies are the same as outlined in this chapter, the refactoring work is more challenging and high-risk, even with proper test coverage—an admittedly rare property of code with severe issues. Anything you can do to catch growing problems early is valuable.

Use Abstraction as a Tool for Thinking

We started this chapter by visiting Luria's compassionate portrait of S.—the man with limitless memory. The typical human memory is radically different from what S. experienced. For starters, most humans don't recall precise information but instead focus on the key elements of a message. The software design principles in this chapter all stem from such human imperfection; design compensates for cognitive bottlenecks, including, but not limited to, our fallible memory.

Still, software design does more than compensate; it enables. A good design allows us to reason about both problems and solutions so that we can refine our code, generalize to patterns, and adapt to new challenges from there. This continuous cognitive process reflects learning and won't happen without an enabling abstraction. Abstraction is key to being able to memorize and understand a domain.

Now that you are familiar with the common code smells, you have the tools to talk about technical issues with your engineering peers. What's missing is the business impact. Refactoring complex hotspots takes time, and adding new features will have to temporarily take a backseat. Communicating this trade-off to non-technical stakeholders—product owners and management—is vital for avoiding stress and aligning expectations across the organization. In the next chapter, you'll take on this challenge. But first, try the following exercises to apply what you've learned in this chapter.

Exercises

The code smells in this chapter are language agnostic, but illustrating them on real-world code means you might have to look at a language you are unfamiliar with. That said, I've tried to identify examples that stick to general programming concepts. As always, remember to check out the Appendix 1, Solutions to the Exercises, on page 267 for pointers and additional advice.

Hollywood's Calling

- Repository: https://github.com/code-as-a-crime-scene/tensorflow
- Language: Python
- Domain: TensorFlow is a platform for state-of-the-art machine learning.
- Analysis snapshot: https://tinyurl.com/tensorflow-hotspots

tensor_tracer.py is a Python file containing several instances of nested logic. Take a look at the code starting at line 2145.[7] There's a common pattern where a function query is used to determine the conditional path, and hence, the behavior to execute.

```python
if self._use_tensor_values_cache() or self._use_tensor_buffer():
    if self._use_temp_cache():
        # Create the temporary tf cache variable by concatenating all
        # statistics.
        graph_cache_var = self._cache_variable_for_graph(graph)
        if graph not in self._temp_cache_var:
            ...
```

The problem is similar to the Law of Demeter violations discussed earlier. How would you refactor this code?

Hint: There's a beautiful solution summed up in the Hollywood Principle[8] of "Don't call us, we'll call you."

Simplify a Simple Button

- Repository: https://github.com/code-as-a-crime-scene/lightspark
- Language: C++
- Domain: Lightspark is an open-source Flash player implementation.
- Analysis snapshot: https://tinyurl.com/lightspark-hotspots

The main hotspot in Lightspark is the C++ file flashdisplay.cpp. Let's turn our investigative eyes to the constructor for the SimpleButton class at lines 5625 to 5661.[9]

```cpp
SimpleButton::SimpleButton(
  ASWorker* wrk,
  Class_base* c,
  DisplayObject *dS,
  DisplayObject *hTS,
  DisplayObject *oS,
  DisplayObject *uS,
```

---

7. http://tinyurl.com/tensorflow-2145
8. https://wiki.c2.com/?HollywoodPrinciple
9. http://tinyurl.com/flash-display-5625

```
   DefineButtonTag *tag)
        // slightly simplified to highlight the relevant section
        // for the exercise
{
        subtype = SUBTYPE_SIMPLEBUTTON;
        if(dS)
        {
                dS->advanceFrame();
                if (!dS->loadedFrom->needsActionScript3())
                        dS->declareFrame();
                dS->initFrame();
        }
        if(hTS)
        {
                hTS->advanceFrame();
                if (!hTS->loadedFrom->needsActionScript3())
                        hTS->declareFrame();
                hTS->initFrame();
        }
        if(oS)
        {
        ...
```

Which design issues can you detect here? Can you suggest a mitigating refactoring, ideally in multiple safe steps as discussed in *Refactor Complex Code via Simple Steps*, on page 73?

CHAPTER 7

Communicate the Business Impact of Technical Debt

Now that you know how to identify hotspots, determine complexity trends, and remediate complicated code, it's a good time to stop and address technical debt. But what is technical debt? Technical debt is a consequence of accidental complexity, resulting in code that's more expensive to maintain than it should be. Just like a financial loan, this means we pay interest. If our code is hard to understand, each modification comes with an increased cost and risk: longer coding time and more bugs. No fun.

You already know how hotspots drive the priorities on *what* to fix, as well as the consequences of bad code, the *why*, in technical terms. To make it relevant to non-technical managers, you need to rephrase the *why* in metrics that carry meaning for the business. Connecting code-level diagnosis to outcomes like time-to-market, customer satisfaction, and road-map risks gives you a vocabulary for communicating tradeoffs to non-technical stakeholders. This enables us, as developers, to make a business case for technical improvements and large-scale refactoring based on business impact. Let's start by diving into why companies are doing such a poor job at managing technical debt today.

Know the Costs and Consequences of Technical Debt

In the late 2010s, we finally got research numbers on the impact of technical debt. The numbers vary depending on which study you read. They all paint a pretty depressing picture: organizations waste 23 to 42 percent of developers' time dealing with the consequences of technical debt and bad code in general (*Software developer productivity loss due to technical debt [BMB19]*).

As a thought experiment, let's consider what 42 percent waste implies. Say we have a department with 100 software engineers. If we waste 42 percent of their time, all else being equal, we end up with an output corresponding to just 58 developers, an efficiency loss that would be unacceptable in virtually any other context than software. Unfortunately, even this estimated productivity loss is overly optimistic: an organization having 100 developers will always require more overhead than another organization that can deliver the same outcome with just 58 people.

Given that our industry faces a global shortage of software developers, wasting half of their time sounds like a poor choice, and you'd expect IT managers around the world to have technical debt at the very top of their agendas. As you've probably witnessed firsthand, this is not really what's happening. Instead, studies confirm that development teams are pushed to introduce even more technical debt as companies keep trading code quality for short-term gains like new features. It's a no-win situation, so let's look into the psychology of the problem so we can change the situation.

Technical Debt Is a Growing Problem

The first edition of *Your Code as a Crime Scene* only discussed technical debt in passing. Back then, in 2014, the term wasn't widely adopted, and most IT managers I spoke to hadn't come across the metaphor. Fast forward a decade, and you're hard-pressed to find a technical manager who isn't conscious of technical debt. Technical debt, as a concept, is now in mainstream use, and my hypothesis is that technical debt will keep gaining importance in the years to come. At the time of writing, in late 2022, the world was heading into an economic downturn, meaning we could no longer compensate for waste by continuously hiring more people. Companies need to get more done with existing or even reduced staff, which makes it more important than ever to pay down technical debt.

Understand Why Short-Term Gains Win Over Sustainable Solutions

Within forensic psychology, almost any model for crime prediction includes the individual's time preferences. Years of research have shown that individuals with short time horizons face higher risks of criminal involvement simply because they can reap the rewards of the crime here and now, whereas the punishment lies in an indefinite future. (See *Time discounting and criminal behavior [ÅGGL16]* for the latest research.)

The omnipresent mismanagement of technical debt stems from a similar mindset; there's a crucial difference in feedback timing on software projects, too:

- Launching a new feature delivers immediate rewards such as providing satisfied customers (or at least less angry ones), securing a new client, or even allowing us to enter a new market. Quick wins on the short time horizon.

- On the other hand, the feedback from growing technical debt is slow, and once we notice the symptoms, it might already be too late to act.

This difference in feedback timing is an open invitation to a decision-making bias known as *hyperbolic discounting*. Hyperbolic discounting happens when we make choices today that our future selves are going to regret. We might have that extra drink at the conference party despite a scheduled business meeting the morning after, or we may choose to add that extra if statement to an already complex function. (See the original write-up on the bias in *Hyperbolic discounting [AH92]*.)

Hyperbolic discounting is frequently used to explain the psychology of addiction. It's also, coincidentally, the best explanation of why companies fail to manage technical debt: just like the addict, we trade our future well-being—a healthy codebase—for the lure of the next quick fix and short-term reward. Or, in the words of Mel Conway: "There's never enough time to do something right, but there's always enough time to do it over" (quote from *How do committees invent? [Con68]*).

To counter the hyperbolic discounting bias, we need to provide timely feedback to prime decision-makers to think about the future in terms of risk. Sounds simple, yet with something as technical as, well, technical debt, there are multiple challenges:

1. *Code is abstract*—If we developers struggle with understanding code ourselves, how can we expect a non-programming manager to understand the intricacies of software complexity? Code was never meant to be a universal language.

2. *Code lacks visibility*—Code is a product of our imagination, meaning it lacks physics. We cannot pick up a large codebase, turn it around, and inspect it for flaws and technical debt.

3. *Code quality is low on the business agenda*—During my decades in the software industry, every company I've worked with paid lip service to the idea that code quality is important. Yet, once a deadline hits the fan, code quality is the first thing to go. It's too easy to dismiss code quality as a

technical concern, and consequently, it fails to get traction at the business level. As you can see in the following image, combining the first two challenges creates a powerful dynamic that feeds into the third challenge.

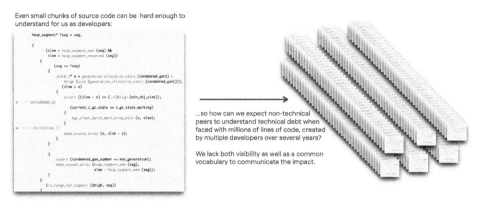

Let's take on the challenge by visiting some brand-new research on code quality.

Know Why Half the Work Gets Done in Twice the Time

The research discussed so far does a good job of quantifying technical debt's general impact. However, even if a hypothetical business manager knows that their industry throws away half of their developers' time, those numbers aren't actionable since a) they don't know what their own waste is, b) they cannot see the future risks, and c) they have no way of measuring it even if they wanted to. Hence, technical debt won't be an immediate concern until they feel the pain, similar to when the doctor tells you to eat more vegetables, cut down on the wine, and get some exercise—hyperbolic discounting deluxe.

In 2022, I teamed up with software researcher Markus Borg in an attempt to change the situation by assessing the business impact of technical debt down to the code level. To ensure a representative sample, we started by collecting data from 39 proprietary codebases spanning a wide range of industry segments, such as retail, construction, infrastructure, brokerage, and data analysis. It's also important to know that the data could generalize across implementation technologies, so the study included codebases implemented in 14 different programming languages (Python, C++, JavaScript, C#, Java, Go, and so on). All companies consented to participate in the study and provided access to their source code repositories and Jira product data. (See the full research paper for details: *Code Red: The Business Impact of Code Quality–A Quantitative Study of 39 Proprietary Production Codebases [TB22]*.)

The dataset for our *Code Red* research collected three key measures for each software module in the included codebases:

1. *A proxy for code quality*—The research used the *Code Health* concept as a proxy for code quality.[1] Code Health is an aggregated metric based on 25+ factors scanned from the source code. These factors are known to make code harder to comprehend, and you met the most important issues—low cohesion, nested logic, bumpy roads, primitive obsession—back in Chapter 6, Remediate Complicated Code, on page 63.

2. *The Time-in-Development per file*—Time-in-Development is the time a developer needs to implement the code associated with a Jira backlog item. The study calculated it as the time between an issue moving to an "In Progress" state until the last commit referencing the Jira issue is completed.

3. *The number of defects per file*—Similar to Time-in-Development, combining version-control information with Jira data makes it possible to calculate the number of defects per file in terms of known, and hence confirmed, bug fixes.

As illustrated from top to bottom on the right side of the following figure, each source code file is categorized as being either Green (healthy code that's easy to understand), Yellow (code with several code smells), or Red (highly complex code). This aggregation of multiple code-level issues is key; we simply cannot measure a multifaceted concept, like code quality, by a single metric. (See the scientific rationale in *Software measurement: A necessary scientific basis* [Fen94].)

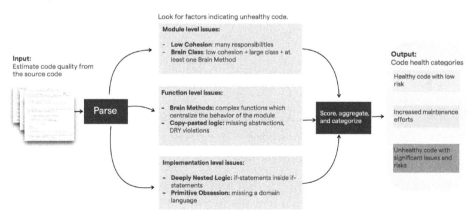

---

1.   https://codescene.io/docs/guides/technical/code-health.html

Now that you know how the study was designed, we're ready to take on the big unknown. You see, everyone in the software industry "knows" that code quality is important, yet—surprisingly—we've never had any studies or numbers to prove the claim. Let's remove the quotation marks and turn "knows" into *knows*.

All Findings Are Statistically Significant

All findings quoted from the Code Red paper are statistically significant. In layperson's terms, the results are unlikely to be just a fluke or randomness in the data. This is important: money, jobs, and people's work satisfaction are at stake when advising on professional software development. The software profession is still a relatively young field that needs more facts and fewer opinions.

Result 1: Implement a Feature Twice as Fast

The first part of the Code Red study looked at throughput in terms of task completion times. The results are quite dramatic, showing that implementing a Jira task in Green code is 124 percent faster than in Red code, as shown in the following figure. And, this relationship holds even for tasks of similar scope and size.

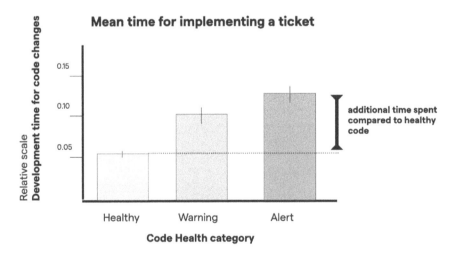

Translated to a business context, this finding relates to speed to market. If your company can implement a new feature in 2.5 months in Red code, then a potential competitor with Green code can get the same capability in less than a month. It's going to be impossible to keep up.

Result 2: Features Can Take an Order of Magnitude Longer

The previous data point on speed to market probably didn't come as a surprise. After all, we "know" that code quality is important, and the graph confirms a productivity cost associated with poor-quality code. However, averages can be misleading, so the next part of the study looked at variations in task completion times. Instead of looking at the mean Time-in-Development, the study investigated the maximum time for implementing a feature across the thousands of modules in the dataset.

As shown in the following figure, the maximum time for implementing a task in Green code doesn't deviate much from its average completion time. Contrast this with the Red code, where a task can vary by almost an order of magnitude.

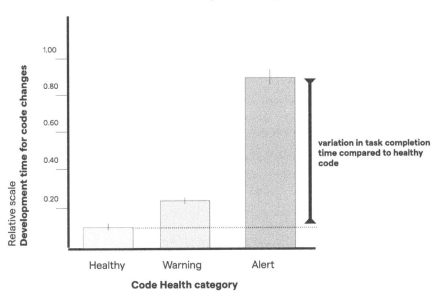

This wide variance leads to uncertainty in completion times, and uncertainty is a property that few people enjoy. Imagine a sales representative who, after checking with the product manager, promises a new customer: "Sign with us, and you'll have this feature in a month." Now, if their code is Red, the risk is the feature takes nine to ten months rather than the estimated one month. Both the sales rep and product manager are going to look really bad.

When we put on our developer hats, we also don't like uncertainty. Uncertainty is causing us stress, overtime, and missed deadlines, a topic which we return to in Learn How Bad Code Causes Unhappiness: The Scientific Link, on page 216.

Result 3: Red Code Is a Bug Magnet

The previous two graphs let you quantify the waste in terms of throughput and uncertainty, but working in unhealthy code is also a high-risk activity in terms of defects. The next figure shows the consequences are quite dramatic: Red code has, on average, fifteen times more defects than healthy code.

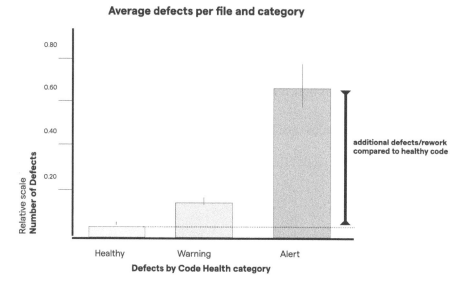

Error-prone code adds another business dimension, namely, customer satisfaction. A high degree of defects will also strike back at the development team in the shape of unplanned work, which in turn causes additional waste via context switches, a topic we'll return to on page 94.

Make the Business Case for Refactoring

Quantifying the inherent risk in low-quality code enables balanced discussions on the tradeoffs between adding more features vs. investing time into paying down technical debt. Even better, you will be able to have those conversations in terms that business people understand. That way, we, as developers, can finally build a business case for refactoring to get everyone on board for the mythical "buy-in."

The first step toward this business case is to assess the health of your codebase, and there are multiple options. You can either keep track of it manually by checking for a combination of code smells from Chapter 6, Remediate Complicated Code, on page 63, or you can automate the task using a code analysis tool. (There's a comprehensive list of options at Wikipedia's list of code analysis tools.[2])

Avoid Technical Jargon

The moment you drop a line like "this code needs refactoring because it has a cyclomatic complexity of 152," you lose the attention of any business manager (and probably most programmers, too). Instead, look to simplify the vocabulary. The three categories—Red, Yellow, and Green—reflect this simplification. There's obviously a range of badness within each category, but those are mere details when reasoning about risk and waste. In fact, this is just like a forensic expert presenting evidence to a jury that probably doesn't want a complete chemistry lesson but clear information. Just like these forensic psychologists, you need to make your message understandable to all without diluting it.

As we did with hotspots, visualizing the results provides a brain-friendly overview that's accessible to non-technical stakeholders. The enclosure diagrams you used in Chapter 4, Hotspots Applied: Visualize Code from the People Side, on page 33 work well in this context, too; you just replace the change frequency data with the selected code quality proxy. The figure on page 92 shows an example from Folly, a C++ component library.[3]

Armed with this data, you're ready to communicate with non-technical stakeholders about something as deeply technical as code. Let's explore each main use case.

Let Refactoring Come with a Business Expectation

Earlier in this chapter, we discussed how code quality gets dismissed as a technical concern, sacrificed on the altar of urgent user-facing work. This becomes painfully obvious in a study of 15 large software organizations, where the benefit of paying down technical debt wasn't clear, with the consequence that most managers wouldn't grant the necessary budget, nor priorities, for much-needed refactoring. (See *Technical debt tracking: Current state of practice: A survey and multiple case study in 15 large organizations [MBB18]*.)

This failure to continuously invest in refactoring isn't from incompetence, ignorance, or even malice. Most business leaders want to do the right thing and value our technical expertise. We simply need to support them by

---

2. https://en.wikipedia.org/wiki/List_of_tools_for_static_code_analysis
3. https://tinyurl.com/folly-code-health

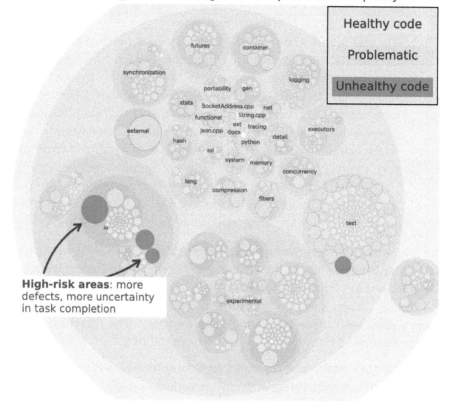

Visualizing the strong and weak parts in the Folly codebase using enclosure diagrams to represent code quality.

translating gains from increasing code quality into concrete business value. The findings from the Code Red study on page 86 provide the foundation: with 15 times fewer bugs and twice the development speed, existing capacity is freed to fuel innovation and product growth. This is a clear and quantifiable advantage to any business, implying that refactoring can now come with a business expectation. Here are the recommended steps:

1. *Get attention*—Start by summarizing the consequences of Red code, preferring the outcome-oriented vocabulary (for example, time-to-market, rework, customer satisfaction) over technical jargon.

2. *Create situational awareness*—Now that the general consequences are understood, give all stakeholders—development, product, management—the same situational awareness of where the strong and weak parts are in your codebase. Make the data easily digestible by visualizing the technical debt as we did for Folly on page 92.

3. *Focus on relevant parts*—Not all code is equally important, so distinguish between low- and high-interest technical debt based on the hotspot criteria. In particular, communicate that even a minor amount of technical debt in a hotspot is expensive due to the high frequency of code changes. It's the engineering equivalent of a payday loan.

4. *Set the expectations*—Explain that moving from Red to Green code gives us all these advantages. In particular, reducing uncertainty in task completion time greatly benefits all organizations.

Of course, it's important that we also deliver on these promises, and we'll look at ways of visualizing the outcome in Fight Unplanned Work, the Silent Killer of Projects, on page 94. Before we go there, let's cover one more use case enabled by the Code Red findings.

Counter Hyperbolic Discounting via Risk-Based Planning

Within psychology, *priming* describes the phenomenon of exposure to some stimulus, which then unconsciously influences future responses and actions. Fighting hyperbolic discounting is largely about priming decision-makers' awareness of long-term risks. You achieve this by incorporating code health views in existing practices such as retrospectives or planning meetings. Let's look at an example from Folly.

Pretend we're working on the Folly codebase, and your development team sits down with the product manager to decide on priorities. Your product manager brings up two features for discussion, as you can see in the following figure.

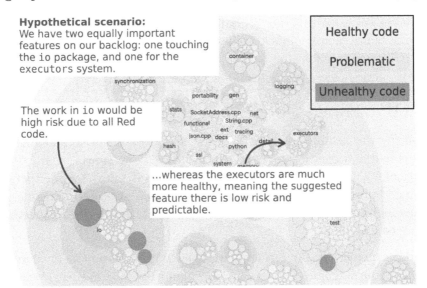

As the preceding visualization shows, one suggested feature involves a high-risk area, whereas the other doesn't. This is vital information for planning with risk in mind, leading to three possible outcomes:

1. *Accept the risk*—We know there's uncertainty in the task completion time, but we could choose to accept the risk. The difference compared to how it usually goes is that the whole team is now aware of the risk and can plan accordingly, avoiding the stress of unrealistic deadlines.

2. *Prioritize low-risk work*—Another alternative is to go ahead with a low-risk feature instead. This is a viable option in all scenarios where multiple features have equal value to your customers.

3. *Mitigate the risk*—Finally, in the best of all worlds, you'd take this as a call to action for refactoring the problematic io package in Folly so that future work is simplified and safe.

Make Technical Debt Tangible to Executives

The lack of technical debt awareness is an issue for higher-level management, too. Perhaps the company executives want to take your product to a new market, but you know that the in-house-built payment system is a mess, making it painful to adapt to other currencies and market rules. Or there's pressure to continue adding capabilities to a legacy codebase that has received little refactoring love over the past decade. Pushing ahead in such situations will likely send your organization spiraling into a death-march project.

Explaining this risk is challenging if your company executives or board members lack deeper technical skills. The techniques and data from this chapter help you communicate the problem to your stakeholders. Visualizations are key.

Fight Unplanned Work, the Silent Killer of Projects

Visualizing the health of your codebase offers an actionable starting point and a potential trigger for paying down technical debt. However, any organization looking to improve its delivery efficiency has to take a broader perspective. In addition to the technical improvements, you also need to reshape the engineering and collaborative strategies to ensure no new bottlenecks are introduced.

All of these changes are investments that take time, meaning we need to bring visibility to the outcome to ensure improvements have a real effect. Measuring trends in unplanned work offers a simple solution by complementing the code-level metrics with a higher-level perspective.

Unplanned work is anything you didn't anticipate or plan for, such as bug fixes, service interruptions, or flawed software designs causing excess rework. By its very nature, unplanned work leads to stress and unpredictability, transforming a company into a reactive instead of a proactive entity. In fact, in *The Phoenix Project: A Novel about IT, DevOps, and Helping Your Business Win [KBS18]*—a wonderful and highly recommended read—Gene Kim describes unplanned work as being "the silent killer of IT companies." Let's see how to use the concept for communicating expectations and future improvements.

Adding More People Cannot Compensate for Waste

 When a company accumulates technical debt, the business increasingly experiences symptoms, commonly in the form of Jira tickets moving at a depressingly slow rate. The gut response is a cry for more developers, more testers, more of everything. Yet losing predictability is a sure sign that more people isn't the solution. In See That a Man-Month Is Still Mythical, on page 198, you will learn how adding more people will probably exacerbate the situation.

Open Up the IT Blackbox by Measuring Unplanned Work

Most organizations track unplanned work indirectly via product life-cycle management tools like Jira, Azure DevOps, or Trello. This makes it possible to calculate the ratio of planned vs. unplanned work over time. You just need to agree on which issue types represent unplanned work.

The figure on page 96 shows an example from a real-world project in crisis. Looking at the trend, you see that the nature of the delivered work has shifted over time, and the organization now spends 60 percent of its capacity on reactive, unplanned work. There's also an overall decline in throughput, meaning less work gets completed than earlier in the year.

Focusing the presentation on trends makes the waste obvious: no organization wants to do worse today than it did yesterday. Let's put the amount of unplanned work into context by quantifying the waste.

Calculate the Untapped Capacity Tied Up in Technical Debt

We can never eliminate unplanned work, but we still need a reliable target for putting our numbers into context. A good baseline for unplanned work is 15 percent, which is what high-performing organizations achieve in terms of

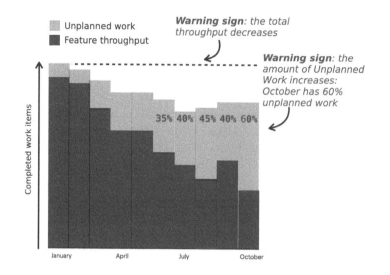

bug fixes. (See *Accelerate: The Science of Lean Software and DevOps: Building and Scaling High Performing Technology Organizations [FHK18]*.) With the 15 percent baseline indicating the acceptable amount of unplanned work, we can now sketch out the following formula:

```
Waste (%) = UnplannedWork% — 0.15
UntappedCapacity ($) = Ndevelopers * AverageSalary * Waste
```

Let's run the formula using the data from the unplanned work trend for the project in crisis in the figure as an example. The figure shows that they spent roughly 60 percent on unplanned work during the last month. Assuming an average European software developer salary, we can estimate the untapped potential by filling in the numbers in our formula:

```
// Assuming an average salary of 5.000 Euros/month.
// With payroll tax and benefits, the employer pays ~7,500 Euros.
// Now, the project had 35 developers.
Waste (%) = 0.60 — 0.15 = 45%
UntappedCapacity: 35 * 7,500 * 0.45 =  118,125€ / month
```

This exercise reveals the potential when unplanned work is minimized: it would mean the equivalent of 15(!) additional full-time developers. These are not new hires; by reducing the amount of unplanned work, you free up developers to focus on actual planned work, which moves your product forward. The added bonus is that those 15 developers come with no extra coordination cost since they are already in the company. How good is that? It's hard to argue with the promise, particularly when it's your data.

Use Quality to Go Fast

Getting more done without hiring more people is a clear competitive advantage. Yet, too many companies in the industry seem to share a commonly held belief that high-quality code is expensive. You detect this mindset each time you hear a "no" as a response to a suggested technical improvement: we might not "have time" for refactoring, test automation, architectural redesigns, and so forth—you know, the usual suspects. It's like there is a supposed tradeoff between speed and quality, where choosing one negatively influences the other.

However, as indicated by the data you met in this chapter, there doesn't seem to be such a tradeoff. In fact, the contrary seems to be true: we need quality to go fast. Use that to your advantage.

Differentiate Remediation Time from Interest Payments

The software industry has seen previous attempts at quantifying technical debt, often by (mis-) using metrics such as the *Software Maintainability Index [WS01]* or *SQALE [LC09]*. While these methods might be valuable to assess the source code itself, they lack the relevance dimension and connection to the actual business impact. Remember, the cost of technical debt is *never* the time needed to fix the code—the remediation work—but rather the continuous additional development work due to technical issues.

Measuring trends in unplanned work lets you quantify this, and combining those trends with code-health visualizations allows you to break down the impact to individual modules to make the data actionable.

Finally, when discussing metrics and outcomes, we also need to touch on the DevOps Research & Assessment (DORA), which established the Four Key Metrics (FKM): change lead time, deployment frequency, mean time to restore, and change fail percentage.[4] In their research, the DORA team showed that these metrics are solid leading indicators for how the organization as a whole is doing.

The DORA metrics work well with this chapter's techniques. As you see in the figure on page 98, FKM focuses on the delivery side, while this book focuses on the earlier steps in the software development cycle: the waste introduced when the code is written. At the end of the day, you need both. It's hard to go fast if you don't go well.

---

4. https://www.devops-research.com/research.html

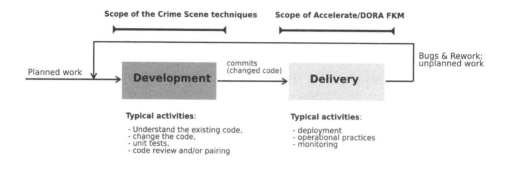

These days, efficient software development is a competitive advantage, enabling companies to maintain a short time-to-market with a mature product experience. Armed with a new vocabulary grounded in research, you can now assess the current waste and—most importantly—know how to communicate it to the business. From here, you're ready to expand the concepts from this first part of the book to the level of software architecture. In Part II, you'll see how the crime-scene techniques scale to the system level. But first, try the following exercises to apply what you've learned in this chapter.

Exercises

The following exercises give you the opportunity to pick up unfamiliar code-bases, assess the technical debt impact, and communicate the findings to a hypothetical non-technical peer.

Understand the Acceptable Risk

- Repository: https://tinyurl.com/github-react-repo
- Language: JavaScript
- Domain: React is a UI library.
- Analysis snapshot: https://tinyurl.com/react-code-health

It's time for your weekly planning meeting on the React core team. You sit in your chair, lean back comfortably, and listen in as the PM shares the latest priorities. Right now, two hypothetical features are on the roadmap, and both are equally important. One feature involves work in the react-devtools-timeline component, while the other is a deeper change to the react-reconciler. Which one would you choose to do first if a predictable delivery is of the essence? Motivate your choice.

Motivate a Larger Refactoring

- Repository: https://tinyurl.com/github-mattermost-repo
- Language: Go
- Domain: Mattermost is a platform for secure collaboration.
- Analysis snapshot: https://tinyurl.com/mattermost-code-health

Let's pretend you're on the Mattermost team. Some parts of the application are more painful to work on than others. Motivate a refactoring in the model package using the steps from Let Refactoring Come with a Business Expectation, on page 91. To keep it simple, focus on one specific file as a refactoring candidate.

Spot the Symptoms of Technical Debt

In this chapter, you saw how technical debt leads to excess unplanned work. However, technical debt impacts other aspects of software development, too. As is often the case with something as technical as code, the organization tends to notice symptoms, not the root cause. What are those symptoms which we have to be attentive to? Yes, it's an open-ended question, so remember to check out Appendix 1, Solutions to the Exercises, on page 267 for one take on the problem.

Part II

Build Supportive Software Architectures

Part I showed you how to identify offending code in your system. Now we'll look at the bigger picture.

In this part, you'll learn to evaluate your software architecture against the modifications you make to your code. The techniques let you identify signs of structural decay, provide refactoring directions, and suggest new modular boundaries in your design. And it all starts with forensics. Let's see what an innocent robber can teach us about software design.

CHAPTER 8

Use Code as a Cooperative Witness

In Part I, we looked at how to detect hotspots in code, which is the ideal starting point. The next step is to look at the bigger picture as we transition from inspecting individual modules to analyzing complete software architectures. Ultimately, you'll be able to assess how well the high-level design of your codebase supports the evolution of the system you're building so you can know if the architecture is more of a hindrance than a help.

To analyze architectures, we need to look beyond individual files and understand how they interact to form a system. We start by taking inspiration from a forensic psychology case study on eyewitness interviews. This case study is applicable beyond police work since it illustrates common memory biases and why we need to support our decisions with objective data. We then apply the concept to software design to visualize how a change to one component leads to a cascade of complex changes in other parts of the code. Let's get going by dipping into the fascinating field of false memories.

Recognize the Paradox of False Memories

Human memory is everything but precise, and it frequently deceives us. Nowhere is that as clear as in the scary studies on *false memories*.

A false memory sounds like a paradox at first: if I remember something and am confident in my memory, how could it be "false"? Well, sorry to potentially disappoint you, but confidence has nothing to do with accuracy or, as we'll soon see, reality.

False memories happen when we remember a situation or an event differently from how it looked or occurred. It's a common phenomenon that is usually harmless. Perhaps you remember rain on your first day of school while, in fact, the sun shone. Under some circumstances, particularly in criminal investigations, when there's life and freedom at stake, false memories can have serious consequences. Innocent people have gone to jail.

There are multiple reasons why we experience false memories. First, our memory is constructive, meaning the information we get *after* an event can shape how we recall the original situation. Our memory organizes the new information together with the old information, and we forget when we acquired each detail or insight.

Our memory is also sensitive to suggestibility. In witness interviews, leading questions can alter how the person recalls the original event. Worse, we may trust false memories even when explicitly warned about potential misinformation. And if we get positive feedback on our false recall, our future confidence in the (false) memory increases.

Keep a Decision Log

In software, we can always look back at the code and verify our assumptions. But the code doesn't record the whole story. Your recollection of why you did something or chose a particular solution is also sensitive to bias and misinformation. That's why I recommend keeping a decision log to record the rationale behind larger design decisions. The mind is a strange place.

Meet the Innocent Robber

The constructive nature of memory implies that our recollections are often sketchy, and we fill out the details ourselves as we recall things. This process makes memories sensitive to biases. This is something Father Pagano learned the hard way.

Back in 1979, several towns in Delaware and Pennsylvania were struck by a series of robberies. The salient characteristic of these robberies was the perpetrator's polite manners. Several witnesses, including both bystanders and clerks, identified a priest named Father Pagano as the robber. Case solved, right?

Father Pagano probably would have gone to jail if it hadn't been for the true robber, Roland Clouser, and his dramatic confession. Clouser appeared during the trial and confessed his deeds, and Father Pagano walked free. Let's look behind the scenes to see why all the witnesses were wrong.

Reduce Bias When Interviewing Cooperative Witnesses

Roland Clouser and Father Pagano looked nothing alike. So, what led the witnesses to make their erroneous statements?

First of all, the offender's key trait was his politeness, which many people associate with a priest. To make things worse, the police had made their speculations known that the suspect might be a priest, a mistake that biased how the witnesses remembered the offender. Finally, during the police lineup, Father Pagano was the only person wearing a clerical collar. (See *A reconciliation of the evidence on eyewitness testimony: Comments on McCloskey and Zaragoza [TT89].*)

A further complication is that—as often happens in these situations—the witnesses wanted to do their best to help the police catch the offender. It's a positive motivation, but also a trait that makes any witness more susceptible to memory biases. Modern investigators need to be aware of these risks when interviewing cooperative witnesses. (See *Forensic Psychology [FW08]* for an overview of eyewitness testimony.) Fortunately, we have learned a lot since then about how easy it is to implant a false memory.

Beware of Implanting False Memories

One of the pioneers in the study of implanting false memories was the psychologist Elizabeth Loftus. Back in 1974, Loftus used a now classic experiment to demonstrate how easily information received after an event affects witnesses. Loftus showed the participants identical films of traffic incidents and then asked them to evaluate how fast the cars went. The one manipulation was to vary the phrasing slightly: different groups were asked how fast the cars went as they either "smashed," "collided," "bumped," "hit," or "contacted" with each other. (See *Reconstruction of automobile destruction: An example of the interaction between language and memory [LP74].*)

Interestingly, all the groups had seen the same films, but the ones asked how fast the cars went as they "smashed" into each other estimated a significantly higher speed than all the other groups. In particular, the groups given the "contacted" phrasing estimated the slowest speed. More fascinating is that many participants in the "smashed" group even remembered seeing shards of broken glass in the film (there weren't any). In other words, varying a single verb in a question posed to eyewitnesses led to very different outcomes. Scary, isn't it?

Law enforcement agencies in many countries have learned valuable lessons and improved their techniques thanks to case studies like Father Pagano and researchers like Loftus. New interview procedures focus on recording conversations, comparing interview information with other pieces of evidence, and avoiding leading questions. These are also things we could use as we look at our code.

In programming, our code is also cooperative—it's there to solve our problems. It doesn't try to hide or deceive. It does what we told it to do. So, how do we treat our code as a cooperative witness while avoiding our own memory's traps?

Reveal the Dynamics of Change

Given that a single verb variation was enough manipulation to bias an eyewitness, imagine how many false assumptions we might make during a regular day. When we program, we're stuck with the same brain and its tendencies toward biases. Sure, in programming, you can go back and recheck the code. The problem is that we have to do that repeatedly—the sheer complexity of software makes it impossible to hold all of the information in our heads. That means our brain works with a simplified view, and as soon as we drop details, we risk missing something critical.

These human imperfections are the main reasons why good software architectures are critical. A good architecture promotes consistency in our designs, making it easier to build up long-term mental models of how the code works. When our architectures fail to accomplish that, changes to the code become risky and error-prone. Let's look at an example.

Recognize That Not All Dependencies Are Equal

If you've worked in the software industry for some time, you're probably all too familiar with the following scenario. You are working on a new feature, which initially seems simple.

In our hypothetical product, you start with a minor tweak to the FuelInjector algorithm, only to quickly realize the Engine abstraction depends on its details. This forces you to modify the Engine implementation, too, but before you can ship the code, you take it for a test run and discover, more or less by chance, that the logging tool still displays the old values. It seems that you also need to change the Diagnostics module. Phew—you almost missed that one.

If you had run a hotspot analysis on this fictional codebase, Engine and Diagnostics probably would've popped up as hotspots. But, the analysis would've failed to tell you that they have an implicit dependency on each other, as shown in the following figure. Changes to one of them mean changes in the other. They're entangled.

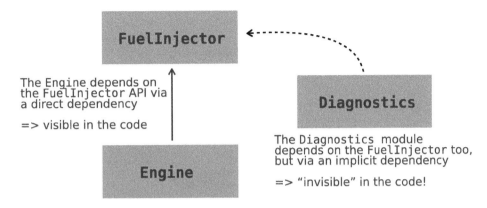

The problem gets worse if there isn't any explicit dependency between them. Perhaps the modules communicate over a network or message bus, or maybe the code represents a classic violation of the *Don't Repeat Yourself (DRY)* principle.[1] In any case, nothing in your code's structure points at the problem, and no dependency graphs or static analysis tools would help you.

If you spend a lot of time with the system, you'll eventually discover these issues, perhaps under a time crunch, when stressed and not really at your best. Let's look deeper at the core of the problem.

Implicit Dependencies Drive Cognitive Load

The nature of the dependencies influences how taxing they become to your working memory, with the main distinction being between implicit and explicit dependencies. While explicit dependencies are visible in the code itself, implicit dependencies require us to keep information in our heads while traversing the codebase. As you've seen throughout the book, our head is a crowded place where memory biases make our software life harder.

Know the Two Types of Accidental Complexity

The previous example reveals a new aspect of how accidental complexity makes your code harder to change: individual modules could be easy enough to reason about in isolation, but the emerging system behavior is anything but simple.

---

1. https://en.wikipedia.org/wiki/Don%27t_repeat_yourself

As the following figure shows, accidental complexity comes in two different forms. A software design aimed at optimizing for understanding needs to address both types of complexity. Keeping the parts and their interactions simple determines the relative ease of change when coding.

The two forms of accidental complexity

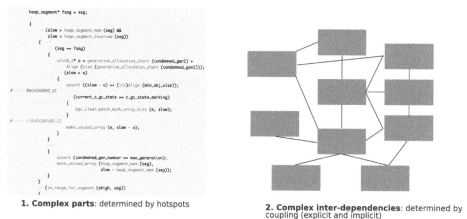

1. **Complex parts**: determined by hotspots

2. **Complex inter-dependencies**: determined by coupling (explicit and implicit)

You have already seen how hotspots help identify complex files. Let's now focus on the second type of complexity by analyzing dependencies. Hotspots rarely walk alone.

\\// **Joe asks:**

ʕ·ᴥ·ʔ **So I Run into Trouble if I Modularize My Code Too Much?**

Yes, there is such a thing as overly decoupled code. Individual functions might look deceptively simple at first, but the complexity is still there, only now it's distributed in the interactions. The root cause tends to be a misunderstanding of modularity. A function or file shouldn't just be a block of code with a name but a meaningful abstraction that represents and encapsulates a concept in the solution domain. It needs to be cohesive.

That said, excess modularization is a rare problem in practice. Most codebases suffer from the opposite problem of too little modularity. (Note that this comes from someone who has analyzed 300+ codebases during the past decade.)

Inspect the Modus Operandi of a Code Change

During the crash course in Learn Geographical Profiling of Crimes, on page 12, you saw how linking related crimes allows predictions, which in turn enables possible counter-steps. We can do the same with code.

In programming, version-control data lets us trace changes over a series of commits to detect patterns. One prominent pattern is called *change coupling*. Change coupling means that two (or more) modules evolve together over time. As such, change coupling implies a temporal dependency, which cannot be detected in code alone; a static snapshot of code lacks the evolutionary perspective.

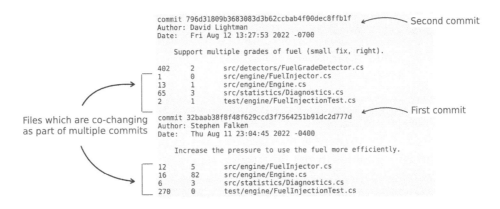

The preceding figure shows the most basic form of change coupling. Files are coupled in time if they repeatedly change together as part of a commit. Let's make it more tangible by visualizing that evolution.

Visualize Change Coupling in a System

Until now, we have been torturing a bunch of open-source systems, so at this point it's only fair to look at my code. Let's peek under the hood of Code Maat to see if we can catch some design mistakes.

It's difficult to show change coupling with a single illustration. A video would work best, but despite recent advances in ebook technology, we're not quite there, so bear with me as I walk you through the evolving frames of the figure on page 110.

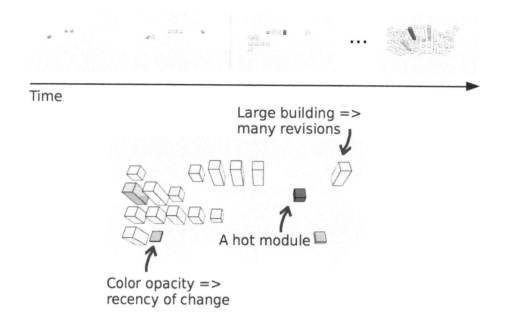

I created the preceding figure by replaying Git data to illustrate how Code Maat evolved. Each time a file changed, the size of its building grew a little so that the tall buildings in the illustration represent the total commits. To identify temporal patterns easily, the algorithm increased the opacity of the building's color every time the corresponding code was changed. As the hotspot cooled down, the opacity decreased gradually.

Looking long enough at this animation could drive you crazy, but not before you would spot some patterns. In the following figure, we highlight two such patterns that illustrate the different types of change coupling.

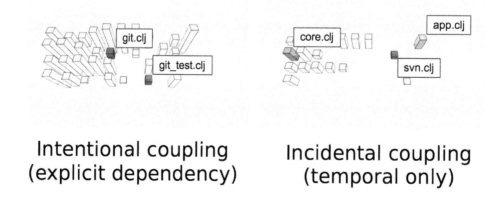

- *Intentional coupling*—git.clj and git_test.clj are frequently changed together. This is hardly surprising, given that the latter is a unit test on the former. In fact, we'd be surprised if the pattern wasn't there: a unit test always has a strong degree of direct coupling to the code under test.

- *Incidental coupling*—The right-hand snapshot is more surprising: core.clj and svn.clj change together. It's interesting information because there isn't any explicit dependency between the two files, yet, as a developer, you need this knowledge so that you remember to inspect both modules when making changes to either one.

A change coupling analysis in itself cannot distinguish between these two types of dependencies; you have to dig into the source code for that information. In the case of the incidental coupling in Code Maat, the dependency is there because the core.clj massages some input data for the SVN parser. This is clearly not a prize-winning design and it's a sign that the responsibilities of the modules aren't well partitioned. Code that changes together should be encapsulated together, so moving the relevant responsibilities from core.clj to svn.clj would resolve this specific problem and limit the blast range of future modifications. Now, let's illustrate another incidental coupling problem by returning to the React codebase.

Analyze Change Coupling in React

Back in Why Are the Files in React Duplicated?, on page 29, we saw that the React team maintains a fork of the codebase on the main branch. The consequence of this decision is that the hotspots come in pairs where much code is duplicated. Applying a change coupling analysis lets us highlight the impact.

The first step is to get a Git log of the development history. You can re-use the log from Create a Git Log for Code Maat, on page 23, or flip back and create one to follow along on the command line. Optionally, you can follow along in the CodeScene analysis online.[2]

The next step is to run Code Maat on the Git log. This time, we specify that we want a coupling analysis:

```
prompt> maat -l git_log.txt -c git2 -a coupling
entity, coupled, degree, average-revs
ReactFiberHydrationContext.new.js, ReactFiberHydrationContext.old.js, 100, 18
ReactFiberReconciler.new.js, ReactFiberReconciler.old.js, 100, 18
ReactFiber.new.js, ReactFiber.old.js, 100, 14
...
```

---

2. https://tinyurl.com/react-change-coupling

I cleaned up the output a bit, removing non-code content such as json and stripping out the leading paths. We now see that the output presents pairs of change-coupled files. The two other columns reveal the percentage of shared commits (degree) and a weighted number of total revisions for the involved files (average-revs). With these numbers, you could filter out files with too few revisions or merely weak coupling to focus on the most important information.

Nonetheless, the data reveals 100 percent coupling between the pairs of new.js and old.js files. We also notice that it's not just a fluke, since the number of revisions where the files were co-committed range between 14 to 18 commits. That's quite some coupling.

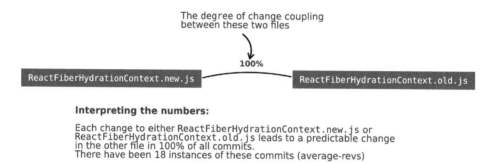

To a developer, this means that each time we touch one of the new.js modules, we must also remember to make a corresponding modification to the old.js module in the pair in 100 percent of all commits.

Our React example reinforces the difference between change coupling and traditional, static dependency techniques: change coupling expands to logical dependencies, meaning the analysis can reveal those implicit dependencies that, otherwise, only experience tells us about. It's exactly the same implicit coupling pattern we saw in the initial example with the FuelInjector and the hidden dependency in Code Maat's design.

Understand the Reasons Behind Temporal Dependencies

Once you've found change coupled modules, the reasons behind the dependencies often suggest places to refactor, too:

- *Copy-paste*—The most common case of change coupling is copy-pasted code, an issue you saw when inspecting the React duplication. The code smell itself is straightforward to address. Extract the common functionality and encapsulate it in a well-named unit.

- *Unsupportive modular boundaries*—Change coupling is related to encapsulation and cohesion. A failure to adhere to these design principles results in shotgun-surgery–style code changes where multiple modules must be changed in predictable but painful patterns. You saw an example of this in the Code Maat case study, where we suggested that the code that changes together gets located within the same module.

- *Producer-consumer*—Finally, change coupling may reflect different roles, such as a producer and consumer of specific information. In that case, it's not obvious what to do, and changing the structure might not be a good idea. In situations like this, we rely on our domain expertise to make an informed decision.

Insights like these are the main strengths of a change coupling analysis. They give us objective data on how our changes interact with the codebase and suggest new modular boundaries.

Just as crime investigators have techniques for reducing bias, change coupling serves a similar purpose when evolving a codebase. It's a way to interview our code about its past, tracing the steps of developers coming before us so that we can benefit from their tacit knowledge.

With the change coupling concept fresh in your mind, you're ready to move on to the next chapter and explore the related use cases, such as legacy modernization, guiding green-field development, and supporting modularization of monolithic applications. But first, try the following exercises to apply what you've learned in this chapter.

Exercises

These exercises let you explore the various facets of change coupling discussed throughout the chapter. We'll focus on the interview style use cases to highlight how quickly we can get deep design insights into previously unfamiliar code.

Language Neutral Dependency Analysis

- Repository: https://github.com/code-as-a-crime-scene/aspnetcore
- Language: C#, JavaScript, TypeScript, PowerShell
- Domain: ASP.NET Core is a framework for building web applications.
- Analysis snapshot: https://tinyurl.com/aspnet-change-coupling

You met ASP.NET Core back in Follow the Law of Demeter, on page 77, where we aimed for loosely coupled designs by limiting the assumptions on our code's dependencies. With change coupling in our tool belt, we can now get feedback on how loosely coupled our designs really are.

One powerful characteristic of change coupling is that it's a language-neutral analysis. This means you can identify dependencies that cross programming language boundaries, for example, changes spanning both front-end and back-end code.

Start by creating a Git log from the aspnetcore repository:

```
prompt> git log --all --numstat --date=short \
        --pretty=format:'--%h--%ad--%aN' --no-renames \
        --after "2020-01-01" > ../git_log.txt
```

Run a coupling analysis on git_log.txt using the same commands as in the React case study on page 111. Now, inspect the resulting change coupling for dependencies spanning language boundaries. You can identify the programming language via the file's extension.

Hint: A good starting point is to look at the PowerShell script InstallAppRuntime.ps1 or the C# file WebAssemblyNavigationManager.cs.

Spot DRY Violations in a Tesla App

- Repository: https://github.com/code-as-a-crime-scene/teslamate
- Language: Elixir
- Domain: A self-hosted data logger for Tesla cars.
- Analysis snapshot: https://tinyurl.com/tesla-change-coupling

TeslaMate is written in Elixir, a powerful functional programming language running on top of Erlang's VM, making it a great choice for scalable and fault-tolerant systems.

TeslaMate is a small application with roughly 20,000 lines of Elixir, and as the preceding visualization shows, the majority of that code represents tests. From a maintenance perspective, the tests must be simple to evolve as the application code changes. Change coupling helps you verify this vital property of maintainable test code.

Navigate to the analysis snapshot linked above and inspect the logical dependencies. Can you detect any change patterns that seem suspicious with respect to tests? Are there any co-changing files that you wouldn't expect to be modified as part of the same commits? See the figure on page 115.

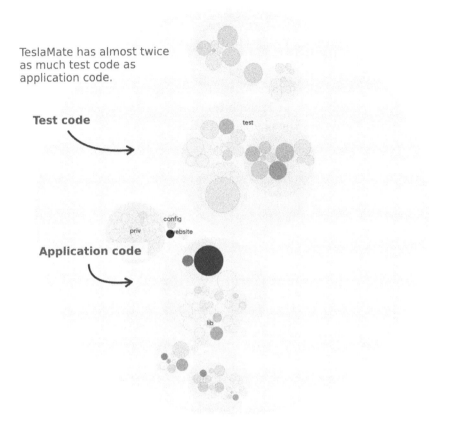

TeslaMate has almost twice as much test code as application code.

Test code

Application code

test

config
priv   website

lib

Hint: This is a harder exercise, so take a look at the solutions on page 271 if you get stuck. You'll also get some hints in the next exercise, meaning you could skip ahead to that one and return here afterward.

Design for a Single Source of Representation

- Repository: https://github.com/code-as-a-crime-scene/teslamate
- Language: Elixir
- Domain: A self-hosted data logger for Tesla cars.
- Analysis snapshot: https://tinyurl.com/tesla-change-coupling

The previous exercise highlights a problem that is common in many different codebases. As developers, we are conscious of adhering to the DRY principle...in application code. When it comes to test code, many of us tend to treat it differently. Often, the arguments go along the lines that "it's only test code" or "duplication makes the tests easier to read."

Code is never "just" test code: if our tests lack quality, they will hold back our overall efforts. And sure, some tests benefit from being a bit more verbose, but it's hard to find an argument for duplicating domain knowledge across multiple files.

Look at the following diff from two of the change-coupled test files, charging_test.exs and driving_test.exs, in TeslaMate. How would you refactor this code, in general terms, to break the change coupling?

Function Comparison   Differences are highlighted .

CHAPTER 9

Architectural Reviews: Support Redesigns with Data

Change coupling, which you explored in the previous chapter, is similar to hotspots in that it reveals information we cannot infer from the code alone. In this chapter, we'll start combining the analyses and have them build upon each other. That way, we enable architectural use cases such as modularizing monoliths, simplifying software designs, or modernizing legacy code. As you'll see, change coupling is an invaluable guide for uncovering patterns in complex software architectures.

To guide your coupling analyses, we need to introduce one more technique, the sum of coupling analysis, which helps identify a starting point for architectural reviews and their related use cases. It's a lot of ground to cover, so let's get started by exploring a failed redesign.

Don't Shoot the Messenger

I once worked on a project where everyone complained about severe problems in the database access layer. Changes were awkward, new features took longer than they should, and bugs swarmed like mosquitoes at a Swedish barbecue.

Learning from mistakes is important, so we decided to redesign the worst parts of the database layer. A small team of developers joined forces and spent two months partly rewriting the database access code. Once finished, something interesting happened. Even though the database layer was objectively in much better shape, developers still complained about how fragile and unstable it was. Changes still broke, and the build pipeline kept broadcasting its alerting red lights. What went wrong? Did we mess up?

While the database improved, it turned out that wasn't where the true problems were. The database was just the messenger subtly warning us about change coupling (and we shot the messenger).

In fact, a deeper inspection revealed that other parts of the system unexpectedly depended on the data storage. The true problem was in automatic system tests, where a minor change to the data format triggered a cascade of failed test scripts. This wasn't obvious to us developers because the scripts didn't explicitly call the database access code but rather fired off raw SQL, effectively short-circuiting any abstractions we came up with. This meant that most build failures were time-consuming false positives in the end-to-end tests. Once we understood the root cause, the tests were changed so that they didn't depend on the internals of the database, a change that finally brought peace to both the team and the build pipeline.

Redesigns are about minimizing risk and prioritizing areas of code that have the largest impact on the work you're doing now. Get it wrong like we did, and you will miss an opportunity to make genuine improvements to your code. Let's see how we can use change coupling to avoid these mistakes and find similar problems earlier.

Use Sum of Coupling to Determine Architectural Significance

In Chapter 8, Use Code as a Cooperative Witness, on page 103, we looked at change coupling as an interview tool for your codebase. The first step in any interview is to know who you should talk to.

As you've already seen, there are multiple reasons for change coupling, and some of the revealed dependencies are both expected and valid. This means that the highest degree of coupling may not be the most interesting. Instead, when striving to make sure our architecture is loosely coupled, we want to focus on the architecturally significant modules. Identifying those is the main purpose of the *sum of coupling* (SOC) analysis.

Sum of coupling is a behavioral code analysis technique that looks at how many times each module has been coupled to any other module in a commit.

As an example, in the figure on page 119, you'll see that the Fortran file login.f changed with both chess.f and dial_up.f in the first commit. The sum of coupling for login.f would be two so far, but over the next commits, the file keeps co-evolving with other modules and ends up with a sum of coupling of five.

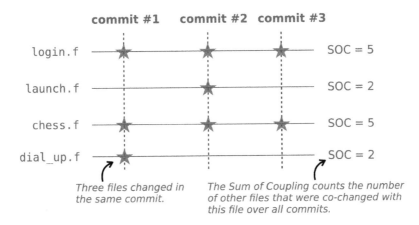

Three files changed in the same commit.

The Sum of Coupling counts the number of other files that were co-changed with this file over all commits.

A sum of coupling can often tell us what our system is *really* about from an architectural perspective. You might think you're working on a system for operational threat responses, but this behavioral analysis reveals that the significant building blocks are around access control, the login module. (The fictional example shown here is modeled on the WOPR computer from the Wargames movie.[1]) Let's apply the technique to a real codebase.

Drive Architectural Reviews by SOC Analysis

A module that changes frequently with others must be central to the system, making a good starting point for our investigation. Let's try it out on TeslaMate, an Elixir application serving as a data logger for Tesla cars.[2]

After cloning the repo and generating a log file as we did in Chapter 3, Discover Hotspots: Create an Offender Profile of Code, on page 21, you're ready to launch the sum of coupling analysis by typing the following command:

```
prompt> maat -l tesla_mate_git.log -c git2 -a soc
entity,                             soc
mix.exs,                            980
lib/teslamate/vehicles/vehicle.ex,  795
lib/teslamate/log.ex,               675
. . .
```

Here, we're requesting the -a soc (sum of coupling) analysis. If you're an Elixir programmer, you'll notice that the first module, mix.exs, is just a definition file for the Mix build tool. That is, it's not part of the application code; hence, it's a false positive we should eliminate in the results. After filtering out the build

---

1. https://en.wikipedia.org/wiki/WarGames
2. https://github.com/code-as-a-crime-scene/teslamate

definition, our data reveals that the most central modules are the Elixir files vehicle.ex and log.ex. This looks promising: the central modules are both core domain concepts (remember, a data logger for a car), which, already at this level, is a testament to the chosen modularity. Let's use this data to drive deeper investigations, focusing on the most coupled module, vehicle.ex.

Squash Sparingly

In Git, a *squash commit* means combining multiple commits into one. Squashing a commit could be the right thing to do if you made a simple mistake that's immediately correctable. Perhaps you forget to remove a print statement—the mother of all debugging—before committing. Facepalm, and a quick one-line deletion. Squash is your friend here.

When restricted to isolated pieces of work, squash commits are just fine. The problems start when we apply them to large commit sets. Hotspots, being a relative metric, aren't impacted. However, a squash effectively erases temporal data, including valuable change coupling information. So, let's learn from George Orwell: rewriting history comes at a price. Avoid it.

Inspect SOC Findings via Change Coupling

At this point, you know that vehicle.ex is the module that is most frequently changed together with other files in the codebase. This means we can zoom in on it and figure out which modules it's coupled to, just like we did in Inspect the Modus Operandi of a Code Change, on page 109.

The figure on page 121 visualizes the coupling as a network of dependencies, and as usual, you can inspect the interactive version online.[3] To clarify the different roles, I've also added an overlay that separates test code from application code. In the next section, we'll see how this information helps us.

Flatten the Learning Curve

Becoming comfortable enough to make significant changes to code we haven't worked on before is no joke. As Mike Gancarz points out in the *Linux and the Unix Philosophy [Gan03]*, the "average learning curve extends further and inclines more steeply than it first appears." Mastery comes hard.

---

3. https://tinyurl.com/teslamate-by-commits

The change coupling for `vehicle.ex`, the most central module as revealed by a sum of coupling analysis.

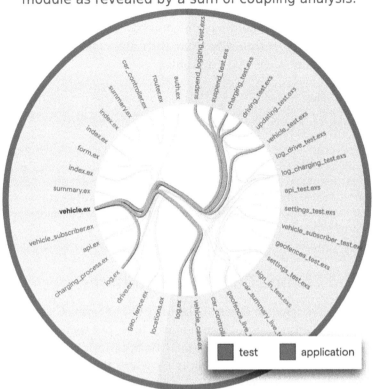

Now, keep Mike's observation in mind and look back at the preceding change coupling visualization of TeslaMate. The analysis is quick and effortless, yet it's capable of explaining how the system evolves, literally at a glance:

- *Test structure*—Changing vehicle.ex means we need to revisit five separate test suites. This tells us that the project doesn't have a one-to-one mapping between application code and test code but rather has chosen a more expressive way of separating test responsibilities.

- *Impact on other subsystems*—Surprisingly, we notice that there's also a logical dependency on a different module, the vehicle_case.ex file. This one would be easy to miss without the change coupling information.

- *Mirrored protocols via Mocks*—Our vehicle.ex evolves together with two(!) log.ex files. One is the real deal, the other a mock object. Again, this teaches us about the design since we now know a change to the log API means updating the test mock too.

Imagine joining the TeslaMate project: deducing all this information from the code would take a while. These analyses provide a head start that speeds up your onboarding while also making sure you don't miss anything critical in the process, such as updating the coupled support package. Change coupling offers a fast track for becoming familiar with any codebase by letting you create a mental model of the code upfront.

> **Joe asks:**
> ## Have I Seen the TeslaMate Code Before?
>
> Indeed, the Spot DRY Violations in a Tesla App, on page 114 explored one of the reasons for the coupling between the test scripts. That exercise was identified using the combination of SOC and change coupling covered in this chapter. This combination directs you to the relevant code, and when inspecting it, you can identify a DRY violation in an unfamiliar codebase within minutes. Change coupling is like a conversation with your local expert but at your pace.

Understand Change Coupling Algorithms

The algorithm we've used so far isn't the only kid in town. Change coupling means that some entities change together over time, but there isn't any formal definition of what *change together* means. One approach is to add the notion of time to the algorithm, so let's look more closely at that variant and see how it compares to the simpler option used so far.

Use a Time-Aware Algorithm

By adding the notion of time to the algorithm, the degree of coupling is weighted by the age of the commits. The idea is to prioritize recent modifications over changes in the more distant past. A relationship thus gets weaker with the passage of time.

Intuitively, adding time awareness to the change coupling algorithms makes sense. After all, recent work seems more important than things that happened in a distant past. Only...it isn't. Before we point out why that's the case, let's just reemphasize that facts like these are why it's so important to base our knowledge on the scientific method rather than intuition.

Research consistently shows that the simpler sum of coupling algorithm used in this chapter performs better than the more sophisticated time-based algorithms. A possible explanation for why time-based algorithms perform worse is that they're based on an assumption that isn't necessarily valid. They assume code gets better over time by refactorings, whereas the proprietary data I have access to via my day job indicates that code deteriorates more often than it improves. As such, those expected refactorings never happen, which is why adding a time parameter doesn't necessarily improve the metric. This allows for a simpler option, so let's explore that.

Keep Your Algorithms Simple

So far, the algorithm you have used is based on the percentage of shared commits, irrespective of recency in time. This option is chosen because when faced with several alternatives that seem equally good, simplicity tends to win. Not only is the measure straightforward to implement, but, more importantly, it's intuitive to reason about and verify.

Interestingly enough, simplicity may win in criminal investigations, too. Back in Find Patterns in Crimes, on page 12, we saw that there's a certain behavioral logic to *where* offenders commit their crimes. Based on simplified versions of that rationale, researchers trained people on two simple heuristics for predicting the home location of criminals:

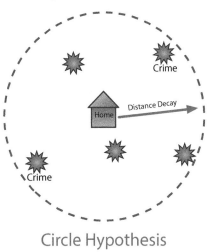

Circle Hypothesis

- *Distance decay*—Criminals do not travel far from their homes to offend. Thus, crimes are more likely closer to an offender's home and less likely farther away.

- *Circle hypothesis*—Many serial offenders live within a circle defined by the criminals' two farthest crime locations.

Like all fascinating studies, the results were surprising: using these simple principles, the participants could predict the likely home location of serial killers with the same accuracy as a sophisticated profiling system. (See *Applications of Geographical Offender Profiling* [CY08].) We build the techniques in this book on the same kind of simplicity and heuristics of behavioral patterns.

Understand the Limitations of Change Coupling

Simplicity might win, but as Rich Hickey reminds us in his classic software talk, there's a difference between simple and easy.[4] The change coupling

---

4. https://www.youtube.com/watch?v=SxdOUGdseq4

algorithm might be simple to reason about, but implementing a watertight and general version is anything but easy.

To start with, the definition of files that change in the same commit takes us far enough to identify unexpected relationships in most systems but becomes too narrow in larger organizations. When multiple teams are responsible for different parts of the system, the temporal period of interest is probably counted in days or weeks—not individual commits. We'll address this problem in Track Change Coupling Across Multiple Git Repositories, on page 155, where we start to group multiple commits into a logical change set based on both timespan and ticket information.

Another shortcoming with the measure is that we're limited to the information contained in commits. We may miss important coupling relationships that occur *between* commits. The solution to this problem requires hooks into our IDE to record precise information on the order in which we interact with each piece of code. Tools like that are under active research.

Yet another matter is moving and renaming modules. While Git appears to track renames, it's all a shallow illusion; Git sees a moved file as a commit deleting one file and adding a new one in a different location. For that reason, Code Maat doesn't track moved or renamed files, but other tools like Code-Scene do. In practice, the lack of rename detection sounds more limiting than it actually is. Problematic modules tend to remain where they are.

Catch Architectural Decay

Now that we have a deeper understanding of the change coupling algorithm, you are ready to put it to use for evaluating software architectures. This will help you simplify your systems by making them easier to understand and maintain. In addition, acting on unexpected dependencies improves the external quality of your code. Just like hotspots, change coupling also predicts software defects and is particularly good at identifying defect-prone modules. More specifically, change coupling shines when it comes to spotting the severe bugs that tend to be classified as major/high priority by an organization. (See *On the Relationship Between Change Coupling and Software Defects [DLR09].*)

There are multiple reasons for this predictive power. For example, a developer may forget to update one of the (implicitly) coupled modules. Often, these omissions happen over system boundaries such as front-end/back-end or between separate services, meaning compilers or linting tools cannot catch the issue. Another explanation for the severity of change coupling defects is when you have multiple modules whose evolutionary lifelines are intimately tied, you risk unexpected feature interactions. Those are some of the worst bugs you can have.

As such, undesired change coupling indicates architectural decay. Let's explore the consequences and what we can do about them.

Design for Continuing Change

Back in Chapter 5, Detect Deteriorating Structures, on page 49, we learned about Lehman's law of increasing complexity. The law states that when our system evolves, we have to continuously work to prevent a "deteriorating structure." This is vital because every successful software product will accumulate more features, and you don't want the codebase to become increasingly harder to work on. The only constant is change.

Lehman has another law of software evolution, too, namely the *law of continuing change*, stating that any program must undergo continual change or it will become progressively less useful over time. (See *On Understanding Laws, Evolution, and Conservation in the Large-Program Life Cycle [Leh80]*.)

There's an interesting tension between these two laws. On one hand, we need to continuously evolve our systems. After all, this is the very reason why we keep adding new features and changes to our existing code: we need to respond to user needs, competitors, and market demands. However, when expanding the system, we are also increasing its complexity unless we actively work to reduce it.

A deteriorating codebase makes it gradually harder to reason about the system. Over time, the pressure of continuing change leads to features becoming entangled and dependent upon each other. At some point, they start interacting in unexpected and surprising ways: you make a tiny change to one feature and an unrelated one breaks. Such bugs are notoriously hard to track down. Worse, without an extensive regression test suite, we may not even notice the problem until later, when it's much more expensive to fix, and the damage is already done.

Let's prevent horrors like that from happening to your code by using change coupling as an early-warning canary so that you can act on architectural problems promptly.

Identify Surprising Change Patterns

A strong software architecture lets you mitigate the tension between continuing change vs. increasing complexity by keeping changes local. That is, code that's expected to co-evolve should also be located together. Similarly, modules that are distant from an architectural perspective shouldn't change together; if they do, we have a telltale sign of architectural decay. Let's look at an example in the following figure.

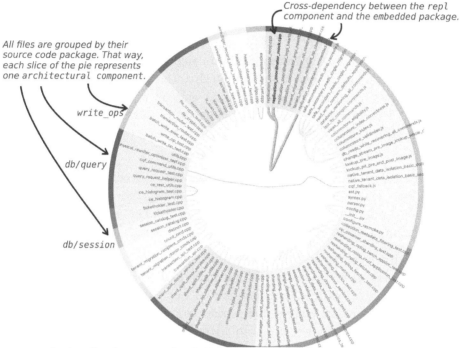

Review the change coupling in MongoDB to identify surprising change patterns.

This figure shows the change coupling in Mongo DB, a document database and popular NoSql choice. By grouping the change-coupled files by their architectural components, you can detect unexpected logical dependencies at a glance. You see an example of that where a programmer working on the replication_coordinator in the REPL—an interactive programming prompt—has to make changes to the embedded package too in 100 percent of all commits. That's as tight as coupling gets.

The more of these inter-component dependencies you detect, the more severe the architectural decay. In the case of Mongo DB, we don't notice any major warning signs, since most change coupling is limited to files within the same physical package. That's good.

Now that we have seen a simple example of how change coupling lets you review architectural fitness, we're ready to turn our eyes to a more severe dependency challenge.

Group by Source Code Folders

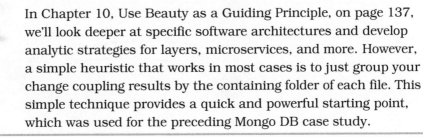

Grouping change-coupled files by their architectural component makes the most relevant information stand out; just look for any change pattern that crosses architectural boundaries and focus your investigation on them. This raises the obvious question: how do I define an "architectural component"?

In Chapter 10, Use Beauty as a Guiding Principle, on page 137, we'll look deeper at specific software architectures and develop analytic strategies for layers, microservices, and more. However, a simple heuristic that works in most cases is to just group your change coupling results by the containing folder of each file. This simple technique provides a quick and powerful starting point, which was used for the preceding Mongo DB case study.

Focus on Change-Coupled Hotspots

Change coupling becomes particularly problematic when it involves hotspots. The high change frequency of hotspots means that the cost of each change multiplies with each dependency. Let's look at an example from Glowstone, an open-source server for Minecraft.[5]

To review the Glowstone codebase, combine analyses on the sum of coupling and change coupling with a hotspot analysis. You can also turn directly to the online analysis to inspect the code.[6]

As you see in the figure on page 128, the analyses reveal that the GlowPlayer.java hotspot is also the class with the highest sum of coupling and several difficult dependencies. The name of this code witness, GlowPlayer, indicates that we found the right module to focus on; a player module sounds like a central architectural part of any Minecraft server. Anything that makes its design hard to understand will hold back future efforts in the codebase, so let's discuss what we can do about the issue.

Break the Dependencies

Change coupling between architectural elements is often due to a mis-partitioning of responsibilities. As we saw back in Design to Isolate Change, on page 68, low cohesion makes it hard to stabilize a design. Adding to that challenge, low cohesion is also a frequent cause of strong change coupling

---

5. https://github.com/code-as-a-crime-scene/Glowstone
6. https://tinyurl.com/glowstone-hotspots-map

The `GlowPlayer.java` hotspot in `Glowstone` is change coupled to three modules in other parts of the system. A warning sign!

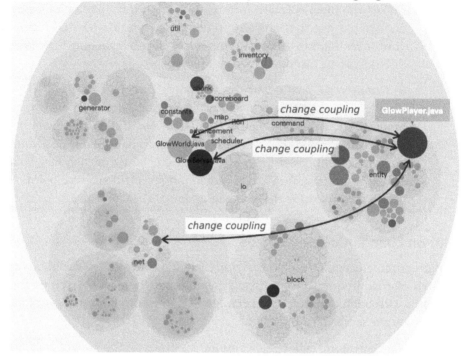

since the code's feature set tends to be spread out across multiple design elements. The consequence is that each time you need to tweak a certain business rule, you end up having to modify three other modules in separate packages.

Getting out of this rabbit hole requires an iterative, multistep process for transforming the design:

1. *Understand*—Focus on identifying the responsibilities that spill over module boundaries.

2. *Encapsulate*—Extract the identified responsibilities into a new and cohesive abstraction. Over time, this allows you to modularize and decouple your architecture, as illustrated in the figure on page 129.

3. *Refactor*—Look for opportunities to simplify the design in the newly extracted code in order to prevent similar issues in the future.

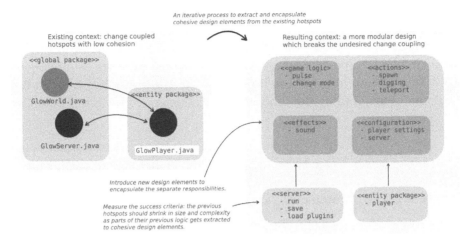

Make no mistake, breaking architectural dependencies is hard work. For guidance at the code level, *Working Effectively with Legacy Code [Fea04]* comes with several dependency-breaking techniques. To modularize a complex hotspot, you might also want to look at the *splinter refactoring pattern* from *Software Design X-Rays: Fix Technical Debt with Behavioral Code Analysis [Tor18]*, which offers a structured way to break up hotspots into manageable pieces that can be divided among several developers to work on. Finally, make it a habit to visualize the iterative decrease in complexity using the techniques from Calculate Complexity Trends from Your Code's Shape, on page 49. That type of running feedback is both motivating and reassuring.

Ultimately, a hotspot with low cohesion and strong dependencies is an architectural warning sign. Such code acts like a magnet for further problems and will become a busier place than an anthill covered in cotton candy. Refactor.

Modularize Monoliths

So far, we have performed more or less ad hoc architectural reviews to illustrate that the techniques are a solid companion any time you find yourself on a new job or in an unfamiliar codebase. But our offender profiling skills become even more useful when applied systematically as part of larger goals, so let's connect the dots by looking at legacy code modernization.

Drive Legacy Modernizations Projects

Legacy modernization projects are high risk. Typically, we aim to replace a working codebase, which earns the company profit, with a new solution that only exists in our imagination. It's a steep mountain to climb.

Once you have made the key decisions around a future platform, scalability requirements, and resiliency strategy, the main challenge that tends to remain is how to prioritize the parts to modernize. A system that has accumulated features over years and decades will contain millions of lines of complex code, all of it in desperate need of modernization. Yet you cannot rewrite it all; it would take years, and by the time you were done, you'd be out of business. You'd be Netscape.[7]

In a way, the challenge is similar to what crime investigators face when thousands of people fit a loose witness description of an offender. Narrowing down the search space via offender profiling gives us an actionable starting point. Here's how you would do that selection in a legacy system:

- *Pull risk forward with hotspots*—Migrating the functionality of a codebase built up over years or even decades takes time. Migrating and modernizing the hotspot areas of the system first is likely to give you the largest benefits in terms of both increased developer productivity and decreased risk for schedule overruns. Once the hotspots are migrated, the remaining work tends to be of lower impact.

- *Break dependencies guided by change coupling*—Most legacy codebases have grown tight dependencies over the years. You attempt to pull out a specific module, and suddenly, half of the database and five dialogs of presentation logic seem to follow. A change coupling analysis lets you discover these potential surprises up front. Focus on breaking those dependencies in the existing codebase to allow for a smooth migration. See the figure on page 131.

In particular, I've found that hotspots also work well for identifying code that we *don't* have to migrate. Rewriting code that we lack familiarity with is a high-risk activity. It's way too easy to introduce bugs or miss important customer scenarios. As discussed earlier, stable code that works is a much-underestimated design property, and we should value such code—there's clearly something right about it.

So if a hotspot analysis reveals that a package hasn't been modified in years, consider keeping the existing code and simply letting the new system interface with it, ideally via an Anti-Corruption Layer.[8]

---

7.   https://www.joelonsoftware.com/2000/04/06/things-you-should-never-do-part-i/
8.   https://dev.to/asarnaout/the-anti-corruption-layer-pattern-pcd

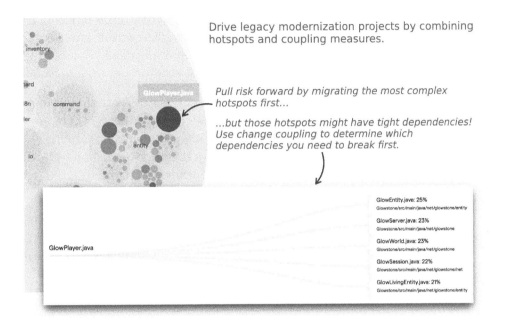

Drive legacy modernization projects by combining hotspots and coupling measures.

Pull risk forward by migrating the most complex hotspots first...

...but those hotspots might have tight dependencies! Use change coupling to determine which dependencies you need to break first.

GlowEntity.java: 25%
Glowstone/src/main/java/net/glowstone/entity

GlowServer.java: 23%
Glowstone/src/main/java/net/glowstone

GlowWorld.java: 23%
Glowstone/src/main/java/net/glowstone

GlowSession.java: 22%
Glowstone/src/main/java/net/glowstone/net

GlowLivingEntity.java: 21%
Glowstone/src/main/java/net/glowstone/entity

GlowPlayer.java

Joe asks:
Are There Situations When You'd Rewrite All Code?

Yes, there are a few situations where I have recommended complete system rewrites in a spare-nothing style. The main motivation in those few cases was never technical but rather related to developer happiness and recruitment. To give you an idea of what I mean, one company had a massive VB6 codebase, a technology that had seen its end-of-lifetime support fly by a decade earlier. Technically, the case could be made that remaining on a legacy language implies security issues and operational expenses since outdated operating systems and runtimes need to be kept around. However, the main issue is that you'll have a hard—almost impossible—time keeping and recruiting a team of skilled programmers. Few people would be thrilled to work on programming's evolutionary dead ends.

Watch Out for the Modernization Pitfalls

Most legacy migration projects start out high on inspiration. You've lived with this legacy codebase that no one really understood. You've fought heroic fights against its main hotspots, and here's your chance to finally move on to greener pastures: a replacement system built with all the latest technological bells and whistles.

I don't want to be the one to kill the party (well, maybe a little bit), but for how long will the new system feel fresh and inspiring? New code can turn to legacy code by the mere utterance of a dreaded word: deadline.

The Majority of Legacy System Modernization Projects Fail

A 2021 report found that 77 percent of businesses that started a legacy modernization project failed to complete them.[9] There are two main causes: first, participants blamed a lack of planning, and second, there was a disconnect in the priorities set by technical people vs. the ones valued by the leadership teams.

The strategies in this chapter are vital input to the planning so you know which risks lie ahead. Complement your analysis with the techniques from Chapter 7, Communicate the Business Impact of Technical Debt, on page 83 to bridge the communication chasm between engineering and leadership. That way, you're all set on a shared modernization goal, increasing your probability of success.

A couple of years ago, I visited an organization that had embarked on a legacy rewrite. The architecture was in place, and development proceeded quickly while making sure the code was clean and dependencies controlled. All was well. However, after the first six months, the directives took a sharp turn: top-level management was going to visit the site, and they wanted a live demo of the system-to-be. Rather than sticking to what worked, they decided to fast-track certain user-facing features and—predictably—sacrificed code quality on the altar of short-term goals.

The project never fully recovered from that early rush. The architecture had been compromised and showed several signs of structural decay and undesired dependencies. Critical hotspots were already getting hard to understand as their complexity trends had skyrocketed close to the looming, artificial deadline. The promise of an easily maintainable new system was gone.

Supervise New Code Continuously

By the time you notice the symptoms of architectural decay and technical debt, it's hard to reverse those trends. Doing an after-the-fact analysis is vital for proceeding with meaningful improvements, but essentially, these actions come too late. So why not make it a habit to perform regular analyses early and continuously?

---

9. https://modernsystems.oneadvanced.com/globalassets/modern-systems-assets/resources/reports/
advanced_mainframe_report_2021.pdf

Code can decay fast, so sit down with the team and walk through the analyses on a weekly basis. This approach has several advantages:

- You spot structural decay immediately.
- You see the structural impact of each feature as you work with it.
- You make your evolving architecture visible to everyone on the team.

Soon, you'll notice that having a shared mental model of the code helps by stimulating design discussions with your peers. Interestingly enough, you can start this process early on. You only need a few weeks' worth of version-control data to detect the main patterns.

Had the modernization project I visited used this approach, the tradeoffs with rushing features to a demo-able state would have been immediately clear to all stakeholders. It could have changed the outcome.

Simplify Your Software Architecture

We've covered a lot of ground in this chapter. Starting from a sum of coupling analysis, you learned to identify architecturally significant modules. We then showed how approaching a codebase from this data-guided perspective offers insights into our design. Often, the critical modules aren't necessarily the ones we'd expect from our formal specifications or high-level sketches. From there, you learned to combine the coupling analyses with hotspots to guide complex, high-risk architectural work.

Until now, we have limited the analyses to individual files. However, and this might be great news, both hotspots and change coupling also scale to the level of architectural building blocks like services, layers, and components. In the next chapter, you'll meet these powerful system-level analyses. We'll approach them via an essential software architectural principle, universal to all good systems. No, it's not performance, dependencies, or any other technical concerns, but rather a deeply psychological value with significant impact: beauty. That will be exciting!

But first, try the following exercises to apply what you've learned in this chapter.

Exercises

This chapter introduced the sum of coupling analysis and connected the dots to the hotspots. The following exercises let you practice those techniques on larger codebases.

Prioritize Refactoring by Combining Hotspots and SOC Analyses

- Repository: https://github.com/code-as-a-crime-scene/mongo
- Language: C++, JavaScript
- Domain: Mongo DB is a document database.
- Analysis snapshot: https://tinyurl.com/mongodb-hotspots-map

When discussing how to Modularize Monoliths, on page 129, we noted how hotspots and change coupling analyses build upon each other by offering complementing information. This combination enables use cases such as prioritizing refactoring targets amongst several hotspots. Let's start with an example.

The following figure shows the development activity over the past year in Mongo DB. As you see, there are many potential hotspots, and you're unlikely to be able to refactor them all. Instead, perform a sum of coupling analysis as you did in Drive Architectural Reviews by SOC Analysis, on page 119 on MongoDB. Look for overlap between hotspots and high SOC—a hotspot is more of a problem when it's coupled to several other files.

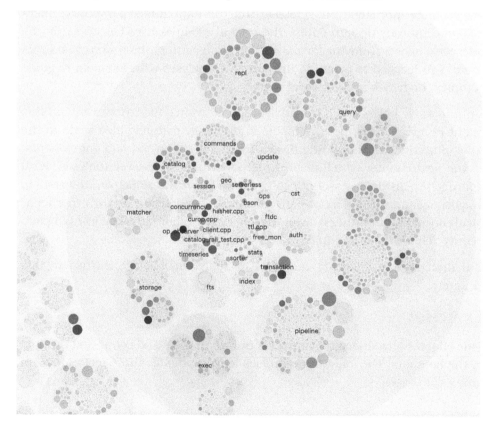

To help you get started, follow these steps:

1. Use the interactive online visualization for identifying hotspots.[10]

2. When generating the Git log needed for the SOC analysis, limit the log to the past year by adding the --after="2021-09-01" argument to the Git command.

3. Mongo DB contains a lot of third-party code, which comes out noisy in the analyses. Filter it out by adding the ":(exclude)src/third_party" pattern to the Git command.

Now, can you identify at least two hotspots that are also high on sum of coupling?

Run in Circles: Use Change Coupling for Design Improvements

- Repository: https://github.com/code-as-a-crime-scene/Glowstone
- Language: Java
- Domain: Glowstone is an open-source Minecraft server.
- Analysis snapshot: https://tinyurl.com/glowstone-hotspot-review

In essence, object-oriented design principles are all about coupling and cohesion. One thing that's rarely discussed in software design literature is that not all coupling is equal; stable dependencies, no matter how "wrong" they are in principle, constitute less of a problem than volatile dependencies that you actively traverse when working on the code. Change coupling helps you identify the true problems.

The following figure shows the change coupling of the ChunkManager.java class based on commit patterns over the past year. By limiting the coupling analyses to the last year, we know that all these logical dependencies are impactful and can start to inspect them.

ChunkManager.java

GlowChunk.java: 36%
Glowstone/src/main/java/net/glowstone/chunk

OverworldPopulator.java: 26%
Glowstone/src/main/java...ne/generator/populators

GlowWorld.java: 25%
Glowstone/src/main/java/net/glowstone

ChunkIoService.java: 22%
Glowstone/src/main/java/net/glowstone/io

Turn to the code for GlowWorld.java and ChunkManager.java: what's the relationship between these two classes? That is, which object is calling the other, and is it a good idea?

---

10. https://tinyurl.com/mongodb-hotspots-map

CHAPTER 10

Use Beauty as a Guiding Principle

By now, you know how to patrol your architectural boundaries by using change coupling. You've also learned to supervise the evolution of your code and use the information as an early warning system when things start to go downhill.

You're now ready to scale the analysis techniques from files to higher-level boundaries such as components and services. Starting from common architectural patterns, you'll see how we can analyze their effectiveness with respect to the way the code is worked on.

We'll start with an analysis of a small system. Once you're comfortable with the ideas, we'll move on to investigate a large web-based application built on multiple technologies like .Net, JavaScript, and CSS. Finally, we'll discuss how you analyze *microservice* architectures. By focusing the case studies on systems built from radically different patterns, you'll learn the general principles behind the analysis methods. That will give you the tools to tackle your current and future systems, no matter what architectural style they might use.

This chapter takes a different starting point from what you otherwise meet in programming books. Instead of focusing on technical principles, we'll use beauty as a reasoning tool. Supported by research, we explore what beautiful code is, why it matters, and how your brain loves it. Let's start by defining beauty—mathematically.

Learn Why Attractiveness Matters

Think about your daily work and the changes you make to your programs. Truth be told, how often do you get something wrong because the program's real behavior doesn't match up with your conceptual model? Perhaps that query method you called had a side effect that you rightfully didn't expect.

Or perhaps there's a feature that breaks sporadically due to an unknown timing bug, particularly when it's the full moon and, of course, just before that critical deadline.

Programming is hard enough without having to guess a program's intent. As we get experience with a codebase, we build a mental model of how it works. When some code then fails to meet our expectations, bad things are bound to happen. Those moments trigger hours of desperate debugging, introduce brittle workarounds, and kill the joy of programming faster than you can say, "null pointer exception." Beautiful code lets you avoid such unpleasant surprises, so let's explore what that is.

View Beauty as a Negative Concept

Beauty is a fundamental quality of all good code. But what exactly is beauty? To find out, let's look at beauty in the physical world.

At the end of the 1980s, scientist Judith Langlois performed an interesting experiment. (See *Attractive faces are only average [LR90]*.) Aided by computers, she developed composite pictures by morphing photos of individual faces. As she tested the attractiveness of all these photos in a group, the results turned out to be controversial and fascinating. Graded on physical attractiveness, the composite pictures won. And they won big.

The controversy stems from the process that produced the apparently attractive faces. When you morph photos of faces, individual differences disappear. As you can see in the following figure, the more photos you merge, the more average the result. That would mean that beauty is nothing more than average!

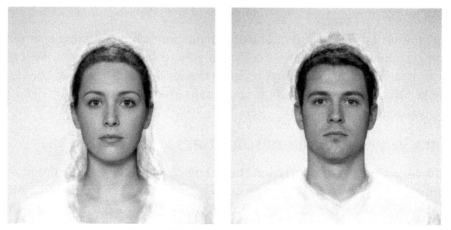

Pictures with kind permission by: The Face research Lab, University of Glasgow

The idea of beauty as averageness seems counterintuitive. In our field of programming, I'd be surprised if the average enterprise codebase would receive praise for its astonishing beauty. But beauty is not average in the sense of ordinary, common, or typical. Rather, beauty lies in the mathematical sense of averageness found in the composite faces.

The composite pictures won because individual imperfections were also evened out with each additional morphed photo. This is surprising since it makes beauty a negative concept, defined by what's absent rather than what's there. Beauty is the absence of ugliness.

Evolution shaped our preference for beauty to guide us away from bad genes. This makes sense since our main evolutionary task was to find a partner with good genes. And back in the Stone Age, DNA tests weren't easy to come by. (In our time, the technology is there, but trust me, a date will not end well if you ask your potential partner for a DNA sample.)

Instead, we tacitly came to use beauty as a proxy for good genes. The theory is that natural selection operates against extremes. This process works to the advantage of the composite pictures that are as average as it gets.

Now, let's see what a program with such good genes would look like.

Use Beauty in Code

Beauty, being the absence of ugliness, translates well to our software world, too. Beautiful code has a consistent level of expression that's easy to follow. Just as deviations from the mathematical average make a face less attractive, so does any coding construct that deviates from the main style of your application or introduces accidental barriers to understanding the code. Examples of such issues include special cases and the code smells covered in Chapter 6, Remediate Complicated Code, on page 63.

These constructs signal bad genes in our programs because they make it harder to form a mental model of the program. That's just how your brain works; when presented with complexity, inconsistencies, or conflicting representations, your brain selects one of the stimuli at the price of other details. You can switch between them, but it will be mentally expensive.

That means you've introduced a cognitive cost as soon as you break the flow of someone reading your code. This cost makes your programs harder to understand and riskier to modify. A broken code reading flow is to blame for many bugs.

Beauty Influences Sentencing

Beauty has a profound impact on all our lives, and often, we're not consciously aware of the beauty bias. You find a good example in the field of forensic psychology, where a growing body of research suggests that appearance alone can impact jurors. More specifically, attractive defendants tend to be perceived as less guilty and, should they be convicted, receive a more lenient sentence than unattractive offenders. It's a finding that seems to hold both for mock jurors, used during experiments, and for real-life judges (source: *The Psychology of Physical Attraction [SF08]*).

These findings are, of course, worrisome and unfair. But sometimes, the attractiveness of offenders works against them. A good-looking criminal may receive a more lenient sentence for a burglary. However, should the criminal use their good looks to swindle victims, the court will likely hand out a harsher sentence. In any case, appearance and not objective facts made the difference, so if you've ever doubted the importance of beautiful code, you now see how profound attractiveness is and how it influences our lives.

Avoid Surprises in Your Architecture

The beauty principle applies to software architectures, too. Since an architectural decision is, by definition, more important than a local coding construct, breaking beauty in a high-level design is even worse.

Consider a codebase that has multiple ways to do interprocess communication, differs in its error-handling policies, or uses several conflicting mechanisms for data access without any obvious benefit. Such a system is hard to learn and work with—particularly since the knowledge built up when working on one part of the codebase doesn't necessarily transfer to other parts.

So, beauty is about consistency and avoiding surprises. Fine. But what you consider a surprise depends on context. In the real world, you won't be surprised to see an elephant at the zoo, but you'd probably rub your eyes if you saw one in your front yard (at least here in Sweden, where I live). Context matters in software, too.

Measure Against Your Patterns

When you use beauty as a reasoning tool, you need principles to measure against. This is where patterns help. All architectures—even the seemingly architectureless *big ball of mud*—have some pattern. If you're fortunate enough to work on a codebase grown with care, those patterns will be obvious in the design and will guide you. If not, you'll have constant battles to fight as you'll be working against, rather than with, your architecture.

Your architectural patterns serve as a frame for evaluating your analysis results, too. Anything supporting the benefits you want to achieve with a certain pattern (for example, loosely coupled components) adds to the beauty, and anything violating those principles falls on the ugly side. To add some technical depth to the discussion, let's apply these ideas to some actual codebase.

Analyze Pipes and Filters Architectures

The architectural pattern *Pipes and Filters* is useful whenever you want to process an input as a sequence of steps, where each step encapsulates a certain transformation. It's a popular pattern in web frameworks. A browser request serves as the input event, triggering a sequence of authentication, validation, and other steps before the result is returned.

The core idea in Pipes and Filters is to "divide the application's task into several self-contained data processing steps" (quotation from *Pattern-Oriented Software Architecture Volume 4: A Pattern Language for Distributed Computing [BHS07]*). Based on that description, we can agree that any Pipes and Filters implementation with coupled processing steps would surprise a maintenance programmer. This is a sure sign of ugliness, which we can detect via a change coupling analysis. Let's see how.

Look at the Implementation

Conveniently for our purposes, Code Maat is modeled as a Pipes and Filters architecture, shown in the following figure. The input stream is the version-control log, which is transformed via a sequence of analysis steps into specific metrics, our results.

A high-level sketch of an architecture built around the Pipes and Filters pattern.

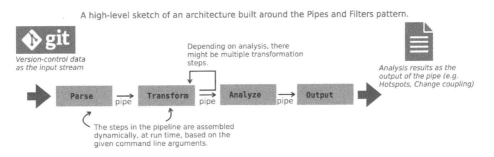

We've already performed a quick file-level analysis of the Code Maat codebase back in Visualize Change Coupling in a System, on page 109. Now, we'll scale that analysis to the overall architecture. Let's start by defining its architectural boundaries.

Specify the Architecturally Significant Components

When analyzing the higher-level architectures, we want to move from individual files to groups of files, each representing an architectural building block. In practice, this is done by aggregating the Git activity across all files within a component, as shown in the next figure.

```
To analyze architectures, map physical files to logical names.
Each logical name should represent an architectural building block of interest.

commit 796d31809b3683083d3b62ccbab4f00dec8ffb1f (HEAD -> main, origin/main, origin/HEAD)
Date:    Fri Aug 12 13:27:53 2022 -0700

    Implement basic stylesheet Resources for react-dom (#25060)

    This feature is gated by an experimental flag and will only be made avai
    experimental builds until some future time.                              Example:
                                                                             These commits reference
    402    2       packages/react-dom/src/__tests__/ReactDOMFizzServer-test.js  the "Client" component.
    1      0       packages/react-dom/src/__tests__/ReactDOMRoot-test.js
    13     1       packages/react-dom/src/client/ReactDOMComponent.js
    65     3       packages/react-dom/src/client/ReactDOMHostConfig.js          "Client"
    2      1       packages/react-dom/src/client/ReactDOMRoot.js
    101    8       packages/react-dom/src/server/ReactDOMServerFormatConfig.js   "Server"
```

Once we have decided upon the level of analysis, we need to tell our analysis tools about those boundaries. If you use Code Maat, you do that by specifying a set of transformations. Open a text editor and type in the following text:

```
src/code_maat/parsers    => Parse
src/code_maat/analysis   => Analyze
src/code_maat/output     => Output
src/code_maat/app        => Transform
```

As you see, each logical name in the transformation corresponds to one Filter in the software architecture. Now, save the text you just entered as code_maat_architecture_spec.txt and run the following analysis:

```
prompt> maat -l code_maat_git_log.txt -c git2 -a coupling \
            -g code_maat_architecture_spec.txt --min-coupling 20
 entity,  coupled,   degree, average-revs
 Analyze, Transform, 28,      83
 Parse,   Transform, 22,      75
```

Compared to earlier analyses, the difference is we specify the transformation file and add the --min-coupling flag to include weaker coupling so we detect all potential architectural violations. As evident from the preceding output, there are temporal dependencies from the Transform components to both the Analyze and Parse steps. Even if those dependencies aren't strong—co-changes in 22 to 28 percent of all commits—they may still be bad enough. Let's see why.

Identify the Offending Code

Once you have identified the architectural violations, the next step is to follow up with a change coupling analysis at the file level and zoom in on the offending components, in this case Transform, Analyze, and Parse. Doing so will reveal the same patterns we uncovered in Visualize Change Coupling in a System, on page 109; parts of the Transform components massage some input data for the SVN parser. Even though there isn't any direct dependency in the source code, this analysis reveals a logical dependency. This hints that some code from the Transform package might belong with the code in Parse instead.

Combine Behavior That Belongs Together

Similar to how we would split a module with too many responsibilities into smaller and more cohesive units, we should look for opportunities to combine code with logical dependencies. This doesn't mean you need to put all code in the same file, but code that changes together should be part of the same architectural component. That way, you turn large, sweeping changes into local modifications that are much easier to test, review, and reason about.

In a small codebase like this, we can go directly to the source to identify the offending code.

```
(defn- parser-from
  [{:keys [version-control]}]
  (case version-control                    ← Conditional logic
    "svn"  svn-xml->modifications          Code which knows how to invoke
    "git"  git->modifications              each parser.
    "git2" git2->modifications             This construct couples this code to
    "hg"   hg->modifications               all known parsers.
    "p4"   p4->modifications
    "tfs"  tfs->modifications
    (throw (IllegalArgumentException.
            (str "Invalid --version-control specified: " version-control
                 ". Supported options are: svn, git, git2, hg, p4, or tfs.")))))
```

If you follow that track, you'll soon find the code above. As you see, the piece of Clojure code determines the version-control system to use. It then returns a function—for example, svn-xml->modifications—that knows how to invoke a parser for that system.

This explains the coupling between the factory function above and the code in Parse. When a parser component changes, those functions have to change as well. It isn't a severe problem in a small codebase, but the general design is questionable because it encourages coupling between parts that should be independent. It's the kind of design that becomes an evolutionary hurdle for the program. If we break that change coupling, we remove a surprise and make our software easier to evolve in the process. That's a big win.

Now that you've seen how to analyze one type of architecture, let's scale up to a more complex system.

Analyze Layered Architectures

The core idea of *layered architectures* is to represent each horizontal responsibility in its own component, a layer. In embedded systems, those layers would be hardware abstractions, device drivers, and protocols with application-level code as the top slice. For a web application, the layers typically encapsulate the UI, request routing, business rules, and data persistence. As shown in the next figure, it's not uncommon to come across architectures that are seven to eight layers deep.

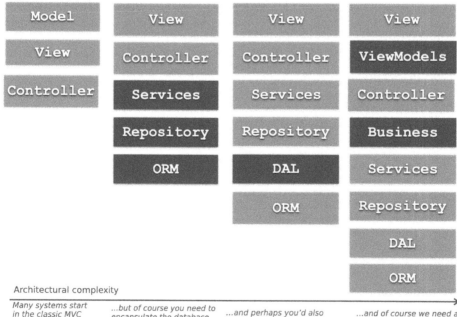

Examples of Layered Architecture: Most real-world layered web applications tend to use many more layers than the canonical MVC, MVP, MVVM patterns suggest.

Architectural complexity

Many systems start in the classic MVC style with three layers...

...but of course you need to encapsulate the database access using Repository patterns and Object-Relational Mappers (ORM).

...and perhaps you'd also like to encapsulate your ORM access with a Data-Access Layer.

...and of course we need a Business layer so we have one place for all our, well, business rules.

In many ways, layered architectures are the IBM of software architecture. No one has ever been fired for building a layered architecture. Layers are the safe bet.

The basic premise of layered architectures is that you can swap out one implementation for another, leaving the rest of the code, located in different layers, unaffected. The canonical example is changing databases, let's say by moving from an Oracle implementation to MySQL. Implement the new code for accessing MySQL, and as long as the original API of the database layer is maintained, it's a plug-and-play replacement. Beautiful.

However, layered architectures often optimize for the wrong evolutionary force. I've been writing code for 25 years, and during that time, I've had to switch database implementation exactly twice. The conclusion is that—on average—a layered architecture is the right choice once a decade. The rest of the time? Not so much.

The horizontal slicing of layers comes at a cost. As we'll soon see, layered architectures optimize for a rare case at the expense of the effort of the day-to-day work we do on its implementation. Let's use change coupling to illustrate the point.

Identify Significant Layers

Our next case study uses nopCommerce.[1] nopCommerce is an open-source product used to build e-commerce sites. It's a competent piece of code consisting of 400,000 lines of C# and JavaScript together with a bunch of SQL scripts and CSS files—a perfect opportunity to see how the analysis method works across multiple languages.

The first step is to identify the architectural principles of the system. nopCommerce is a web application built around the *Model-View-Controller* *(MVC)* pattern.

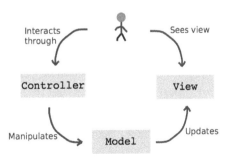

Model-View-Controller is a pattern for implementing user-interface applications. As we saw in the figure earlier in this section, each implementation looks different. One common variation is introducing a service layer encapsulating the business logic and having the Controller delegate to that layer. This is how it's done in nopCommerce.

---

1. https://github.com/code-as-a-crime-scene/nopCommerce

Define Each Layer as an Architectural Boundary

As we did for our Pipes and Filters analysis, we will map each architectural part to a logical name. Here's an example of a transformation for nopCommerce:

```
src/Presentation/Nop.Web/Models                    => Models
src/Presentation/Nop.Web/Views                     => Views
src/Presentation/Nop.Web/Controllers               => Controllers
...
src/Libraries/Nop.Services                         => Services
src/Libraries/Nop.Core                             => Core
...
src/Presentation/Nop.Web/Areas/Admin/Models     => Admin Models
src/Presentation/Nop.Web/Areas/Admin/Views      => Admin Views
src/Presentation/Nop.Web/Areas/Admin/Controllers => Admin Controllers
...
```

I derived this transformation from the nopCommerce documentation.[2] I also looked at the source code to identify the Model-View-Controller layers you see below the src/Presentation/Nop.Web folder. (When analyzing your own system, you're probably already familiar with its high-level design.)

Before we turn to the analysis, note nopCommerce consists of two applications: one administration application and one application for the actual store. We specify both in our transformation since they're logical parts of the same system and have to be maintained together. In particular, we'd like to know about any potential dependencies between them. Let's look at them.

Identify Expensive Change Patterns

The mechanical steps for investigating logical dependencies in a layered system are no different from what we did in analyzing architectural change coupling on page 142. Performing those steps on the nopCommerce repository reveals some strong change coupling:

```
prompt> maat -l nopcommerce_git_log.txt -c git2 -a coupling \
           -g nopcommerce_architecture_spec.txt
 entity,            coupled,       degree, average-revs
 Admin Controllers, Admin Models, 64,      813
 Admin Controllers, Admin Views,  60,      1141
 ..
 Admin Controllers, Controllers,  45,      885
 ...
```

---

2.   https://docs.nopcommerce.com/en/index.html

To ease the interpretation, the following figure visualizes the nopCommerce change coupling. The interactive graph for this analysis is also available online.[3]

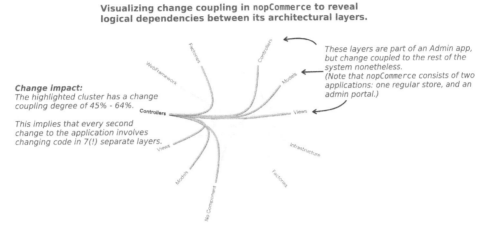

Visualizing change coupling in nopCommerce to reveal logical dependencies between its architectural layers.

These layers are part of an Admin app, but change coupled to the rest of the system nonetheless. (Note that nopCommerce consists of two applications: one regular store, and an admin portal.)

Change impact:
The highlighted cluster has a change coupling degree of 45% - 64%.

This implies that every second change to the application involves changing code in 7(!) separate layers.

Now, take a closer look at the highlighted cluster. The raw change coupling data and/or the interactive visualization show that the architectural elements within that cluster are tightly coupled. Their degree of change is between 45 and 64 percent. Put differently, this implies that in half of the changes you'd do in the nopCommerce codebase, you have to be prepared to traverse and change multiple layers. Is that really a separation of concerns? Well, let's dig into it.

Understand Why Layers Represent a Disarrangement of Concerns

There's a simple idea behind all those layers we, as a community, tend to put into business applications. That idea is a *separation of concerns*, allowing us to change our minds and swap one layer for another with a different implementation. This flexibility often comes at the cost of making application changes more complex than they should be. Let's take a step back and look at how applications grow.

The most common work in virtually any application is implementing or enhancing a feature, together with bug fixes. This is something we do on a daily basis. What we are *not* doing is replacing databases, ORMs, or service layers. These types of architectural changes are rare, yet they are the driving force behind a layered application. With layers, we optimize for infrequent events at the expense of making change difficult in our daily tasks. Think back to the change coupling in nopCommerce: if we have to modify code in

3.   https://tinyurl.com/nopcommerce-arch-coupling

seven layers to add a feature, I'd like to go out on a limb and claim that the architecture isn't supporting change. We seem to be working against, rather than with, our architecture.

In Isolation, an Architecture Is Never Good or Bad

Back in Know Why Half the Work Gets Done in Twice the Time, on page 86, we saw how we can assess code health, meaning we can distinguish between good and bad code. When it comes to software architectures, there is no such thing as a generally applicable "good" architecture. An architecture is good when it supports the properties we—as an organization— value in the system. These properties are going to change as the business and organization evolve, but the one property that always remains fundamental is changeability, our ability to implement new features and make improvements. Change coupling allows you to evaluate and visualize how well your architecture supports change.

Migrate Away from Layers

In practice, layered architectures rarely deliver upon their promise. Instead, you'll often find that each modification you make to the code ripples through multiple layers, as shown in the following figure. Such modification patterns indicate that the layers aren't worth the price you pay. Perhaps they even make your code *harder* to change.

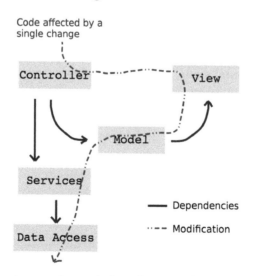

These days, many teams choose to break apart their monolithic architectures into microservices. A common motivation for those decisions is to create a loosely coupled architecture where changes can be local, avoiding the ripple effects inherent in layered architectures.

We'll look at microservices soon, but let's be clear that unless you have additional requirements that motivate the overhead of operating a distributed system, you are probably better off with a modular monolith.

Package by component is one such pattern that I have seen work particularly well as an alternative to layers. I discuss the pattern in more depth in *Software Design X-Rays: Fix Technical Debt with Behavioral Code Analysis [Tor18]*, but the gist of it is to slice your architecture into components that combine application logic with data-access logic inside the same building block. See the following figure.

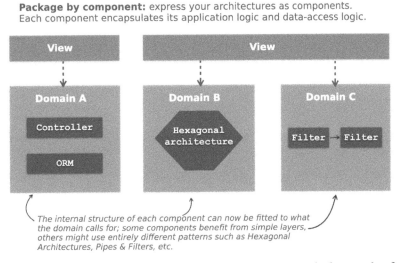

Package by component: express your architectures as components. Each component encapsulates its application logic and data-access logic.

The internal structure of each component can now be fitted to what the domain calls for; some components benefit from simple layers, others might use entirely different patterns such as Hexagonal Architectures, Pipes & Filters, etc.

Following the package-by-component pattern lets you rebalance the forces. In a layered architecture, there's no distinction between how you implement features of various scope and complexity; even the simplest change has to follow a complex path. It's one size fits none. The beauty of packaging by component is that you can now let the local design of each component vary, depending on what their respective domains call for.

Further, rearchitecting toward components could also serve as a first step toward a service-based architecture and, eventually, if the problem calls for it, microservices. Decomposing a tightly coupled application is hard, which is why most systems benefit from these intermediate steps as a way of mitigating the technical risk. (See *Software Architecture: The Hard Parts: Modern Trade-Off Analyses for Distributed Architectures [FRSD21]* for in-depth material on the trade-offs.)

Should you decide to take the step and rethink your architecture, then the techniques from Modularize Monoliths, on page 129 are there to guide you during those migrations. As illustrated in the following figure, you would start with the largest impact—the main hotspots—and use change coupling to identify and break dependencies.

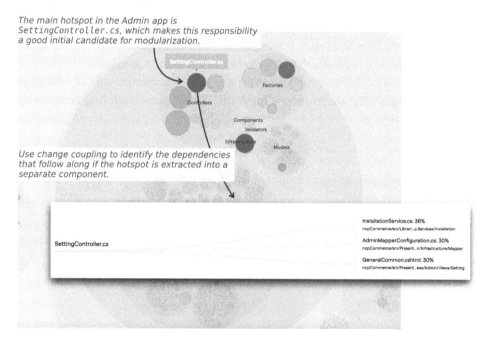

The main hotspot in the Admin app is SettingController.cs, which makes this responsibility a good initial candidate for modularization.

Use change coupling to identify the dependencies that follow along if the hotspot is extracted into a separate component.

SettingController.cs

InstallationService.cs: 36%
nopCommerce/src/Librari..p.Services/Installation

AdminMapperConfiguration.cs: 30%
nopCommerce/src/Present..n/Infrastructure/Mapper

GeneralCommon.cshtml: 30%
nopCommerce/src/Present..ess/Admin/Views/Setting

Joe asks:
But What Comes First: Component Extraction or Dependency Breaking?

I recommend that you start the decomposition in the existing structure. Dependency breaking is simpler that way. Once you have decoupled the relevant code, move on to extract and reshape your new building block into the desired structure.

However, *tactical forking* offers another possible path.[a] With this pattern, you duplicate the codebase into a new, isolated component, and then start to remove all the code that isn't needed. You flip the problem on its head. Tactical forks might be useful when your potential component has strong and inconsistent dependencies or as an optional path if you get stuck during the dependency breaking.

---

a. https://faustodelatog.wordpress.com/2020/10/16/tactical-forking/

Make Patterns the Foundation of Attractive Codebases

So far, I've criticized a couple of patterns where various layering patterns, in particular, took a hit. This does not mean that patterns—architectural or design—don't work. Quite to the contrary.

Software patterns are context-dependent and do not, by some work of magic, provide universally good designs. You can't take the human out of the design loop. Instead, think back to earlier in this chapter, where we saw how the most attractive facial patterns were the ones that connected with the most people. Patterns offer a way for your software design to connect with other developers. As such, these are the main advantages of patterns in a software architecture:

- *Patterns are a guide*—Our architectural principles will likely evolve together with our system. Remember, problem-solving is an iterative process. Agreeing on the right set of initial principles is challenging, and this is where the knowledge captured in patterns helps.

- *Patterns share knowledge*—Patterns come from existing solutions and experiences. Since few designs are truly novel, we'll often find patterns that apply to our new problem as well.

- *Patterns have social value*—When the architect and design theorist Christopher Alexander formalized patterns, the intent was to enable collaborative construction using a shared vocabulary. As such, patterns are more of a communication tool than a technical solution.

- *Patterns are reasoning tools*—You learned about chunking back in Meet Your Brain on Code, on page 63. Patterns are a sophisticated form of chunking. Pattern names serve as handles for knowledge stored in our long-term memory. Patterns optimize our working memory and guide us as we evolve mental models of the problem and solution space.

Analyze Microservice Systems

Since 2015, *microservice* architectures have rapidly gained popularity and are now mainstream. This means that many of tomorrow's legacy systems will likely be microservice architectures. Let's stay a step ahead and see what we would want to analyze when we come across such systems.

Microservices are based on an old idea: keep each part small and orthogonal to others, and use a simple mechanism to glue everything together (for example, a message bus or an HTTP API). In fact, these are the same principles on which UNIX has built since the dawn of curly braces in code.

A microservice architecture attempts to encapsulate each responsibility or business capability in a service. This principle implies that a microservice architecture is attractive when it allows us to modify and replace individual services without affecting others. In fact, in his seminal *Building Microservices, 2nd Edition [New21]*, Sam Newman highlights *independent deployability* as a key principle for microservices.

The concept of independently deployable services implies we need to keep our microservices loosely coupled. A fundamental architectural principle like that should be monitored, and change coupling is a valuable tool for the task.

Consequently, changes that ripple over boundaries and affect multiple services are the main warning signs, as shown in the following figure. When we analyze microservices, we want to consider each service an architectural boundary. That's what we specify in our transformations. As soon as we detect change patterns across multiple services, we know that ugliness is creeping into our system. Let's approach the topic by starting with the desired properties.

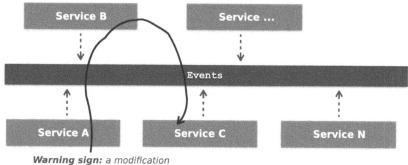

Warning sign: a modification which impacts multiple services!

Think About Change in Microservice Systems

The essential property of any microservice system is a set of small and independent services with decoupled lifetimes. Building such systems comes with several advantages:

- *Independent development*—In essence, each microservice is like an application in its own right. This allows you to scale an organization by having a team take responsibility for one or more services. These services can now be developed and maintained with a level of independence that just isn't possible in a monolith where code from multiple teams has to deploy simultaneously.

- *Fine-grained scalability*—All systems have a hot path where response times are more critical than in other parts. Isolating such critical code in its own microservice allows you to dynamically spin up more instances of the critical resource to meet demands. Contrast this to a monolith where it's all or nothing; even parts of the system that are executed less frequently would get scaled up. Don't pay for what you don't use.

- *Testability*—If you manage to keep the services loosely coupled, for example, via asynchronous messaging, then each team can spin up their minimal version of the system and easily simulate external input and error conditions.

These reasons are often the main driving forces behind microservices today, and the benefits are real. Microservices can enable organizations to deliver faster while scaling the engineering teams. However—and this is important—developing and operating a microservice architecture will always be significantly more time-consuming than the corresponding monolith. Hence, the first rule of microservices is don't do them. At least not until you really have to. If you have to use microservices, the second rule is to make sure they are kept independent. Tight coupling is the cardinal sin of any microservice system and is a surefire way to have ugly surprises further down the road.

The following visualization shows an example of tightly coupled services. The data is from a real-world online gaming system, but I've scrambled the service names to keep the actual product anonymous. As you see, virtually any change you'd like to make in the system requires modifying multiple services. Independent deployability becomes virtually impossible since everything depends on everything else.

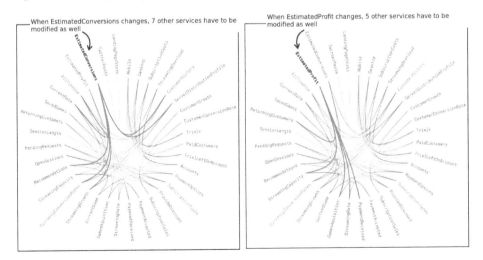

Building a tightly coupled microservice system gives you the worst of two worlds: you have all the drawbacks of a monolith but with the operational overhead of a distributed system. Don't do this.

The most common reason for tight coupling is inappropriate service boundaries. Microservices need to be based on business capabilities, much like we'd do with the monolithic package-by-component pattern discussed earlier. The rationale for this principle is that changes (new features or bug fixes) come at the domain level. Having a 1:1 mapping between domain concepts and architectural building blocks lets us keep changes local, allowing us to deliver quickly and safely, with a minimum of coordination overhead.

> \]// **Joe asks:**
> ⤳ᶠ
> ## Alright, So What's Wrong with the Service Boundaries in This Example?
>
> Looking at the names of the services, you'll see that they are way too granular. Those names would be a good fit for objects and classes but are a huge red flag when representing fundamental architectural building blocks. This system is more like a mesh of distributed objects, with the undesired consequence that tweaking a certain business capability requires the team to modify whole clusters of services. Quite expensive.

Build a Mental Model of Your Emerging Services

When you manage to strike a balance between your service boundaries, teams, and business capabilities, most changes and extensions will be straightforward and predictable since they can be kept local to a service. Sweet. However, while each service might be easy enough to reason about in isolation, the emerging system behavior is anything but simple. This often proves to be particularly painful when debugging.

When something goes wrong, you have to understand the sequence of events leading up to the failure. With multiple services involved—some you might not even be aware existed—these tasks become more detective work than engineering practice. Today's powerful logging and diagnostics tools do help, but the core challenge remains: building a mental model of the system.

For that reason, change coupling is a valuable addition to the distributed system engineer's toolbox since the analysis reveals information we cannot spot in the code itself. As an example, take a look at the figure on page 155. This type of information comes in handy when trying to understand how the pieces in a complex system fit together.

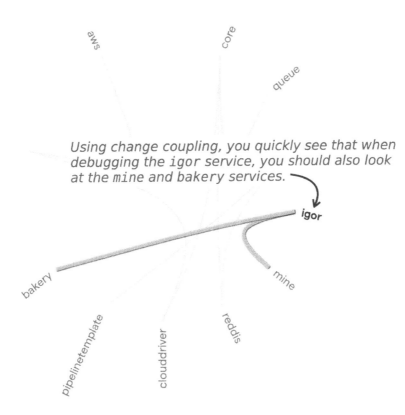

Using change coupling, you quickly see that when debugging the igor service, you should also look at the mine and bakery services.

Even if you're familiar with the codebase, change coupling delivers new insights and occasionally lets you spot warning signs of problematic dependencies. Over time, your mental model of the system becomes even richer. However, a complicating factor when analyzing microservices is that they tend to be located in separate Git repositories. It's a common model, so let's look at that scenario in the following section.

Track Change Coupling Across Multiple Git Repositories

When microservices are contained in separate Git repositories, the technique used so far won't work. There's simply no relationship between commits in separate repositories. To resolve this, we need to use one additional data source: product management tools.

Virtually all organizations use some kind of product or project management software like Jira, Azure DevOps, or Trello. Piecing together the information from these tools with the Git data allows us to raise the analysis to the level of logical change sets rather than individual commits.

The following figure shows how the practice of *smart commits* lets you preserve change information across multiple services. From here, you can merge all commits referencing the same tickets into the logical change set. The change coupling algorithm itself remains the same. It's more complex to implement, but the resulting information makes it worth every minute.

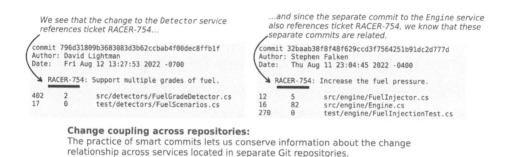

Change coupling across repositories:
The practice of smart commits lets us conserve information about the change relationship across services located in separate Git repositories.

We'll return briefly to microservices in Part III to consider the organizational forces operating on our architecture, as we Visualize Organizational Friction, on page 222. But let's leave services behind for now and look at a less pleasant architectural style.

Reverse-Engineer Your Principles from Code

So far, we have seen examples from widely different architectural styles. Conveniently, we used the same steps to analyze all kinds of architectures, define our boundaries, measure the change patterns, and look for any signs of ugliness violating our system principles. Sounds simple, but what if we don't have any existing principles on which to base our reasoning? What if we inherited a legacy nightmare without any obvious structure or style? Well, our focus changes. Let's see how.

Make Sense of Big Balls of Mud

All codebases, even the worst spaghetti monsters, have some principles. All programmers have their own style. It may change over time, but we can find and build upon consistencies.

When you find yourself wading through legacy code, take the time to step back. Look at the records in your version-control system. Often, you can spot patterns. Complement that information with what you learn as you make changes to the code. Perhaps most of the database access is located in an inaptly named utility module. Maybe each subscreen in the GUI is backed by its own class. Fine—you just uncovered your first principles.

As you start to reverse-engineer more principles, tailor the analyses in this chapter accordingly. Look for changes that break the principles. The principles may not be ideal, and the system may not be what you want. But at least this strategy allows you to assess how consistent the system is. Used that way, the analyses will help you improve the situation and make code changes more predictable over time.

Don't Confuse Familiarity with Beauty

I'm not sure how much the philosopher Friedrich Nietzsche knew about coding, but his classic observation that "if you gaze into the abyss, the abyss gazes also into you" clearly indicates that he had a good grasp on how our code influences us. In modern psychology, there's a related phenomenon called the *mere-exposure effect*. The mere-exposure effect is the fact that we humans tend to develop a stronger preference the more often we see something. That something could be abstract symbols, human faces, or a particular coding style.

Like so many other cognitive biases, the mere-exposure effect makes sense from an evolutionary perspective. It shaped firm attachments to people close to us, people we depended on to put food on the table and offer shelter for the night.

Despite the evolutionary survival value, these phenomena make it hard to spot flaws and inefficiencies in systems we are intimately familiar with. Biases like the mere-exposure effect are another reason why we need objective measures like change coupling to get that much-needed separate perspective.

The Mere-Exposure Effect and Programming Languages

Isn't it interesting how we become attached to certain programming languages? In the majority of cases, it's not like a freshly minted developer sits down to learn the top 20 languages and makes an active choice from there. Rather, our first professional job tends to make that choice for many of us ("We're a Java shop"). Yet, that first language tends to become part of our identity. We're now C programmers, C# developers, or possibly Clojure hackers. While there's more to it, mere exposure is likely to play a significant role in shaping our attachment.

Analyze Continuously and Early

Now, you have a set of new skills that allow you to analyze everything from individual design elements all the way up to architectures. With these techniques, you can detect when your programs start to evolve in a direction your architecture cannot support.

The key to these high-level analyses is to formulate simple rules based on your architectural principles. Once you've formulated those rules, run the analyses frequently so the results can serve as an early warning system.

Before we move on to the people side of code, we need to look at one more software design element in the next chapter: automated tests. But first, try the following exercises to apply what you've learned in this chapter.

Exercises

The mechanical steps in an architectural change coupling analysis are simple, but interpreting the results requires a bit of practice and experience. The following exercises give you the opportunity to practice on various architectural problems.

Explore Microservice Coupling: DRY or WET?

- Repository: https://github.com/code-as-a-crime-scene/magda
- Language: Scala, JavaScript, TypeScript
- Domain: Magda is a data catalog system for organizations.
- Analysis snapshot: https://tinyurl.com/magda-arch-coupling

Microservices can become coupled for multiple reasons. Not all dependencies are as direct as the ones we looked at in Think About Change in Microservice Systems, on page 152, where the service boundaries were way too granular. Another common reason for coupling is shared code. This is a hard trade-off: do we encapsulate shared responsibilities as the Don't Repeat Yourself (DRY) principle tells us, or do we instead duplicate code and Write Everything Twice?

The figure on page 159 shows the change coupling at a service level in the Magda system. With the previous discussion in mind, are there any warning signs? Bonus points if you can make the case for being either DRY or WET here.

Decompose a Monolith

- Repository: https://github.com/code-as-a-crime-scene/nopCommerce
- Language: C#

- Domain: nopCommerce is an eCommerce solution.
- Analysis snapshot: https://tinyurl.com/nopcommerce-hotspots-map

Architectural change coupling in the Magda system:
Are there any signs of potential problems?

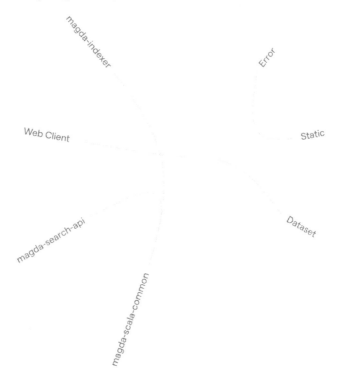

In Migrate Away from Layers, on page 148, you saw how hotspots and change coupling let you surface information that guides architectural decomposition. Apply the same strategy to identify a dependency of concern if you were to extract the OrderController.cs and related functionality into a separate component. See the figure on page 160.

Beautify Ugly Code

In this exercise, you won't explore any particular repository. Instead, you'll take a look at a common design problem.

Earlier in the chapter, we discussed the beauty principle at the level of software architectures. But the concept of beauty being the absence of ugliness is also

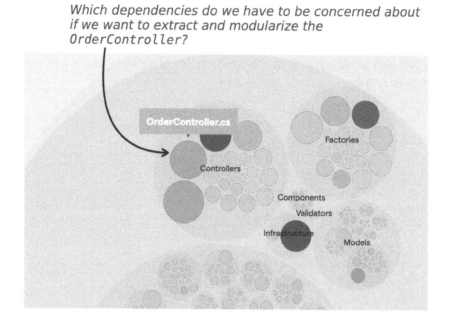

Which dependencies do we have to be concerned about if we want to extract and modularize the OrderController?

useful for identifying refactoring options, too. Consider the following piece of code:

```
void persistStatusChange(
  final Status newStatus,
  final Boolean notifyClients) {

  persist(newStatus);

  if (notifyClients) {
    sendNotification(allClients, newStatus);
  }

}
```

Notice how the boolean parameter controls the execution flow of the method? The technical term is *control coupling*, and it's a common ugliness that tends to sneak into code.

The main problem with control coupling is that it breaks encapsulation. The client now "knows" that we have logic for notifying clients. Control coupling, by definition, also leads to lower cohesion as control-coupled methods have at least two responsibilities as designated by the true/false execution paths.

But what if you really need to notifyClients? Good question. How would you refactor the previous code? Feel free to check out the Appendix 1, Solutions to the Exercises, on page 267, as there are several options.

CHAPTER 11

Expose Hidden Bottlenecks: Delivery and Automation

With the architectural review covered, you know how to investigate an evolving system with respect to its core patterns. Building on that, we'll now use the same techniques for inspecting the supporting code that enables us to implement and ship new tasks without compromising quality: test automation.

Automated tests are still a relatively young discipline, and we, as a community, might not yet have captured all the patterns needed to ensure that our tests remain maintainable. Adding to that challenge, in many organizations, tests are still added as an afterthought, almost like a hidden architectural layer. In those situations, the systems often become hard to reason about and more painful to maintain than necessary.

In this chapter, we'll cast a light on these hidden architectural layers. You'll see how to set up an early warning system for detecting when automated tests go wrong. In the process, you'll also learn about problem-solving and how it relates to programming, testing, and planning. Let's see what hidden secrets we can uncover in our systems.

Understand What's in an Architecture

If someone approaches you on a dark street corner and asks if you're interested in having a software architecture, chances are they'll pull out a diagram. It will probably look UML-like, with a cylinder for the database and lots of boxes connected by lines. It's a structure—a static snapshot of an ideal system.

But architecture goes beyond structure, and we should treat architecture as a set of principles rather than a specific collection of modules. Let's think of architecture as principles that help us reason through and navigate large-scale systems. Breaking these principles is expensive since it makes the system harder to understand. It introduces ugliness.

As an example, consider the war story from Don't Shoot the Messenger, on page 117, where the automated system tests depended upon the data storage. Like so many other failed designs, this one started with the best intentions.

The first iterations went fine. But we soon noticed that new features started to become expensive to implement. What ought to be a simple change suddenly involved updating *multiple* high-level system tests. Such a test suite is counterproductive because it makes change harder. We found out about these problems by performing a change coupling analysis. However, we also made sure to build a safety net around our tests to prevent similar problems in the future. Let's see why it's needed.

View Automated Tests as an Architectural Layer

Automated tests becoming mainstream is a promising trend. When we automate mundane tasks, we humans can focus on real testing, where we explore and evaluate the value of the features we deliver. Test automation also makes changes to the system more predictable. We get a safety net when modifying software, and we use the scripts to communicate knowledge and drive additional development. Test automation—at all levels—is a prerequisite for *continuous delivery*, allowing us to ship high-quality software daily.

While we all know these benefits, we rarely discuss the risks and costs of test automation. Automated tests, particularly on the system level, are notoriously hard to get right. And when we fail, these tests become time sinks, halting all real progress.

Test scripts are architecture, too—albeit an often neglected aspect. Like any architectural boundary, a good test system should encapsulate details and avoid depending on the internals of the code being tested. We want to refactor the implementation without affecting the tests themselves. If we get this wrong, we rip increasingly larger holes in the safety net that a test suite could provide.

In addition to the technical maintenance challenge, as the figure on page 163 shows, such tests lead to significant communication and coordination overhead. We developers now risk breaking each other's changes.

There are two reasons why this happens. First, work tends to be organized along architectural boundaries, allowing multiple developers to work on separate features in parallel. However, with excess change coupling to the test

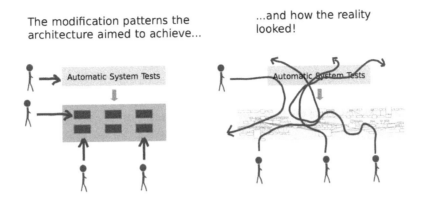

layers, the tests become coordination bottlenecks. Second, if the tests are expensive to change, our tasks will take longer to complete. The longer a task is open, the more likely someone else will touch the same code, and we might end up with conflicting changes to the code.

The architecture we choose must support the kind of changes we make, and automated tests are no different from any other subsystem. Let's see how you inspect those properties.

Profile Targets in Test Code

While hotspots help us discover isolated maintenance bottlenecks, limiting our investigations to them would be a mistake. The unhealthy code in hotspots frequently spills over to other, potentially more distant, parts of the system.

These challenges are similar to the developments of geographical offender profiling. Early profiling implementations relied on the distance decay concept: criminals do not travel far from their homes to commit offenses. However, subsequent research suggests that we can improve the precision of the profile if we also consider *opportunity structures*. Within criminology, opportunity structures represent the attractiveness of potential targets. For example, a remote and poorly lit area might be more attractive to a burglar since it minimizes risk. (See *The usefulness of measuring spatial opportunity structures for tracking down offenders [Ber07]* for a summary of the improved profiling precision.)

Software development is obviously different since we drive the changes to our code guided by a purpose. Nevertheless, there are similarities too: our starting point might be a hotspot, but unless we manage to maintain a clean test architecture, we will leave multiple additional targets for code crimes in our wake. Like the traveling criminal offender, these issues might be harder to detect since they are spatially distributed and might involve multiple teams. So, given a change to your application code, what else needs to be updated, and how expensive are those revisions?

Fortunately, you can answer these questions using the same techniques applied when analyzing software architectures. The only difference is in the level of analysis, where we focus on just two main boundaries: the production code and the test code. Let's look at an example from the well-known Java framework.

Specify Your Architectural Boundaries

Spring Boot is a back-end framework that helps Java developers create stand-alone applications such as microservices.[1] The project has invested in test automation at multiple levels: unit tests for driving the low-level design, integration and system tests for making sure the code works, and a smoke test suite to catch regressions. See the following figure:

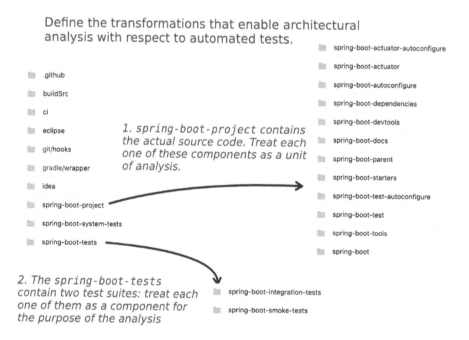

Define the transformations that enable architectural analysis with respect to automated tests.

1. *spring-boot-project* contains the actual source code. Treat each one of these components as a unit of analysis.

2. The *spring-boot-tests* contain two test suites: treat each one of them as a component for the purpose of the analysis

Interpret the Results

To analyze the codebase, we start by defining the architectural boundaries of interest. As shown in the preceding figure, we let these boundaries follow

---

1. https://github.com/code-as-a-crime-scene/spring-boot

the structure of the source code and make sure to also include the system-level tests. From here, we perform the same change-coupling analyses as in the previous chapter. Let's jump to the result.[2]

Take a look at the following figure, showing the change coupling across the Spring Boot components. What does this information tell us about the maintenance effort with respect to test automation?

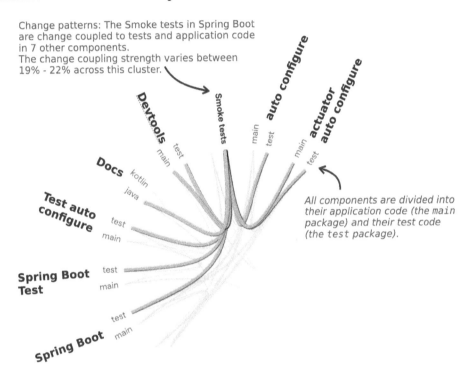

Well, there do seem to be significant dependencies since seven separate components appear to co-evolve with the smoke tests. That in itself can actually be a good sign; it could signal that the tests are being kept up-to-date, with new smoke tests being written as the code evolves. However, if that's not the case, then these results indicate that the smoke tests are coupled to the internals of the implementation.

Even if you're part of the project, it might be hard to have the full picture. Let's look at a technique that helps us diagnose a potential problem and then serves as a safety net for future test automation.

2. https://tinyurl.com/springboot-arch-coupling

Change Coupling at the Commit Level Might Not Be Enough

In many organizations, a separate team writes system-level tests. This means that the commit-level change coupling won't find the relevant dependencies. Similarly, some developers might put off integration and system-level tests until the rest of the code is written. The solution in both scenarios is to use higher-level information to transform individual commits into logical change sets, as we learned in Track Change Coupling Across Multiple Git Repositories, on page 155.

Create a Safety Net for Your Automated Tests

Remember how we monitored structural decay back in Supervise New Code Continuously, on page 132? We're going to set up a similar safety net for automated tests.

Our safety net is based on the change ratio between the application code and the test code. We get that metric from an analysis of change frequencies, just like the hotspot analyses you did back in Part I.

Monitor Tests in Every Iteration

To turn our change frequencies measure into a trend analysis, we need to define a sampling interval. I recommend obtaining a sample point in each iteration or, if you're delivering continuously, at least once per week. In case you're entering an intense period of development (for example, around deadlines—they do bring out the worst in people), perform the analysis daily as part of the build pipeline.

To acquire a sample point, you specify your transformations and run a hotspot analysis at that level. Try it out on one of your repositories. If you use Code Maat, you simply run a revisions analysis with a file specifying your architectural transformations.

```
prompt> maat -l git_log.txt -c git2 -a revisions -g src_test_boundaries.txt
entity,n-revs
Code,153
Test,91
```

The preceding example shows that in this development period, we modified the application code in 153 commits and the test code in 91. If we continue to collect sample points at regular intervals, we'll soon be able to spot trends. Let's look at some common patterns to see what they tell us.

Think About Tests via Their Modification Patterns

The following figure shows the typical patterns you can expect to encounter. Each case shows how fast the test code evolves compared to the application code. Note that we're talking about system-level tests now.

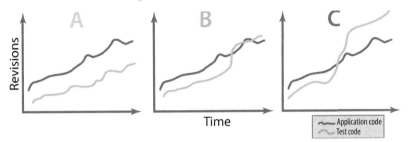

In Case A, you see an ideal change ratio. The test code is kept alive and in sync with the application. Most of the effort is spent in the application code.

Case B is a warning sign. The test code suddenly had more reasons to change. When you see this pattern, you need to investigate. Sure, there might be legitimate reasons for the sudden burst in test activity: perhaps you're focusing refactoring efforts on your test code. That's fine, and the pattern is expected. But if you don't find any obvious reason, you risk having your development efforts drown in test-script maintenance, a problem that we will look at in more depth soon.

Case C means horror. The team spends too much effort on the tests compared to the application code. You recognize this scenario when you make what should be a local change to a module, and suddenly, your build breaks with several failing test cases. These scenarios seem to go together with long build times (counted in hours or even days). That means you get the feedback spread out over a long period, making the problem even more expensive to address. Ultimately, the quality, predictability, and productivity of your work suffers.

Avoid the Automated-Test Death March

Over the past decade, I have seen way too many test automation attempts gone wrong. If you run into the warning signs we examined in the previous section, be sure to run a coupling analysis on your test code and combine it with a hotspot analysis to identify the issues you need to address.

But don't wait for warning signs. Once our tests start slowing us down, it's time-consuming to get back on track. There's much you can do upfront. To illustrate the point, let's look at code health, the concept we discussed back in Know Why Half the Work Gets Done in Twice the Time, on page 86, but this time, use it to compare the test against the application code.

For this case study, we're back to Spring Boot, and you see in the following visualization that it seems to be a healthy codebase. No red flags. That's promising, but do you see how the test files seem to be both larger and more problematic than the application code? That's a warning sign. Let's look at the code of AbstractServletWebServerFactoryTests.java, one of the hotspots in the tests.

A Code Health visualization of the Spring Boot component.

Note how there's more Yellow/Problematic code in the tests compared to the application code (the main package).

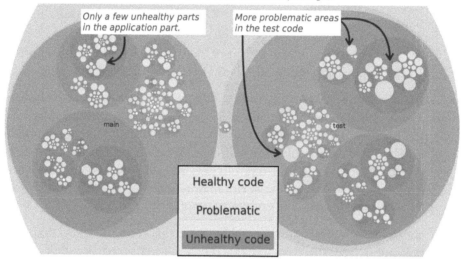

As you'll see in the following figure, there's a clear duplication of both code and knowledge across the tests. (This is only one example; there are more to come in the exercises.) The problem here is that each time we change the relevant parts of the application code, we need to update multiple tests. If you forget one, you break the build. It's obviously less of a problem in unit tests, which can be run fairly fast, but it's disastrous in any high-level tests, such as integration of system tests.

Duplicated logic in the AbstractServletWebServerFactoryTests.java test suite.
Only difference is the arguments passed to the getSsl method.

Reduce Duplication via Parameterized Tests

We'll return to the topic of code duplication in just a minute, but before we go there, how would you refactor this code?

The following figure shows a possible refactoring that removes the duplication. The refactoring is based on *parameterized tests*, which simply lets you re-use the same test logic with multiple input arguments. This design lets you separate the commonalities—the test logic—from the concept that varies, the SSL certificate used as an input argument. It's a separation that's the basis of good software design, yet it's frequently violated in tests. Let's spend some time examining why that happens.

Parameterized tests let you execute the same test logic but with different inputs. Let's use it to provide the different SSL certificates. That is, use it to encapsulate the concept that varies so we can re-use the test logic without duplication.

```
@ParameterizedTest
@ArgumentsSource(SslArgumentsProvider.class)
void clientAuthenticationWithSsl(final Ssl certificateForTest)
{
  AbstractServletWebServerFactory factory = getFactory();
  addTestTxtFile(factory);
  factory.setSsl(certificateForTest);
  this.webServer = factory.getWebServer();
  ...
```

Understand Why Test Code Isn't Just Test Code

Even if test automation—and its distant relative, Test-Driven Development (TDD)—are in widespread use today, both are fairly recent additions to mainstream software development. Consequently, we as a community might not yet have learned what good tests are, what works, and what doesn't. Let's illustrate the point with a prominent example, which you can also view interactively.[3]

Roslyn is the implementation of the C# and Visual Basic compilers, together with an API for writing tools. It's a large-scale codebase with six million lines of code. The .Net team has also invested heavily in test automation.

Let's peek under the hood in the visualization on page 170.

---

3. https://tinyurl.com/roslyn-code-health

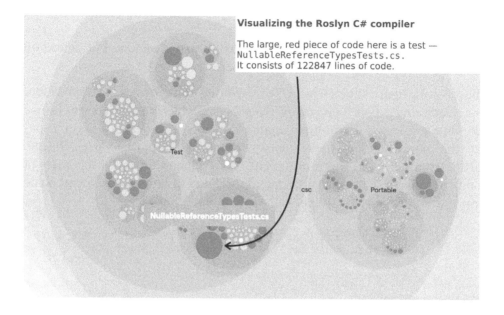

Visualizing the Roslyn C# compiler

The large, red piece of code here is a test —
NullableReferenceTypesTests.cs.
It consists of 122847 lines of code.

As you see, the tests have a massive piece of red code: NullableReferenceType-sTests.cs. That test suite alone consists of more than 120k lines of code! A quick scan of the source code reveals several instances of duplication, which makes the code harder to understand, not easier.

```
[Fact]
public void TestMeetForNullableAnnotationsIsAssociative()
{
    foreach (var a in s_AllNullableAnnotations)
    {
        foreach (var b in s_AllNullableAnnotations)
        {
            foreach (var c in s_AllNullableAnnotations)
            {
                var leftFirst = a.Meet(b).Meet(c);
                var rightFirst = a.Meet(b.Meet(c));
                Assert.Equal(leftFirst, rightFirst);
            }
        }
    }
}

[Fact]
public void TestMeetForNullableFlowStatesIsAssociative()
{
    foreach (var a in s_AllNullableFlowStates)
    {
        foreach (var b in s_AllNullableFlowStates)
        {
            foreach (var c in s_AllNullableFlowStates)
            {
                var leftFirst = a.Meet(b).Meet(c);
                var rightFirst = a.Meet(b.Meet(c));
                Assert.Equal(leftFirst, rightFirst);
            }
        }
    }
}

[Fact]
public void TestEnsureCompatibleIsAssociative()
{
    Func<bool, bool> identity = x => x;
    foreach (var a in s_AllNullableAnnotations)
    {
        foreach (var b in s_AllNullableAnnotations)
        {
            foreach (var c in s_AllNullableAnnotations)
            {
                foreach (bool isPossiblyNullableReferenceTypeTypeParameter in new[] { true, false })
                {
                    var leftFirst = a.EnsureCompatible(b).EnsureCompatible(c);
                    var rightFirst = a.EnsureCompatible(b.EnsureCompatible(c));
                    Assert.Equal(leftFirst, rightFirst);
                }
            }
        }
    }
}
```

These three nested loops create a context which is identical to the one in TestEnsureCompatibleIsAssociative.

Confusingly, the structure of the intervening test, TestMeetForNullableFlowStatesIsAssociative, looks similar too but is different, a fact which is likely to mislead any code reader.

different nesting context

same nesting context

Now, you might think that I pulled out an extreme case with the Roslyn hotspot just to make my point. And you'd be correct. I did. But I did it for a reason. Over the past decade, I've probably analyzed 300-plus codebases. During all those analyses, I observed that we developers are fairly conscious of the DRY principle...in application code. When it comes to test code, well, not so much. Consequently, some of the worst technical debt I find tends to be in tests, similar to what we found in the Roslyn platform.

We already discussed the fallacy of treating test code as "just test code." From a productivity perspective, the test scripts you create are every bit as important as the application code you write, and technical debt in automated tests spells just as much trouble. We'd never accept a 120k-line monstrosity in our application code, would we?

> **Joe asks:**
> ## What Else Could You Achieve with 120,000 Lines of Code?
>
> Finding a single test suite with 120,000 lines of code is astonishing. To help you put it into perspective, the complete source code for the Apollo 11 Guidance Computer measures a mere 115,000 lines of code.[a] Implementing nullable reference types in C# seems to be a harder problem than landing on the moon. Respect.
>
> ———————
> a.   https://github.com/code-as-a-crime-scene/Apollo-11

Of course, there's always the counterargument that if we abstract our tests too much, they become harder to understand. That's absolutely true. But it's also true that there's a whole gulf of abstractions between "not at all" and "too much." Perhaps there's a mid-point where we can pay attention to the abstraction level in our tests without going completely overboard with abstraction acrobatics? Again, parameterized tests, which we met in Reduce Duplication via Parameterized Tests, on page 169, are a much-underutilized tool for striking this balance.

Encapsulate the Test Criteria

Virtually all automated tests contain assertions used to verify the test outcome. (If your tests don't, then it's likely they are there merely to game the code coverage metrics; see Reverse the Perspective via Code Coverage Measures, on page 176.) In many codebases, these assertions tend to be repetitive and leaky abstractions. Let's see this in action by inspecting another Roslyn test suite, EditAndContinueWorkspaceServiceTests.cs (see the figure on page 172).

The preceding figure reveals chunks of large and non-trivial assertion blocks that are duplicated across the test suite. Again, this is an exceedingly common test smell. The problems with this testing style are a) the intent of the test becomes harder to understand and b) the duplication makes it very easy to miss updating the test criteria in all places when it changes.

The duplicated-assertion-blocks smell is a classic example of a lack of encapsulation. The solution is straightforward: encapsulate the test criteria in a custom assert with a descriptive name that can communicate without the need for the code comment, and re-use the custom assert when your tests call for it. Test data has to be encapsulated just like any other implementation detail.

Weigh the Use of Code Duplication in Tests

We programmers have become conditioned to despise copy-paste code, for good reasons. We all know that copy-paste makes code harder to modify. There's always the risk of forgetting to update one or all duplicated versions of the copied code. But there's a bit more to the story.

No design is exclusively good. Design always involves tradeoffs. When we ruthlessly refactor away all signs of duplication, we raise the abstraction level in our code, and to abstract means to take away. In this case, we're trading ease of understanding for locality of change.

Change coupling offers a way of distinguishing the copy-paste you don't want from the code duplication you can live with. If you identify clusters of test scripts that change together, my bet is that there's some serious copy-paste code to be found. This is high-impact copy-paste, which needs to be refactored.

Finally, be aware that reading code and writing code put different requirements on our designs. It's a fine but important distinction. Just because two code snippets look similar doesn't mean they should share the same abstraction. (Remember, DRY is about knowledge, not code.)

Distinguish Between Code and Knowledge Duplication

Consider the distinction between concepts from the problem domain and concepts from the solution domain. If two pieces of code look similar but express different domain-level concepts, we should probably live with the code duplication. Because the two pieces of code capture different business rules, they're likely to evolve at different rates and in divergent directions. On the other hand, we don't want any duplicates when it comes to code that makes up our technical solution.

Tests balance these two worlds. They capture many implicit requirements that express concepts in the problem domain. If we want our tests to also communicate that to the reader, the tests need to provide enough context. Perhaps we should accept some duplicated lines of code and be better off in the process.

Design for Human Problem-Solving

So far, we have explored several common test code smells. Often, these smells seem obvious in retrospect. So, why not choose the right abstractions from the beginning? That would be great, wouldn't it? Unfortunately, you're not likely to get there. To a large degree, programming is problem-solving. As the following figure illustrates, human problem-solving requires a certain degree of experimentation.

Human problem-solving is an inherently iterative process. We learn by doing, observing the outcome, and using that feedback to refine our understanding of the problem.

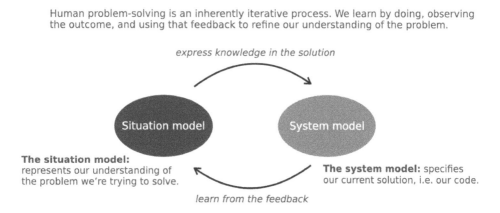

express knowledge in the solution

Situation model   **System model**

The situation model: represents our understanding of the problem we're trying to solve.

The system model: specifies our current solution, i.e. our code.

learn from the feedback

The preceding figure presents a model from educational psychology. (See *Understanding and solving word arithmetic problems [KG85].*) We programmers face the same challenges as educators: we have to communicate knowledge to all the programmers who come to the code after we've left. That knowledge is built by an iterative process between two mental models:

- The *situation model* contains everything you know about the problem, together with your existing knowledge and problem-solving strategies.

- The *system model* is a precise specification of the solution—in this case, your code.

You start with an incomplete understanding of the problem. As you express that knowledge in code, you get feedback. That feedback expands your situation model, which in turn makes you improve the system model. It means that human problem-solving is inherently iterative. You learn by doing. It also means that we cannot know up front where our code will end up.

This model of problem-solving lets us define what makes a good design: a good design is any solution where the two mental models are closely aligned. That kind of design is easier to understand because you can easily switch between the problem and the solution. Tests that are easy to understand form a fundamental building block by supporting rapid feedback.

Plan for Continuous Feedback

To reinforce our brain's problem-solving capabilities, we also need a process that supports learning. *Continuous delivery* is the most promising approach for rapid feedback. (See *Continuous Delivery: Reliable Software Releases Through Build, Test, and Deployment Automation [HF10]*.)

Continuous delivery practices enable teams in high-performing organizations to consistently implement and ship new tasks multiple times a day. Achieving that speed without compromising quality requires several high-discipline practices where automation on all levels is key. However, I have often found that many organizations meet this rapid development speed with skepticism. Hopefully, you're not there, but if you are, then this section is for you.

The most common objection against the idea of completing multiple tasks in a single day goes along the "we're different" track of arguing. There is value to that objection as it gets to the essence of what makes continuous delivery work; if your features tend to take weeks or even months to implement, how can you possibly ship them in less than a day? Impossible?

True, customer-facing features might indeed take weeks to complete. The trick—as always with software development—is to divide and conquer. Let me share the strategies that I've seen work.

Long-Running Tasks Are an Invitation to Disruptions

All software development is prone to unplanned work. The most obvious examples are incoming support issues or production failures that we need to act on immediately. The longer your task duration, the more likely you will become interrupted. A trail of interrupted tasks leads to more and more work in parallel, which is one of the most common bottlenecks in software organizations.

Divide and Conquer for Continuous Feedback

To pull this off, we need to rethink how we plan our tasks. And just to be clear: that doesn't mean some big up-front ceremony involving half the company and then some. Planning is intrinsic to all human action, and its extent should depend on the complexity of the problem we're trying to solve. Further, planning should be a continuous activity driven by feedback from what we learn as we code.

One of the most common planning mistakes is to scope your tasks to represent product features. Yes, it works for minor features and tweaks, but it quickly breaks down for any interesting product capability. Instead, the trick is to decouple the development tasks from the customer-facing features. That way, a long-running feature can be implemented as a series of short-running tasks, and test automation is the key enabler. Here are some tips on how to make it work:

1. *Dead code is your friend*—Test drive your code to ensure it does what you want, but push off integrating the new code into the application flow. Initially, the only user of your new code would be the automated tests. It's essentially dead code for now, and dead code is perfectly safe to merge at any time.

2. *Enable feature flags once the feature is completed*—Build up towards your features task by task. At some point, you might add high-level tests such as component or integration tests. Only integrate the new feature into the application flow once you have evidence that it works. This is also the point where you'd protect it with a feature flag.

3. *Decouple deployment from release*—There are two main advantages to separating deployment from release. First, it lets you choose when to release a feature, so you can time that with other activities, such as marketing events. Second, it offers a simple way of rolling back behavior in case something doesn't work as expected. Use both to your advantage.

The majority of all work happens as iterations within the first item in the list above. Sure, it might require that you keep the new code separate from the existing application code. It's always a tradeoff, but more often than not, this results in a better design by forcing us to decouple different aspects of our feature set.

Viewed from the outside, splitting features into smaller development tasks isn't a big change for our product owners and managers. The road map still has to be prioritized, and that's typically done at the feature level. However, for us as developers, completing a stream of small tasks that build upon each other gives a much better fit with how code evolves. There's nothing like the feedback you get from a running system.

Reverse the Perspective via Code Coverage Measures

Most organizations that invest in continuous delivery and test automation also implement *code coverage* metrics. Code coverage tells you how much of your code is executed via automated tests. It's a useful yet frequently misused metric, where the problems tend to start the moment we make code coverage a KPI with a minimum required threshold, such as "all code must have at least 80 percent coverage."

Instead, the level of coverage you need is context-dependent. A complex hotspot that you look to refactor? I'd like to be close to full coverage in that case. A stable piece of code where we only make a minor change? Well, perhaps it's enough to only cover the impacted logic.

This means that the specific figure you get is secondary. While it's possible to write large programs with full coverage, it's not an end in itself, nor is it meaningful as a general recommendation. It's just a number.

For that reason, I don't bother analyzing coverage until I've finished the initial version of a module. But then it gets interesting. The feedback you get is based on your understanding of the application code you just wrote. Perhaps there's a function that isn't covered or a branch in the logic that's never taken?

To get the most out of this measure, try analyzing the cause behind low coverage. Sometimes, it's okay to leave it as-is, but more often, you'll find that you've overlooked some aspect of the solution. Used this way, code coverage becomes a valuable feedback loop for spotting misalignments between your problem and solution models.

Joe asks:
What Can I Do to Increase My Code Coverage?

There's a strong correlation between good design and ease of testing: if your code is hard to test, you have a design problem, not a test problem. As such, the refactorings we explored in Chapter 6, Remediate Complicated Code, on page 63 will help you to get even the most complex hotspots under test. Let me share a story.

Namespace	Line Coverage
deep-learning.predictions.inputs	32
deep-learning.predictions.layers	40
deep-learning.predictions.gradient-descent	11
deep-learning.predictions.back-propagation	52

A couple of years ago, I decided to implement a deep learning network from scratch—no libraries, no framework. It was an obvious toy program to explore how those networks achieve their perceived magic. As a challenge, I decided to do it in functional programming with an artificial constraint: no conditional logic. No if statements, for loops, and so forth. I also wrote tests as I went along, and when I finally looked at the coverage report, it came out at 100 percent since there was only a single path through the code. It's obviously not a general solution, but a lot can be gained from keeping our code as conditionless as possible.

Understand the Costs of Automation Gone Wrong

Automation and delivery practices go hand-in-hand. When things go wrong, the most obvious problem is that teams spend more time keeping tests up and running than developing new features. That's not where you want to be. Remember Lehman's law of continuing change? Without new features, your software becomes less useful.

Another, less obvious, cost is psychological. Consider an ideal system. There, a broken test would be a loud cry to pause other tasks and focus on finding the bug causing the test to fail. But when we start to accept failing tests as the normal state of affairs, we've lost. A failing test is no longer a warning signal but a potential false positive. Over time, you lose faith in the tests and blame them. As such, a failed test-automation project costs more than just the time spent on maintaining test environments and scripts.

In this chapter, you learned techniques and strategies for catching such problems. This treatment completes the architectural outlook, but you'll continue to build on the analysis techniques in Part III as you discover how to add social analyses on top of your technical investigations. When you complete that, you'll have come full circle, and you'll be able to diagnose any codebase, whether it's a small project run by a handful of people or a massive enterprise work spanning multiple development teams. You'll start this journey in the next chapter, where you'll see how your organization impacts the code you're writing. But first, try the following exercises to apply what you've learned in this chapter.

Exercises

The following exercises let you detect and remediate bottlenecks in test development. Note that all issues are from real-world code and illustrate some common patterns you'll likely encounter in other codebases.

Act on Hotspots in the Test's Test

- Repository: https://github.com/code-as-a-crime-scene/junit5
- Language: Java
- Domain: JUnit is a legendary test library with a rich history.
- Analysis snapshot: https://tinyurl.com/junit-change-coupling

An architectural hotspot analysis offers a wonderful way of prioritizing the parts of a larger system that require our attention.

The figure on page 179 visualizes the architectural hotspots in JUnit5, effectively reflecting where the development efforts have been focused over the past year. The junit-jupiter-engine component stands out: there have been 53 commits to that code. Since JUnit is heavy on testing, it's worth looking at the interior of the junit-jupiter-engine.

Investigate the change coupling and focus it on the test files belonging to junit-jupiter-engine. Can you identify any test coupling that looks suspicious and potentially indicative of technical debt?

Uncover Expensive Change Patterns in Test Code

- Repository: https://github.com/code-as-a-crime-scene/aspnetcore

- Language: C#

- Domain: ASP.NET Core is a framework for building web apps, IoT apps, and mobile back ends.

- Analysis snapshot: https://tinyurl.com/aspnet-change-coupling

In Profile Targets in Test Code, on page 163, we learned how to use change coupling as an early warning system for when our tests become expensive to maintain. We performed the analyses at the architectural level. Once we noticed the high-level warning signs, we dug deeper with a file-level change coupling analysis.

With this in mind, investigate the test files in ASP.NET Core. Can you detect any suspicious change patterns?

Refactor Test Code

- Repository: https://github.com/code-as-a-crime-scene/spring-boot
- Language: Java
- Domain: Spring Boot is a framework for creating stand-alone applications.
- Analysis snapshot: https://tinyurl.com/springbot-xray-coupling

In this chapter, we discussed the importance of monitoring our test code. As the following figure shows, the test-code portion grows more rapidly than the application code in Spring Boot. This might not be a problem in itself, but we should always look for signs of trouble so that we can act early.

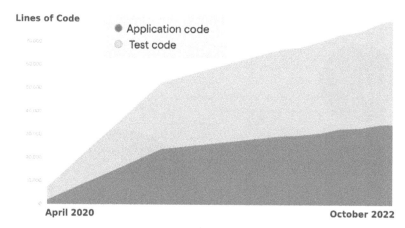

One such sign is DRY violations. Earlier, we looked at duplicated test criteria, a common reason tests become hard to maintain. However, tests also tend to contain other types of duplicated logic. So let's revisit the test hotspot AbstractServletWebServerFactoryTests.java in Spring Boot, but this time, looking at a trickier form of duplication in the following code:

```
void serverHeaderCanBeCustomizedWhenUsingSsl() throws Exception {
    AbstractServletWebServerFactory factory = getFactory();
    factory.setServerHeader("MyServer");
    factory.setSsl(getSsl(null, "password", "src/test/resources/test.jks"));
    this.webServer = factory.getWebServer(new ServletRegistrationBean<>(new ExampleServlet(true, false), "/hello"));
    this.webServer.start();
    SSLConnectionSocketFactory socketFactory = new SSLConnectionSocketFactory(
            new SSLContextBuilder().loadTrustMaterial(null, new TrustSelfSignedStrategy()).build());
    PoolingHttpClientConnectionManager connectionManager = PoolingHttpClientConnectionManagerBuilder.create()
            .setSSLSocketFactory(socketFactory).build();
    HttpClient httpClient = this.httpClientBuilder.get().setConnectionManager(connectionManager).build();
    ClientHttpResponse response = getClientResponse(getLocalUrl("https", "/hello"), HttpMethod.GET,
            new HttpComponentsClientHttpRequestFactory(httpClient));
    assertThat(response.getHeaders().get("Server")).containsExactly("MyServer");
}


void serverHeaderIsDisabledByDefaultWhenUsingSsl() throws Exception {
    AbstractServletWebServerFactory factory = getFactory();
    factory.setSsl(getSsl(null, "password", "src/test/resources/test.jks"));
    this.webServer = factory.getWebServer(new ServletRegistrationBean<>(new ExampleServlet(true, false), "/hello"));
    this.webServer.start();
    SSLConnectionSocketFactory socketFactory = new SSLConnectionSocketFactory(
            new SSLContextBuilder().loadTrustMaterial(null, new TrustSelfSignedStrategy()).build());
    PoolingHttpClientConnectionManager connectionManager = PoolingHttpClientConnectionManagerBuilder.create()
            .setSSLSocketFactory(socketFactory).build();
    HttpClient httpClient = this.httpClientBuilder.get().setConnectionManager(connectionManager).build();
    ClientHttpResponse response = getClientResponse(getLocalUrl("https", "/hello"), HttpMethod.GET,
            new HttpComponentsClientHttpRequestFactory(httpClient));
    assertThat(response.getHeaders().get("Server")).isNullOrEmpty();
}
```

The code in this comparison has issues that go beyond the glaring duplication. Despite being just a few lines, it's hard to interpret the code's intent and understand the test variations. Let's get down to the code: how would you refactor these tests?

Part III

Meet the Social Side of Your Code

Here we expand our vision into the fascinating field of social psychology. Software development is prone to many of the social fallacies and biases we meet in our everyday life. They just manifest themselves in a different setting.

In this part, you'll learn to analyze the communication and interaction between developers. We'll also cover the perils of multiple authors working on the same module and introduce techniques to predict post-release defects. Best of all, we'll pull it off from the perspective of your code. This is your codebase like you've never seen it before!

CHAPTER 12

Meet Norms, Groups, and False Serial Killers

As far as technology goes, you now have what you need to uncover the mysteries of your codebase. However, large-scale software projects are more than technical problems. Software development is also a social activity. Programming involves social interactions with our peers, customers, and managers. Those interactions range from individual conversations to important decisions made in large groups.

Just as you want to ensure that your software architecture supports how you evolve your system, you also want to ensure that how you organize your work aligns with how the system is structured.

How well you and your team fare with these social aspects influences how your system looks. That's why social psychology is just as important to master as any programming language. In this final part of the book, you'll learn about social biases, how to predict bugs from the way you work, and how to build a knowledge map of your codebase. And just as before, we'll mine supporting data from our version-control systems.

We'll start with the social biases. These biases may lead to disastrous decisions, so you want to be aware of and recognize them. We'll then learn how to gather objective data on the social aspects of software development to inform our decisions about team organization, responsibilities, and processes. Let's start in the middle of a criminal investigation.

Learn Why the Right People Don't Speak Up

In the early 1990s, Sweden had its first serial killer. The case led to an unprecedented manhunt. Not for an offender—he was already locked up—but for the victims. There were no bodies.

A year earlier, Thomas Quick, incarcerated in a mental institution, started confessing to one brutal murder after another. The killings Quick confessed to were all well-known unsolved cases.

Over the course of some hectic years, Swedish and Norwegian law enforcement dug around in forests and traveled across the country in search of hard evidence. At the height of the craze, they even emptied a lake. Yet not a single bone was found.

This striking lack of evidence didn't prevent the courts from sentencing Quick to eight of the murders. They judged his story as plausible because he knew detailed facts only the true killer could've known. Except, Quick was innocent. Both he and the investigators fell prey to powerful cognitive and social biases.

The story about Thomas Quick is a case study of the dangers of social biases in groups. The setting of his story is different from what we encounter in our daily lives, but the biases aren't. The social forces that led to the Thomas Quick disaster are present in any software project.

Understand Process Loss in Teams

We'll get back to the resolution of the Quick story soon. But let's first understand social biases so we can prevent our own group disasters from happening.

When we work together in a group to accomplish something—for example, to design that amazing web application that will knock Google Search down—we influence each other. Together, we sometimes turn seemingly impossible things into reality. Other times, the group fails miserably. In both cases, the group exhibits what social scientists call *process loss*.

Process loss is the theory that groups, just as machines, cannot operate at 100 percent efficiency. The act of working together has several costs that we need to keep in check. All teams exhibit process loss, but the reasons for it differ depending on the tasks we perform. In a software development context, where our tasks are complex and interdependent, most of our process loss is due to communication and coordination overhead, as shown in the figure on page 185. Consequently, studies on groups frequently find that they perform below their potential.

So, why do we choose to work in groups when it's obviously inefficient? Well, the task is often too big for a single individual. Today's software products are so large and complex that we have no other choice than to build an organization around them. We must remember that as we move to teams and hierarchies, we pay a price: process loss.

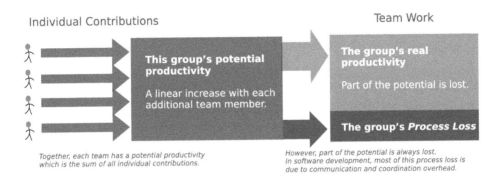

Together, each team has a potential productivity which is the sum of all individual contributions.

However, part of the potential is always lost. In software development, most of this process loss is due to communication and coordination overhead.

When we pay for something, we expect a return. We know we'll lose a little efficiency in all team efforts; it's inevitable. (You'll learn more about minimizing coordination and communication overhead in subsequent chapters.) What's worse is that social forces may rip your group's efforts into shreds and leave nothing but broken designs and bug-ridden code behind. Let's see what we can do to avoid that.

Watch Out for Motivational Process Loss

Excess coordination overhead might well be the leading cause of process loss, but poor leadership with unclear goals is a strong runner-up. When our goals aren't clearly tied to the project outcome, teams suffer a loss of motivation.

As a technical leader, make sure to communicate the background for each task or feature request. Explain how they benefit the customers and the company, and remember to share the end-user feedback with the rest of the team to close the motivational loop. Contextual information like this is just as important as any technical requirements.

Learn About Social Biases

Pretend for a moment that you've joined a new team. On your first day, the team gathers to discuss two design alternatives. You get a short overview before the team leader suggests you all vote for the best alternative.

It probably sounds a little odd to you. You don't know enough about the initial problem, and you'd rather see a simple prototype of each suggested design to make an informed decision. So, what do you do?

If you're like most of us, you start to look around. You look at how your colleagues react. Since they all seem comfortable and accepting of the proposed decision procedure, you choose to go along with the group. After all, you're fresh on the team and don't want to start by rejecting something everyone else believes in. As in Hans Christian Andersen's fairy tale, "The Emperor's New Clothes," no one mentions that the emperor is naked. We'll get to why that's the case soon, but let's first address an important question about the role of the overall culture.

Recognize the Connection Between Technology Choice and Culture

Different cultures vary in how sensitive they are to certain biases. Most research on the topic has focused on East-West differences. But we don't need to look that far. To understand how profoundly culture affects us, let's look at different programming communities.

Take a look at the code in the speech balloon of this image. It's a piece of APL code. APL is part of the family of array programming languages. The first time you see APL code, it will probably look just like this figure: a cursing cartoon character or plain line noise. But there's a strong logic to it that results in compact programs. This compactness leads to a different mindset.

The APL code calculates six lottery numbers, guaranteed to be unique, and returns them sorted in ascending order.[1] As you see in the code, there are no intermediate variables to reveal the code's intent. Contrast this with how a corresponding Java solution would look.

Object-oriented programmers value descriptive names like randomLotteryNumberGenerator. To an APL programmer, *that's* line noise that obscures the real intent of the code. We need more names in Java, C#, or C++ because our logic—the stuff that does something—is spread out across multiple functions and classes. When our language allows us to express all of that functionality in a one-liner, our context is different, affecting how we and our community think.

Different cultures have different values that affect how their members behave. Remember that when you choose a technology, you also choose a culture.

Understand Pluralistic Ignorance

Earlier in our fictional example about joining a new team, you fell prey to *pluralistic ignorance*. Pluralistic ignorance happens when everyone privately

---

1.   http://en.wikipedia.org/wiki/APL_(programming_language)

rejects a norm but thinks everyone else in the group supports it. Over time, pluralistic ignorance can lead to situations where a group follows rules that all of its members reject in private.

We fall into this social trap when we conclude the behavior of our peers depends on beliefs that are different from our own, even if we behave identically. That's what happened around Andersen's naked emperor. Because everyone praised the emperor's new clothes, each individual thought they missed something obvious. That's why they chose to conform to the group behavior and play along with the praise of the wonderful clothes they couldn't see.

Another common social bias is to mistake a familiar opinion for a widespread one. If we hear the same idea repeatedly, we come to think of that opinion as more prevalent than it actually is. As if that wasn't bad enough, we fall prey to the bias even if it's the *same* person who keeps expressing that opinion (source: *Inferring the popularity of an opinion from its familiarity: A repetitive voice can sound like a chorus [WMGS07]*).

This means that one individual constantly expressing a strong opinion is enough to bias your whole software development project. It may be about technology choices, methodologies, or programming languages. Let's see what you can do about it.

Challenge Biases with Questions and Data

Most people don't like to express deviating opinions, but there are exceptions. One case is when our minority opinion aligns with the group's ideal. That is, we have a minority opinion, but it positively deviates from the group norm; the group has an ideal it values, and we take a more extreme position and value it even more. In that setting, we're more inclined to speak up, and we'll feel good about it when we do.

Within our programming world, such "good" minority opinions may include desired attributes such as automated tests and code quality. For example, if we view writing more tests as a good thing, testing everything must be even better (even if it forces us to slice our designs into unfathomable pieces). And since code quality matters, we must write code of the highest possible quality all the time (even when prototyping throwaway code).

Given what we know about pluralistic ignorance and our tendency to mistake familiar opinions for common ones, it's easy to see how these strong, deviating opinions may move a team in a more extreme direction.

Social biases are hard to avoid. When you suspect them in your team, try one of the following approaches:

- *Ask questions*—By asking a question, you make others aware that everyone doesn't share the proposed views.

- *Talk to people*—Decision biases like pluralistic ignorance often grow from our fears of rejection and criticism. So, if you think a decision is wrong but everyone else seems fine with it, talk to your peers. Ask them what they like about the decision.

- *Support decisions with data*—We cannot avoid social and cognitive biases. What we can do is to check our assumptions with data that either supports or challenges the decision. The rest of this book will arm you with several analyses for this purpose.

If you're in a leadership position, you have additional possibilities to guide your group toward good decisions:

- Use outside experts to review your decisions.
- Let subgroups work independently on the same problem.
- Avoid advocating a specific solution early in the discussions.
- Discuss worst-case scenarios to make the group risk-aware.
- Plan a second meeting up front to reconsider the decisions of the first one.

These are useful strategies for avoiding *groupthink* (source: *Group Process, Group Decision, Group Action [BK03]*). Groupthink is a disastrous consequence of social biases where the group suppresses all forms of internal dissent. The result is group decisions that ignore alternatives and the risk of failure, giving a false sense of consensus.

As you've seen, pluralistic ignorance often leads to groupthink. This seems to be what happened in the Thomas Quick case.

Witness Groupthink in Action

Let's get back to our story of Thomas Quick. Quick was sentenced for eight murders before he stopped cooperating in 2001. He no longer wanted to share his bizarre stories, nor did he have any new crimes to confess. Without Quick's confessions, there was little to do—remember, there was no hard evidence in any of the murder cases. It took almost ten years for the true story to unfold.

What had happened was that Thomas Quick was treated with a pseudoscientific version of psychotherapy back in the 1990s. The therapists managed to restore what they thought were recovered memories. (Note that the scientific support for such memories is weak at best.) The methods they used are almost identical to how you implant false memories. (See Recognize the Paradox of False Memories, on page 103.) Quick also received heavy doses of benzodiazepines, drugs that may make their users more susceptible to suggestion. Coincidentally, the moment Quick was weaned off benzodiazepine, he stopped cooperating with investigators for his alleged crimes.

The murder investigation started when the therapists told the police about Quick's confessions. Convinced by the therapists' authority that repressed memories were a valid scientific theory, the lead investigators started to interrogate Quick.

These interrogations were, well, peculiar. When Quick gave the wrong answers, he got help from the chief detective. After all, Quick was fighting with repressed memories and needed all the support he could get. Eventually, Quick got enough clues to the case to create a coherent story. That was how he was convicted.

By now, you can probably see where the Thomas Quick story is heading. Do you recognize any social biases in it? To us in the software world, the most interesting aspects of this tragic story are in the periphery. Let's look at them.

Understand the Role of Authorities

Once the Quick scandal, with its false confessions, was made public, many people started to speak up. These people, involved in the original police investigations, now told the press about the serious doubts they'd had from the very start. Yet few of them had spoken up ten years earlier when Quick was originally convicted.

The social setting was ideal for pluralistic ignorance—particularly since the main prosecutor was a man of authority and was convinced of Quick's guilt. He frequently expressed that opinion and contributed to the groupthink.

From what you now know about social biases, it's no wonder that a lot of smart people decided to keep their opinions to themselves and play along. Luckily, you've also got some ideas for avoiding having similar situations unfold in your own teams. Let's add one more item to that list by discussing a popular method that often does more harm than good—brainstorming.

Move Away from Traditional Brainstorming

If you want to watch process loss in full bloom, check out any brainstorming session. It's like a best-of collection of social and cognitive biases. That said, you can be productive with brainstorming, but you need to change the format drastically. Here's why and how.

The original purpose of brainstorming was to facilitate creative thinking. The premise is that a group can generate more ideas than its individuals can on their own. Unfortunately, research on the topic doesn't support that claim. On the contrary, research has found that brainstorming produces *fewer* ideas than expected and that the quality of the produced ideas may suffer as well.

There are several reasons for the dramatic process loss. For example, in brainstorming, we're told not to criticize ideas. In reality, everyone knows they're being evaluated anyway, and they behave accordingly. Further, the format of brainstorming allows only one person at a time to speak. That makes it hard to follow up on ideas since we need to wait for our time to talk. In the meantime, it's easy to be distracted by other ideas and discussions.

To reduce the process loss, you need to move away from the traditional brainstorming format. It turns out that even if a truly inspirational group leader can increase a team's creativity, they cannot fully eliminate the biases inherent in brainstorming. (Besides, there might not always be an abundance of inspirational leaders eager to join your internal meetings.)

Instead, the solution is much simpler: move brainstorming sessions to computers instead of face-to-face communication and keep the contributions visible but anonymous. In that setting, where social biases are minimized, digital brainstorming may actually deliver on its promise. (See *Idea Generation in Computer-Based Groups: A New Ending to an Old Story [VDC94]* for a good overview of the research.) As a positive side effect, *Inspiring group creativity: Comparing anonymous and identified electronic brainstorming [SAK98]* shows that good group leadership—if you have it—has a stronger impact when team members can contribute anonymously to collective problem-solving.

Now you know what to avoid and what to do instead. Before we move on, take a look at some more bias-reducing tools.

Discover Your Team's Modus Operandi

Remember the geographical offender-profiling techniques you learned back in Learn Geographical Profiling of Crimes, on page 12? One of the challenges with profiling is linking a series of crimes to the same offender. Sometimes, there's DNA evidence or witnesses. When there's not, the police have to rely on the offender's *modus operandi*.

A modus operandi is like a criminal signature. For example, the gentleman bandit you read about in Meet the Innocent Robber, on page 104 was characterized by his polite manners and concern for his victims.

Software teams each have their unique modus operandi, too. If you manage to uncover it, it will help you understand how your team works. It will not be perfect and precise information, but it can guide your discussions and decisions by opening new perspectives. One way to do that is by using commit messages.

Use Commit Messages as a Discussion Basis

Some years ago, I worked on a project that was running late. On the surface, everything looked fine. We were four teams, and everyone kept busy. Yet, the project didn't make any real progress regarding completed features. Soon, the overtime bell began to ring.

Luckily, there was a skilled leader on one of the teams. He decided to find out the root cause of what was holding the developers back. I opted in to provide some data as a basis for the discussions. Here's the type of data we used:

```
commit9593c2ee9546f2d9ea2d24ff56743a70b4af2a01
Author: XX
Date:    Wed Aug 6 13:27:06 2014 -0400

    SERVER-14680 remove broken unit test  ⟵ Process information

commit6a81ce76079c72b7f7c78170ac33f7a7c2772922
Author: XX
Date:    Tue Aug 5 09:43:54 2014 -0400

    SERVER-14783 switch maxSyncSourceLagSecs to Seconds

commit8130d43a0dbc51413fd460efc4bb27108c1ea315
Author: YY
Date:    Wed Jul 30 11:59:05 2014 -0400

    SERVER-14680 initial topocoord unit tests (plus some bug fixes the tests found)

commit35f827aef4ddfcf9acb9e4b90cb200ff29183b7c
Author: XX
Date:    Mon Aug 4 14:42:58 2014 -0400              Info on where we
                                                    spent our time
    SERVER-14714: Add stack trace signal handler
    SERVER-14181: Dump dbtest & python processes, add timeout
                                     ↖The features we worked on
```

This data is useful, but there's another consideration. Until now, you've focused on techniques that deal with the code you're changing. However, a version-control log has more information. Every time you commit a change, you provide social information. Have a look at the following *word cloud*:

This word cloud was created from the commit messages in the Glowstone repository[2] you saw in Chapter 9 by using the following command:

```
prompt> git log --pretty=format:'%s'
Fix QueryHandler responds on 127.0.0.1 for wildcard address (#1134)
use ASM10 opcode for compatibility with latest Java
handle signature response
1.19 protocol and features (#1139)
...
```

The command extracts all the commit messages. You have several simple alternatives for visualizing them. This one was created by pasting the messages into WordArt.[3]

If you look at the commit cloud, you can see that certain terms dominate. What you'll learn right now is not scientific, but it's a useful heuristic: the words that stand out tell you where the team spends their time. Looking back at the preceding figure as an example, it seems that bug fixes are the recent dominant activity in the Glowstone project. This could very well be a symptom of technical debt, as indicated by the issues you discovered back in Focus on Change-Coupled Hotspots, on page 127.

Let's return to the project you saw at the beginning of this section. When we checked the word cloud, we saw two prominent words. One of them highlighted

---

2. https://github.com/code-as-a-crime-scene/Glowstone
3. https://wordart.com/

a supporting feature of less importance where we surprisingly spent a lot of time. The second one pointed to the automated tests. It turned out the teams spent a significant portion of their workdays maintaining and updating tests. This finding was verified by the techniques you learned in Profile Targets in Test Code, on page 163. We could then focus our energy on dealing with the situation.

What story does your own version-control log tell?

Read the Story in Your Team's Commit Cloud

Commit clouds are a good basis for discussions around your process and daily work. The clouds present a distilled version of your team's daily code-centered activities. They give you a different perspective on your development, which stimulates discussions.

Consider the following word cloud, which reflects the development activity from TeslaMate.[4] "Bump" dominates and could be filtered away since it merely indicates that the third-party dependencies are being kept up to date. If you instead look to the right, you see terms from the problem domain like "Charge," "Car," and "Drive." That's a good sign.

We *want* to see words from our domain in a commit cloud, like in the preceding TeslaMate cloud. What we *don't want* to see are words that indicate quality problems in our code or process, such as "Bug" or "Crash." When you find those types of indications, you want to drill deeper.

Commit messages have even more to offer. A new line of research proposes that commit messages convey something about the team itself. A team of

---

4. https://github.com/code-as-a-crime-scene/teslamate

researchers found this out by analyzing commit messages in different open-source projects with respect to their emotional content. The study compared the expressed emotions to factors such as the programming language used, the team location, and the day of the week. (See *Sentiment analysis of commit comments in GitHub [GAL14]*.)

Among other findings, the results of the study point to Java programmers expressing the most negative feelings and distributed teams the most positive.

The study is a fun read. But there's a serious topic underpinning it. Emotions play a large role in our daily lives. They're strong motivators that profoundly influence our behavior, often without making us consciously aware of why we react the way we do. Our emotions affect our creativity, teamwork, and productivity. With that in mind, it's surprising that we don't pay more attention to them. Studies like this are an important step in the right direction.

Data Doesn't Replace Communication

Given all the fascinating analyses, it's easy to drown in technical solutions to social problems. But no matter how many innovative data analyses we have, they're no replacement for actually talking to the rest of the team and taking an active role in the daily work. The methods in this chapter can help you ask the right questions.

Mine Organizational Metrics from Code

In this chapter, you learned about process loss and that groups never perform at their maximum potential. Teamwork and organizations are investments we pay for, and they should be considered as such.

You also learned that groups are sensitive to social biases. You saw that there are biases in all kinds of groups—software development included—and you need to be aware of the risks.

That leads us to the challenges of scaling software development. As we go from a small group of programmers to interdependent teams, we increase the coordination and communication overhead, increasing the risk of biased decisions. The relative success of any large-scale programming effort depends more on the project's people than on any single technology.

Over the coming chapters, you'll learn about fascinating research findings that support this view. As you'll see, if you want to know about the quality of a piece of software, look at the organization that built it. You'll also learn how to mine and analyze organizational data from your version-control system.

As you proceed, please keep the social biases in mind to help you make informed decisions and challenge groupthink. In the next chapter, you'll explore how the number of programmers affects code quality. But first, try the following exercises to help you put into practice what you've learned in this chapter.

Exercises

These exercises help you drill into modus operandi analysis and follow up on the findings. They focus on large-scale, real-world codebases, so several correct answers and directions might exist. Please make sure to check out Appendix 1, Solutions to the Exercises, on page 267 for alternative approaches.

Identify the Team's Modus Operandi

- Repository: https://github.com/code-as-a-crime-scene/mongo
- Language: C++, JavaScript
- Domain: Mongo DB is a document database.
- Analysis Snapshot: n/a

The most important topic in this chapter was social biases; they have probably wrecked more projects than bad code alone. Those biases are fairly easy to spot in workplace situations once you know about them, but they are still notoriously hard to prevent. Getting objective data can help focus group conversations on issues that would otherwise be hard to surface.

Let's pretend you're part of the Mongo DB team, and it's time for a retrospective. Create a word cloud from the commit activity. Are there any terms in that cloud that would make a good starting point for a conversation?

Drill into the Main Topic

- Repository: https://github.com/code-as-a-crime-scene/mongo
- Language: C++, JavaScript
- Domain: Mongo DB is a document database.
- Analysis Snapshot: n/a

Isn't it a bit suspicious that the term "Test" stands out in the Mongo DB word cloud? Sure, if tests are added as an afterthought, this could very well signal progress. But if not, we might fall into the traps outlined in Chapter 11, Expose Hidden Bottlenecks: Delivery and Automation, on page 161.

Explore the raw commit messages in the Git log with respect to tests. Are there any warning signs?

CHAPTER 13

Discover Organizational Metrics in Your Codebase

In the previous chapter, you learned about social biases and how they affect group decisions and interactions with other developers. You also discovered that the social aspects of software development are just as important as the technical ones. Now, you'll see what that means in practice.

You'll start by examining the classic software "laws" of Brooks and Conway and see how they fare against modern research. Based on those findings, you'll explore organizational metrics that let you analyze the quality of your code from the team's perspective. This is an important perspective; getting the organizational side of software wrong has wrecked more codebases than even VB6. Let's start with an example from a failed software project.

Kill a Project: A How-to Guide

I once joined a project that was doomed from the very beginning. The stakeholders wanted the project completed within a timeframe that was virtually impossible to meet. Of course, if you've spent some time in the software business, you know that's standard practice. This case was different because the company had detailed data on an almost identical project, and they tried to game their data.

The historical records indicated that the project could be completed in roughly one year using their five in-house developers. This time, however, they had internal pressure to get it done in just three months. That's a quarter of the time. So, how do you take a project that you know will need a year and compress it down to just one-fourth of that time? Easy—you just throw four times as many developers on the project. Simple math, right? And indeed, the organization went ahead with that proposal. There was just one slight problem waiting around the corner: this tactic doesn't work and never has. Let's see what happened next.

Don't Scale the Wrong Dimension

The in-house team had already fleshed out the software architecture, which, unsurprisingly, was a layered architecture. That architecture might have worked for the original small team, but 15 additional consultants joined the project, and quicker than you can say, "process loss," all developers were organized into four separate feature teams (see the following image).

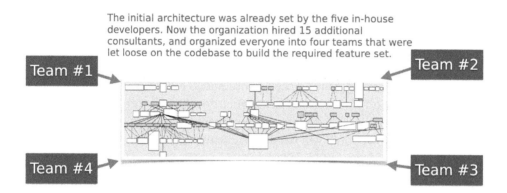

The initial architecture was already set by the five in-house developers. Now the organization hired 15 additional consultants, and organized everyone into four teams that were let loose on the codebase to build the required feature set.

I wasn't there from the start but joined later for the inevitable postmortem analysis and a desperate rescue attempt because—and here's the spoiler alert—this project didn't finish in three months.

So how long did they need? Well, it's a fair guess that the initial, data-based timeline of one year should still hold. After all, they now had four times as many people. Instead, the project actually needed two years until its initial release. And the only reason they managed to complete it after two years was because a) they cut the scope aggressively and b) they scaled down the team.

The idea that you can get much more done with a smaller team still seems counterintuitive to many organizations, yet it shouldn't come as a surprise to anyone who has read *The Mythical Man-Month*. Let's revisit that classic.

See That a Man-Month Is Still Mythical

If you pick up a 40-year-old programming book, you expect it to be hopelessly dated. Our technical field has changed a lot over the decades. But, the people side of software development is different. The best book on the subject, *The*

\\/
ʳʸⳆ
Joe asks:
Isn't That Type of Overstaffing Super Obvious?

Well, everything is obvious in retrospect; hindsight bias is a thing, after all. The problem is that only symptoms reach the surface, which is why it's so hard to diagnose the root causes. As an example, when joining that project, I interviewed the lead developers. All of them remarked that the code was hard to understand. Initially, this was surprising. Sure, a hotspot analysis had revealed some accidental complexity, but the code wasn't *that* hard to understand. I've seen worse. Much worse.

Then it occurred to me: the code was hard to understand because even if you write a piece of code today, three days later, it will look completely different because five other developers have worked on the code in parallel. This volatility of the codebase makes it impossible to maintain any stable mental model of how the code works. You'll find yourself in a constant onboarding mode, only interrupted by painful merges and critical bug reports.

Mythical Man-Month: Essays on Software Engineering [Bro95], was published in the 1970s and describes lessons from a development project in the 1960s. Yet the book hasn't lost its relevance.

In a way, that's depressing for our industry, as it signals a failure to learn. But it goes deeper than that. Although our technology has advanced dramatically, people haven't really changed. We still walk around with brains that are biologically identical to the ones of our ancestral, non-coding cavemen. That's why we repeatedly fall prey to the same social and cognitive biases, with broken software covering our tracks.

You saw this in the story of the doomed project we just discussed. It's a story that perfectly embodies the essence of what we now know as *Brooks's Law* from *The Mythical Man-Month: Essays on Software Engineering [Bro95]*: "Adding manpower to a late software project makes it later."

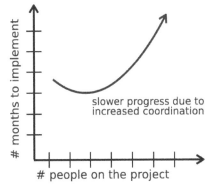

The rationale behind Brooks's Law is that intellectual work is hard to parallelize. While the total number of hours available increases linearly with the number of people available, the additional communication effort increases at a more rapid rate. This combinatorial explosion of possible communication paths is illustrated in the figure on page 200.

The essence of Brooks's Law:
The number of possible communication paths
increase with $(n^2 - n) / 2$

n is the number of people on the team.

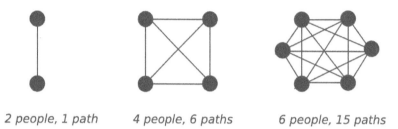

2 people, 1 path   4 people, 6 paths   6 people, 15 paths

At some point, each additional person becomes a net loss for the overall productivity; the extra hours available get consumed by increased coordination needs. Run it too far, and you create an organization that gets little done besides administrating itself (aka the Kafka management style).

As indicated earlier, these types of failures might appear obvious, making them easy to write off as incompetent management decisions. However, process loss is exceedingly common, and unless we're actively monitoring our code from the team's perspective, we will step into these traps. Over the years, I've seen multiple companies and products with strong forward trajectories keep falling victim to Brooks's Law. Surprisingly, success itself might lay the ground for future failures. Let's look at one more case study.

The diagram on page 201 tells the story of overtime, stress, and wasted budgets. On the left-hand Y-axis, you have the number of *story points* delivered per week divided by the number of developers in the team. The right-hand Y-axis shows how the team scaled up over a year.

This project got off to a great start, delivering its minimum viable product (MVP) in late 2018. In an attempt to capitalize on this initial success, the organization tried to scale up its development organization, which you can see reflected in the growing number of authors. However, as you see in the diagram, each time the number of authors grows, the development output decreases: there seems to be an inverse correlation between people and productivity. It's Brooks's Law in its essence, and when that happens, what scales isn't your delivery output but your process loss. Avoid doing this in your projects.

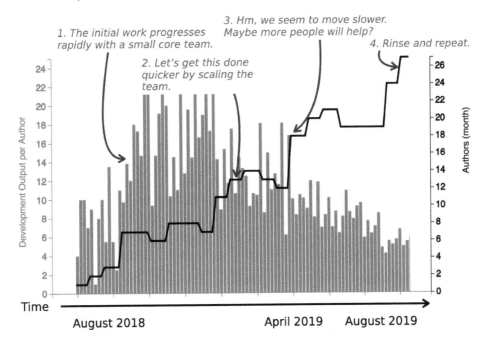

Scaling the team without architectural support and proper processes increases the process loss.

1. The initial work progresses rapidly with a small core team.

2. Let's get this done quicker by scaling the team.

3. Hm, we seem to move slower. Maybe more people will help?

4. Rinse and repeat.

Visualize Brooks's Law

Even though Brooks's Law is 50 years old, organizations still fall victim to it. Far too often, neither the architecture nor the organization can accommodate the growing number of people. A simple way of avoiding the problem is to use the technique presented in this section: fetch a simple output metric from product management tools like Jira, divide it by the number of people on the team, and plot the time series. The moment you notice that the number of people added outpaces the development output, it's time to put on the brakes.

Social psychologists have known for decades about the perils inherent in scaling a team. Group size alone has a strong negative impact on communication. With increased group size, a smaller percentage of group members take part in discussions, process loss accelerates, and the larger anonymity leads to less responsibility for the overall goals. So, let's understand the consequences of larger groups by visiting a murder case with implications for software organizations, too.

Understand Diffusion of Responsibility

A famous and tragic criminal case illustrates how group size impacts our sense of responsibility. Back in 1964, Kitty Genovese, a young woman, was assaulted and killed on her way home in New York City. The attack lasted for 30 minutes. At least a dozen neighbors heard her screams for help. Yet no one came to help, and not one called the police.

The tragedy led to a burst of research on responsibility. Why didn't anyone at least call the police? Were people that apathetic?

The researchers who studied the Kitty Genovese case focused on our social environment. Often, the situation itself has a stronger influence on our behavior than personality factors do. In this case, each of Kitty Genovese's neighbors assumed someone else had already called the police. This psychological state is now known as *diffusion of responsibility*, and the effect has been confirmed in experiments. (See the original research in *Bystander intervention in emergencies: diffusion of responsibility [DL68]*.)

Software development teams aren't immune to the diffusion of responsibility. With increased group size, more quality problems and code smells will be left unattended.

Skilled people can reduce these problems but can never eliminate them. The only winning move is not to scale—at least not beyond the point your codebase can sustain. The takeaway is that if you see something that looks wrong, be it a quality problem or organizational trouble, just bring it up. Chances are that the larger your group is, the fewer the number of people who will react, and you can make a difference.

Analyze Hotspots for Coordination Issues

As we discussed in the first parts of this book, it's virtually impossible to maintain a holistic view of a large codebase. We just can't fit all the details in a single brain. This means that while we recognize when we suffer from quality problems, we don't necessarily know the root causes or how deep potential problems go. There are too many moving parts.

These root causes frequently go beyond technical difficulties and include an organizational component. On many projects, the organizational aspects alone determine success or failure. We'll soon see how to shine a light on these factors, but let's first discuss some related aspects from the open-source projects we use in the case studies.

Know the Difference Between Open-Source and Proprietary Software

So far, we have used real-world examples for all our analyses. The problems we have uncovered are all genuine. But when it comes to the people side, it gets harder to rely on open-source examples because many open-source projects don't have a traditional corporate organization. This means we need to extrapolate to a corporate context when interpreting the results of the analyses, but only a little bit. The context and conclusions might differ, but the analyses and problems are identical. Let's look at what we know.

Open-source projects are often self-selected communities that tend to rely on loosely coordinated participation. This is important since research on the subject has found that the more developers who are involved in an open-source project, the more likely that the project will succeed (source: *Brooks' versus Linus' law: an empirical test of open source projects [SEKH09]*).

Despite the number of contributors being a long-term success factor, open-source projects aren't immune to Brooks's Law. A large-scale study of 201 projects found a strong negative relationship between team size and developer productivity. Further, this negative impact of team size could be explained by the respective team's collaboration structures (see *Big Data=Big Insights? Operationalising Brooks' Law in a Massive GitHub Data Set [GMSS22]*).

There are other aspects to consider beyond productivity. In a study on Linux, researchers found that "many developers changing code may have a detrimental effect on the system's security" (source: *Secure open source collaboration: an empirical study of Linus' law [MW09]*). More specifically, with more than nine developers, the modules are sixteen times more likely to contain security flaws. These results neatly summarize the fact that open source cannot evade human nature; we pay a price for parallel development in that setting, too. With that in mind, let's get started with the organizational analyses.

Analyze Your Hotspots for Multiple Authors

Adding more people to a project isn't necessarily bad as long as we can divide our work meaningfully. The problems start when our architecture fails to sustain all the developers. To identify the problem, we inspect our hotspots for contribution patterns indicative of coordination issues.

To demonstrate this analysis, we'll move back to the Folly codebase that you looked at in Make the Business Case for Refactoring, on page 90. Folly works as a representative example because it has many active contributors, including 695 authors. As a reminder, have a look at the figure on page 204.

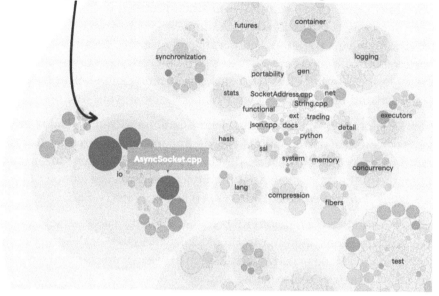

A hotspot map over the Folly codebase, showing a cluster of large, complex files in the async package.

We know from our previous visit to the codebase that it contains some challenging hotspots. To see the organizational impact, we need to collect information about the contributors. As you see in the following figure, this information is available in Git since each commit contains information about the programmer who made the change.

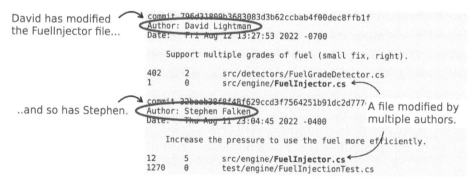

Just as we calculated change frequencies to determine hotspots, let's now calculate the author frequencies to figure out how many developers each hotspot attracts. The first step is to generate a Git log from the Folly repository:[1]

---

1. https://github.com/code-as-a-crime-scene/folly

```
prompt> git log --all --numstat --date=short \
  --pretty=format:'--%h--%ad--%aN' --no-renames \
  --after='2021-08-01' > git_folly_12_months.txt
```

It's the same command you've used before, only we're restricting the data range to the last 12 months, using the -after flag. This is because contributors are volatile, and we want to make sure that whatever problems we detect are current, not something that happened years ago. Looking at the past 12 months should give us a good indication of any potential coordination bottlenecks.

From here, we'll discover which files are shared between multiple programmers. It's a simple algorithm: group all commits by file and sum up the number of unique authors. We can automate this step via Code Maat's authors analysis:

```
prompt> maat -l git_folly_12_months.txt -c git2 -a authors
entity,    n-authors,    n-revs
build/fbcode_builder/getdeps/builder.py,   13, 38
folly/io/async/test/AsyncSSLSocketTest.cpp,12, 15
folly/io/async/test/AsyncSocketTest2.cpp,  10, 17
build/fbcode_builder/getdeps.py,            9, 28
build/fbcode_builder/getdeps/manifest.py,   9, 22
folly/io/async/AsyncSSLSocket.cpp,          9, 10
...
```

The preceding results show the files in Folly, sorted by their number of authors. The interesting information is in the n-authors column, which shows the number of programmers who have committed changes to the module.

Interestingly, builder.py, the file with the most potential coordination needs, isn't application code but is part of the build system. As with test code, this type of supporting code can become a time sink, so you should inspect the module and make sure there isn't any unwarranted complexity in the code.

The rest of the list confirms that the problematic hotspots in the async package also seem to be coordination magnets. Another way of viewing this is that the hotspot AsyncSSLSocketTest.cpp has been modified by 12 developers over the past year. This implies that any technical debt in that module will likely be expensive since it impacts a whole group of people. We'll look at this topic more closely in the next chapter. Before going there, we should visit another classic software observation related to Brooks's Law.

Spot Conway's Law in Your Code

Brooks wasn't the first to point out the link between organization and software design. A decade earlier, Melvin Conway published his classic paper that included the thesis we now recognize as *Conway's Law* (see *How do committees invent? [Con68]*):

> Any organization that designs a system (defined more broadly here than just information systems) will inevitably produce a design whose structure is a copy of the organization's communication structure.

Conway's Law has received a lot of attention over the years, so let's keep this brief. Basically, you can interpret Conway's Law in two ways. First, you can interpret it in the cynical (and fun) way, as in the The Jargon File:[2] "If you have four groups working on a compiler, you'll get a 4-pass compiler."

The other interpretation starts from the system you're building: given a proposed software architecture, how should the optimal organization look to make it happen? When interpreted in reverse like this, Conway's Law becomes a useful organizational tool. Let's see how you can use it on existing systems.

Use Conway's Law on Existing Systems

As you learned in Understand That Typing Isn't the Bottleneck in Programming, on page 4, we spend most of our time modifying existing code. Even though Conway formulated his law around the initial design of a system, the law has important implications for the continued maintenance of existing code.

Thanks to the great work of Matthew Skelton and Manuel Pais of *Team Topologies [SP19]* fame, there has been a growing interest in organizational design. *Team Topologies* presents a valuable contrast to the traditional static view of an organization. Instead, the authors state that we need a dynamic model "that takes into consideration how teams grow and interact with each other." More specifically, *Team Topologies* uses Conway's Law as a driver for team design. That is, the modularity of a software design needs to align with the responsibilities of the development teams. So, let's find out where your communication dependencies are.

Visualize Conway's Law

Your first aim is to figure out a way of quickly checking how well-aligned your organization is with the system you're building. So let's look at a new type of *communication analysis*, a litmus test for Conway's Law.

The basic idea of the communication analysis is to identify dependencies between different authors, as seen from the code. The actual algorithm is

---

2. http://catb.org/~esr/jargon/html/C/Conways-Law.html

similar to what you used for change coupling. As a starting point, look at the scenario in the following figure.

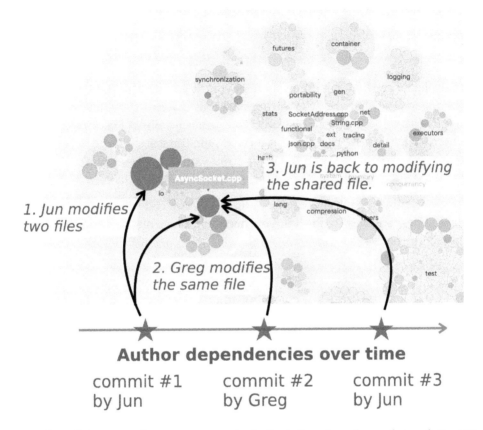

Author dependencies over time

commit #1
by Jun

commit #2
by Greg

commit #3
by Jun

Based on this scenario, we can conclude that there's a dependency between the peers Jun and Greg since they commit to the same file. In isolation, this dependency is neither good nor bad. Rather, it all depends on the context:

- *Cohesive Teams*—If Jun and Greg are on the same team, then working on the same parts of the code might even be desirable since it indicates a team that carries meaning: the members share the same context.

- *Inter-Team Dependencies*—However, should Jun and Greg be on different teams, the shared file could indicate a coordination bottleneck. In other words, it's an invitation to conflicting changes, complex merges, and bugs.

To investigate the whole codebase, move back to the Folly repository and run a communication analysis. You can re-use the Git log from the previous step since you want to maintain the shorter time window to avoid having historical organizational patterns bias the results.

```
prompt> maat -l git_folly_12_months.txt -c git2 -a communication
author,        peer,            shared,  average, strength
poponion,      Kelo,            1,       1,       100
dmitryvinn,    Dmitry Vinnik,   1,       1,       100
...
Alberto,       Sing,            2,       3,       66
Zsolt,         John,            4,       8,       50
...
```

Alright, let's see what this analysis tells you. If you look at the last line, you see a dependency between the authors Zsolt and John. They have made four commits (shared) to the same files, and the average number of commits for both authors is eight. These numbers let us calculate the strength of the dependency, which is 50 percent ((4 / 8) * 100). Or, in other words, every second time one of them makes a commit, chances are they touch the same file.

This data lets you evaluate Conway's Law in your codebase if you also add the team perspective. To do that, you need to diverge slightly and inspect an anomaly in the results.

Resolve Author Aliases

Looking back at the preceding communication results, you might have spotted that one pair, dmitryvinn and Dmitry Vinnik, might be the same physical person using two committer names. Unfortunately, Git is notorious for making it way too simple to introduce aliases: perhaps you made a couple of commits on your laptop at home, while others were done from your computer at work. Unless you take care with unifying your author info across your machines, you'll likely end up with two names in the Git logs.

Resolving aliases is a mundane task, but Git helps via a feature called *mailmap*.[3] To use the feature, add a .mailmap file to the root of your repository and specify the mapping from the alias to the preferred name for each committer. Here's what it looks like for dmitryvinn:

The proper name and email that we want in the Git log   *The alias we want to get rid of*

```
Dmitry Vinnik <some@email.com> dmitryvinn <some_other@email.com>
```

Specifying this mapping resolves the author alias. Now that you have a clean Git log, you can scale from individuals to teams.

---

3.   https://git-scm.com/docs/gitmailmap

Scale from Individuals to Teams: A Social Network in Code

Conway's Law is about the architectural alignment of your organizational units, yet your analyses execute at the level of individuals. This is, of course, due to Git operating at the level of individual authors. One way of solving this is to post-process the Git log and simply replace each author's name with their organizational team, as shown in the next figure.

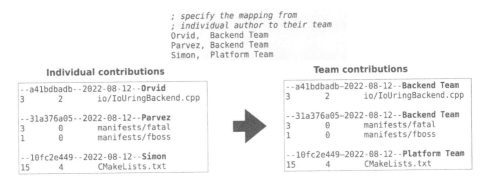

Once that's done, you'd run the same analysis on the post-processed Git log, which now contains teams—there's no algorithmic difference. With that step done, you're ready to evaluate our organization's alignment with Conway's Law:

- *Most communication paths should be between members of the same team*—This pattern indicates that the team carries meaning from an architectural perspective. People on the same team work on the same parts of the code.

- *Contributions across teams should be limited*—Any path that crosses team boundaries indicates a potential coordination bottleneck. While the occasional inter-team contribution might be a positive sign of a helpful colleague, these paths should be significantly rarer than intra-team dependencies.

Following these principles, you'd expect results similar to the top figure on page 210, which shows an organization that's well aligned with Conway's Law.

The top visualization uses links to indicate the dependencies between people. Each link indicates developers that have made commits to the same part of the code. Let's contrast this ideal alignment with the excess inter-team coordination shown in the bottom figure on page 210.

The bottom visualization might look spectacular from an aesthetic perspective, but let me assure you that the only spectacular aspect of the project it

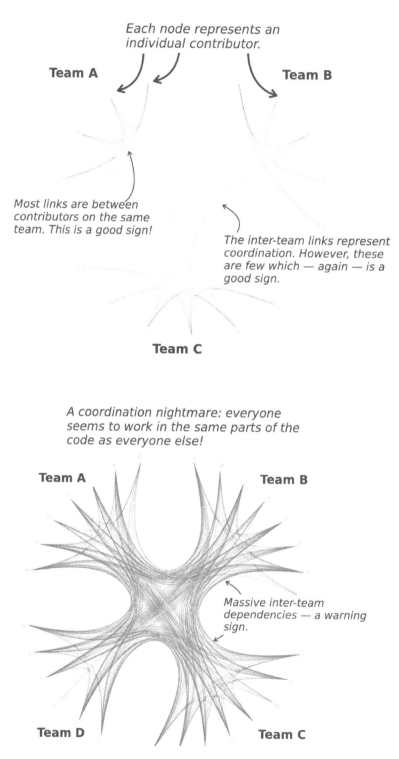

Each node represents an individual contributor.

Team A

Team B

Most links are between contributors on the same team. This is a good sign!

The inter-team links represent coordination. However, these are few which — again — is a good sign.

Team C

A coordination nightmare: everyone seems to work in the same parts of the code as everyone else!

Team A

Team B

Massive inter-team dependencies — a warning sign.

Team D

Team C

represents is the scale of its failure. Remember the project that the stakeholders attempted to complete in three months, rather than the more realistic time frame of one year, by hiring four times as many developers? This is what their resulting inter-team communication paths looked like. You also can see that despite having four teams on the org chart, in practice, those teams don't have any natural boundaries in the code. Rather, what you have is one gigantic team where everyone works everywhere with artificial organizational boundaries around them.

Viewed in this light, the communication analysis comes to represent a social network where individuals in different teams intersect with the code they're building.

Act on Inter-Team Dependencies

In this chapter, you learned that the number of authors behind a module correlates with the number of post-release defects in that code. You saw how this is a consequence of the increased communication overhead that comes with parallel work, as highlighted by Brooks's Law. From there, you transitioned to Conway's Law and saw that how you organize your work impacts the code. You learned that your project organizations must align with how the system is structured.

Identifying a problem is one thing, but mitigating it is immensely more challenging. One typical action is to rearrange the teams according to communication needs. Because those needs will change over the course of a longer project, you'll probably need to revisit these topics at regular intervals. Done right, such a rebalancing of project teams has been found to minimize communication overhead. (See *The Effect of Communication Overhead on Software Maintenance Project Staffing [DHAQ07].*)

Sometimes, it's easier—and indeed more appropriate—to redesign the shared parts of the system to align with the organization's structure. This alternative is close to what Conway himself suggests in his classic paper since he concludes that "a design effort should be organized according to the need for communication" (source: *How do committees invent? [Con68]*).

Often, both the teams *and* the software architecture need to be adjusted to remove bottlenecks. There's no quick fix, but fortunately, you're now close to having all the pieces you need. You already know how change coupling reveals dependencies. If you can complement that with the social context from this chapter, you can pinpoint where in the architecture the undesired coordination happens and which teams are impacted. This would then inform the rearchitecting steps. In the next chapter, you'll connect the remaining dots as you explore how technical problems cause organizational issues. But first, use the following exercises to try out what you've learned in this chapter.

Exercises

Five decades after its publication, projects still run headfirst into the wall erected by Brooks's Law. It would be easy to dismiss this as a failure to learn in an industry that refuses to absorb its own history. Doing so would possibly give you part of the explanation but doesn't really help in addressing the root cause. Instead, you went below the surface explanation in this chapter to identify ways of measuring and visualizing the warning signs. The harder the problem is, the more important objective data is. The following exercises give you the opportunity to continue this exploration so you're ready to act early should you face a similar situation in the future.

Find the Reason Behind the Decrease in Output

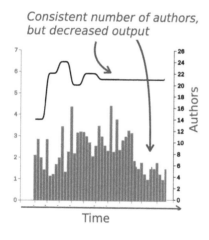

Consistent number of authors, but decreased output

To visualize Brooks's Law, we pulled some task information from tools like Jira and divided the output metrics, for example, story points or features completed, with the number of developers. The project that fell victim to Brooks's Law looked like a crocodile gap: the author number went up as the output moved in the opposite direction.

Now, look at the picture to the right. The development output decreases, yet the number of authors remains static. What could the possible explanations be?

As always, when it comes to these more open-ended questions, remember to also check out Appendix 1, Solutions to the Exercises, on page 267.

Restrict the Analyses to Parts of a Mono-Repo

- Repository: https://github.com/code-as-a-crime-scene/roslyn
- Language: C#, Visual Basic .NET
- Domain: Roslyn is a compiler platform.
- Analysis snapshot: https://tinyurl.com/roslyn-social-fragmentation

Frequently, your team might be responsible for a smaller part inside a larger mono-repo. Focusing on just "your" parts of the code lets you personalize the analysis. This comes in handy when integrating this information into your workflow. For example, pulling up a hotspot map over your team's contributions offers a simple way of focusing retrospectives around the system you're building.

Let's try to restrict the analysis scope on the Roslyn codebase. Back in Understand Why Test Code Isn't Just Test Code, on page 169, we discovered a massive 120k-line test hotspot. Here's how you start the investigation:

```
prompt> git log --all --numstat --date=short \
        --pretty=format:'--%h--%ad--%aN--%aE' \
        --no-renames --after='2020-08-01' \
        -- src/Compilers/CSharp/Test > git_roslyn_log.tx
```

The core of this Git command is the same as you've used before, with the difference that you use a double-dash (--) to restrict the log to the content under src/Compilers/CSharp/Test. This option allows you to zoom in on the parts of interest in a larger codebase.

Using this Git log, run an authors analysis. How many authors touch the NullableReferenceTypesTests.cs hotspot?

CHAPTER 14

See How Technical Problems Cause Organizational Issues

You've now seen how getting the people side of software development wrong can wreck any project. It's also easy to confuse the resulting issues with technical problems, such as code that's hard to understand. You might be surprised to see that the reverse is true as well: how you write code impacts the people side of the organization. Technical decisions are never merely technical.

In this chapter, you'll explore this intersection of people and code in more depth. By pulling together pieces from previous chapters and complementing them with new behavioral code analysis techniques, you'll be able to build up a holistic perspective of any codebase. Ultimately, technical design qualities like coupling and cohesion can be understood by their impact on the people organization. Let's start the investigation by exploring the consequences of unhealthy code on the team's morale.

Have Your Code Motivate Retention

Quick, how many of your core teammates could leave your company before the codebase becomes impossible to maintain? Five or ten? As you'll see in Measure the Truck Factor in Unhealthy Code, on page 226 later in this chapter, each developer leaving takes a piece of the collective knowledge with them. Working in a setting where you no longer have complete knowledge of the code can be frustrating for a developer and devastating to the business.

Surprisingly, few companies realize that offering a healthy work environment is the best way to retain developers. This means more than workplace flexibility, how friendly your managers are, or even if you get that ping-pong table for the cafeteria. While those parts of your environment are fundamental, they are also easily understood and visible in any organization. Instead, I'm referring to the more subtle environment where you spend most of your time: the source code.

The quality of your code is important since it directs the type of work you can do, which in turn connects directly to how meaningful you perceive that work to be. This is highlighted in a report from the management consulting firm McKinsey, identifying the future promise of meaningful work as a top motivator for people switching jobs.[1] Now, you'll explore this link by returning to the impact of unhealthy code.

Learn How Bad Code Causes Unhappiness: The Scientific Link

Throughout the book, you've discovered the technical reasons for the importance of staying on top of emerging hotspots, tricky dependencies, and coordination bottlenecks in the code. However, technical problems rarely stop at their technical impact: these quality issues have a strong effect on the team's well-being, too. When code is difficult to understand or maintain, it leads to a higher attrition rate as developers become frustrated with the codebase and its resulting organizational chaos. Eventually, they decide to leave the company for greener pastures...and code.

This relationship between poor code and developer dissatisfaction is made clear in *On the unhappiness of software developers [GFWA17]*, a large study with 1318 participants, where a team of researchers identified the main reasons for unhappiness among developers. The top three reasons are 1) feeling stuck in problem-solving, 2) being under time pressure, and 3) working with bad-quality code. Given what we learned back in Chapter 7, Communicate the Business Impact of Technical Debt, on page 83, it's easy to see how technical debt can influence morale:

1. *Red code makes you stuck*—Let's say you attend a daily meeting where the team discusses a recent production crash. You volunteer to fix the issue. After all, you have a good idea of what's causing the failure. You can probably wrap up a fix in a couple of hours, tops. However, you soon find yourself in messy code. Trying to decipher the code's intent is hard, and narrowing down the bug proves more challenging than expected. You start to feel stuck.

---

1. https://tinyurl.com/mckinsey-great-attrition

2. *The unpredictability in unhealthy code leads to time pressure*—As you saw in Know Why Half the Work Gets Done in Twice the Time, on page 86, fixing a bug in complex code can take an order of magnitude longer than a similar fix in healthy code. It's easy to see how this causes time pressure: you thought you could fix an issue in a couple of hours, but you end up spending days trying to nail down the failure. Soon, your personal pressure spreads to the organization: after all, you have a production crash waiting for a fix.

3. *Waste and distractions make you dislike complex code*—The code that causes you to get stuck is frustrating to work with. You suffer the most when you "meet bad code that could have been avoided in the first place," which is a lovely summary of accidental complexity. (The quote is from *Happiness and the productivity of software engineers [GF19]*, which is a great read on developer productivity.)

Altogether, this implies that paying down technical debt goes deeper than reducing risk and waste: you also improve the team's morale, motivation, and happiness. This, in turn, lets you focus more on solving actual business problems and building the next cool feature, the thing that probably attracted you to that workplace in the first place. That is, you'd like to spend time on the essential, not the accidental.

Refactor to Improve Morale

If the increased risks and excess waste from unhealthy code aren't enough to persuade your organization to invest in improvements, this research on developer happiness delivers another strong motivator for refactoring problematic code. Each demoralized developer leaving a company takes a piece of the collective knowledge with them. With enough attrition, any codebase will become hard to maintain, which eventually leads you toward the inevitable rewrite trap. Ensuring your code is healthy is far less expensive than losing staff.

Discover How Code Smells Lead to Coordination Problems

In addition to causing stress and frustration for individuals, unhealthy code also results in coordination problems across development teams. The main culprit is a lack of cohesion.

In Meet Your Brain on Code, on page 63, you saw that cohesion is one of the most important design qualities, allowing you to think about your code in terms of knowledge chunks. Now, you'll build on that by examining how the failure to build cohesive modules turns hotspots into coordination bottlenecks.

Understand How Hotspots Attract Multiple Authors

In the previous chapter, you identified a cluster of coordination magnets in the Folly codebase. Look at the next figure as a reminder of the hotspots attracting many authors.

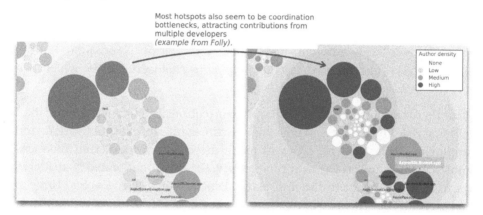

Most hotspots also seem to be coordination bottlenecks, attracting contributions from multiple developers *(example from Folly)*.

> **Joe asks:**
> # I Haven't Seen the Coordination Visualization Before— Is It New?
>
> No, it's actually the same type of D3.js visualization you learned about in Create Your Own Visualizations, on page 38. You can use the same technique and scripting to visualize the author density of each piece of code. Visualizing this critical organizational factor makes it easier to communicate potential problems by making them tangible to everyone on the team.

The overlap between hotspots and coordination problems is common. In most cases, the root cause is a technical problem—the lack of proper modularity—which means that no amount of reorganization can improve the situation. In fact, attempts to reallocate team responsibilities or introduce stronger code ownership would only shift the bottleneck to a new and potentially worse problem. You'll look at those tradeoffs in Recognize Dependencies Between

Teams, on page 223, but for now, let's get to the core of the problem by doing a quick inspection of the AsyncSSLSocket.cpp hotspot. Feel free to read the code in the next figure or jump to the online summary to confirm the issues.[2]

```
ssize_t bytes;
uint32_t buffersStolen = 0;
auto sslWriteBuf = buf;
if ((len < minWriteSize) && ((i + 1) < count)) {
    // Combine this buffer with part or all of the next buffers in
    // order to avoid really small-grained calls to SSL_write().
    // Each call to SSL_write() produces a separate record in
    // the egress SSL stream, and we've found that some low-end
    // mobile clients can't handle receiving an HTTP response
    // header and the first part of the response body in two
    // separate SSL records (even if those two records are in
    // the same TCP packet).

    if (combinedBuf == nullptr) {
      if (minWriteSize_ > MAX_STACK_BUF_SIZE) {
        // Allocate the buffer on heap
        combinedBuf = new char[minWriteSize_];
      } else {
        // Allocate the buffer on stack
        combinedBuf = (char*)alloca(minWriteSize_);
      }
    }
    assert(combinedBuf != nullptr);
    sslWriteBuf = combinedBuf;

    memcpy(combinedBuf, buf, len);
    do {
      // INVARIANT: i + buffersStolen == complete chunks serialized
      uint32_t nextIndex = i + buffersStolen + 1;
      bytesStolenFromNextBuffer =
          std::min(vec[nextIndex].iov_len, minWriteSize_ - len);
      if (bytesStolenFromNextBuffer > 0) {
        assert(vec[nextIndex].iov_base != nullptr);
```

Heuristic: a comment block close to a special case — denoted by an if-statement — indicates a separate responsibility which would be better expressed in its own function.

Notice how multiple chunks of Deep Nested Logic work to form the Bumpy Road code smell.

The preceding code snippet shows only a fragment of the code. In total, AsyncSSLSocket.cpp has more than 100 functions, many of them being of similar complexity. Putting it all together, this combination of code smells points to a *God Class*. The God Class is a design smell used to describe classes that compulsively collect responsibilities and contain at least one God Function. Such code tends to centralize the system's behavior, which impacts the organizational dynamics: programmers working on independent features are now frequently forced into the same part of the code, as illustrated in the figure on page 220. Hotspots are the traffic jams of the software world.

So, at this point, you know that you have a technical problem on your hands. You are also aware of the impact on the team and can prove that the code causes congestion with multiple developers working on it. When these unfortunate stars line up, you'll likely experience severe organizational problems. Let's summarize them in the next section so that you know what to watch out for.

---

2. https://tinyurl.com/folly-async-spot-review

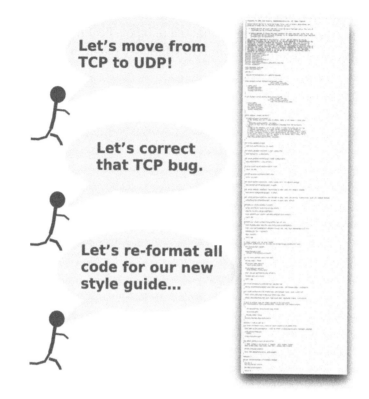

Be Aware of the Technical Factors That Doom a Project

The coordination problems you saw in the previous section explain many cost overruns faced by organizations today. On average, large IT projects run 45 percent over budget, and truly large projects are confronted with overruns of around 200 percent. These are extreme numbers. Worse, empirical research shows that IT projects, in general, are much riskier than decision-makers assume. (See *The Empirical Reality of IT Project Cost Overruns [FBLK22]* for a summary of current research and deeper insights into how projects underestimate risk.)

So why do we, as an industry, keep underestimating the risk? After all, our track record regarding predictable IT delivery isn't exactly rosy. Again, looking at what you've learned so far, the main challenge is that while the symptoms of a doomed project might be visible, the root causes tend to remain opaque, hidden, and obscure. This is true for code quality problems, as you discovered in Chapter 7, Communicate the Business Impact of Technical Debt, on page 83, and now you've seen how organizational problems also tend to fly under the radar.

The complicating factor is that these technical and social issues interact. In particular, the technical problem of low cohesion is intimately tied to Brooks's Law. As you saw in See That a Man-Month Is Still Mythical, on page 198, intellectual work is hard to parallelize. If your software design encourages people on different teams to work on the same parts of the code, you worsen the problem with waste and missed deadlines.

This link to Brooks's Law has been empirically proven in an impressive study of one of the largest pieces of software ever written: Windows Vista. The project investigated the links between product quality and organizational structure. The researchers found that organizational metrics outperform traditional measures, such as code complexity or code coverage, when it comes to predicting defects. In fact, the organizational structure of the programmers building the software is a better predictor of defects than any property of the code itself! (Read about the research in *The Influence of Organizational Structure on Software Quality [NMB08]*.)

One of these super-metrics is the number of programmers who worked on each component. The more parallel work occurs, the more defects you have in that code. This is exactly the type of analysis you performed on Folly in the previous chapter. Grounded in that research, you can predict where the defect-dense parts are. As an example, the AsyncSSLSocket.cpp from Folly with nine active contributors is more likely to contain defects than a file with less parallel work. These attraction points in code become more severe when their contributors are also on separate teams, so let's take a deeper look at that dimension.

Pay Attention to Conflicting Non-Functional Requirements Across Teams

Since teams tend to be organized around business areas, they might have different non-functional requirements on the code, for example, concerning performance or memory consumption. This can quickly cause conflicting changes to the code, which in turn lead to excess rework. Let me share an example so that you can avoid this problem.

A couple of years ago, I interviewed a team responsible for a high-throughput, back-end system. The team complained that another team constantly broke their services. Not broke in the sense that they introduced bugs, mind you, but rather that the services frequently slowed to a crawl, leading to a longer response time for their clients.

The root cause was indeed a heavily congested part of the code—a shared library. It turned out that the second team re-used the shared library for a single-user desktop application with very different performance characteristics than the back-end, which had to scale to many parallel users. Speaking to the desktop team revealed that they, too, shared a frustration. They were frustrated over the hard-to-understand code resulting from relentless performance optimizations by the other team.

The solution? Even if the code required by the teams was functionally equivalent, it is clear that a shared library wouldn't work due to the different contexts of its usage. When you're faced with these situations, consider duplicating the library, deleting what isn't needed anymore, and letting the code evolve in different directions. Just because two pieces of code look the same doesn't mean they should be shared.

Visualize the Pain of Shared Code

The two teams sharing code eventually recognized the proper solution. While both teams had felt the pain of the shared library, they hadn't considered duplicating the shared code; as developers, we're conditioned to despise copy-pasted code. In this case, the feature space was virtually identical, but the non-functional performance characteristics were entirely different.

Make it a habit to perform the analysis from Analyze Your Hotspots for Multiple Authors, on page 203 each time you notice the symptoms of parallel work. That way, you can visualize, explain, motivate the impact, and make the case for a redesign if the problem calls for it.

Visualize Organizational Friction

You've seen how individual hotspots turn into coordination magnets. However, cohesion is a multifaceted concept. Low cohesion can also appear as files that look deceptively simple, yet the emerging system behavior is anything but simple. The figure on page 223 illustrates this issue.

Working on such a codebase, the moment you start to change a specific feature, you soon realize you have to modify three other files located in other packages and, of course, also update that shared service registry at the top level. That's painful.

Strong dependencies spell enough trouble for an individual developer, but like most design issues, this one gets worse in a team context. Let's consider the resulting organizational symptoms.

Example of a design with High cohesion:

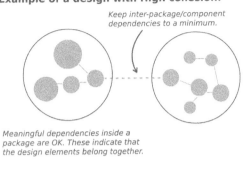

Keep inter-package/component dependencies to a minimum.

Meaningful dependencies inside a package are OK. These indicate that the design elements belong together.

This is what it would look like with Low cohesion:

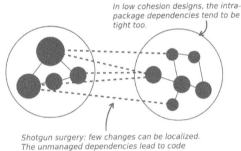

In low cohesion designs, the intra-package dependencies tend to be tight too.

Shotgun surgery: few changes can be localized. The unmanaged dependencies lead to code changes rippling across modular boundaries.

Recognize Dependencies Between Teams

Software architecture is never a purely technical concern. Rather, your software design determines your team's collaboration patterns:

- In a cohesive design where each business rule is properly encapsulated, most changes remain local and obvious.

- When you fail to adhere to that principle, you'll find that business responsibilities are spread out across multiple modules.

Trying to fit multiple teams into a tightly coupled architecture is probably harder than drinking the whole ocean with a straw. (I'm glad you asked: assuming an eight-hour working day, emptying the ocean would take an estimated six million billion years.[3])

Your organization will experience different symptoms depending on your attempted team structure. Consider feature teams, a common organizational pattern. Without cohesive components, feature teams will step on each other's digital toes, leading to a similar situation as you previously saw with shared

3. https://tinyurl.com/quora-drink-ocean

code. The next figure illustrates this disconnect between the features being worked on vs. the patterns emerging from the architecture.

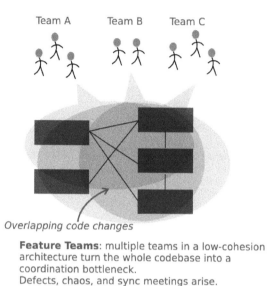

Overlapping code changes

Feature Teams: multiple teams in a low-cohesion architecture turn the whole codebase into a coordination bottleneck.
Defects, chaos, and sync meetings arise.

Again, no amount of reorganization will eliminate the problem of low cohesion. To illustrate why that's the case, let's say you decide to put an end to parallel work by assigning each team a clear area of responsibility. That would give you component teams with clear areas of ownership. Effectively, each component team could work in isolation on "their" part of the code. While it does indeed remove coordination in the code itself, this structure would cause complex handovers and turn each interface into a bottleneck, as shown in the next figure.

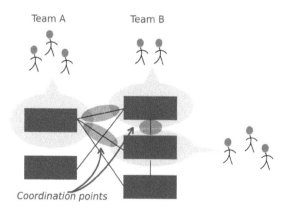

Coordination points

Component Teams: Strong code ownership doesn't help as long as components are logically coupled; now each interface becomes a handover point.

To summarize, an architecture with low cohesion doesn't lend itself well to partitioning work across multiple teams. While you notice the organizational symptoms—an excess number of meetings, low morale, and unclear statuses—your end users are also impacted. The technical problem of low cohesion inevitably leads to defects. Worse, these defects will be hard to debug as the task involves multiple teams, each with an isolated view of what the system looks like. (See *Software Defect-Proneness Prediction with Package Cohesion and Coupling Metrics Based on Complex Network Theory [ZZC20]* for empirical evidence on the link between cohesion and defect reduction.)

Streamline Teams and Architecture

Resolving a misaligned architecture often requires redesigning the impacted parts of the system to align with the organization's structure. This alternative is close to what Conway himself suggests in his classic paper as he concludes that "a design effort should be organized according to the need for communication" (source: *How do committees invent? [Con68]*).

The redesign would involve breaking dependencies by combining separate files into new modules and creating new entities that can capture a specific domain concept in a focused abstraction. This type of redesign is technically demanding yet necessary to mitigate the otherwise disastrous impact of an architecture that isn't properly aligned with your organization. The techniques you learned throughout Part II of the book can help you with this challenging task. In essence, it's all about making iterative refinements to high-impact parts, as you learned in Drive Legacy Modernizations Projects, on page 129.

Rearchitecting a codebase is no joke, though. It's a long-running, complex process. When embarking on such a task, make sure to regularly measure and communicate progress to the team. Not only will that serve as feedback to help ensure you solve the right problem, but it also motivates the team and provides confidence to non-technical stakeholders about the forward movement. A powerful way of getting this feedback is by performing regular change coupling analyses at the architectural level, just as you did in Chapter 10, Use Beauty as a Guiding Principle, on page 137. As exemplified in the figure on page 226, grouping the change coupling results by team lets you focus the visualizations on the core information.

Finally, it's worth pointing out that, in some situations, the architecture could be just fine, yet the organization experiences coordination issues. When that's the case, the typical action is rearranging the teams according to communication needs. Because those needs will change over the product's life cycle, you need to revisit these topics at regular intervals. Done right, such a rebalancing of

Break dependencies between teams via architectural refactoring

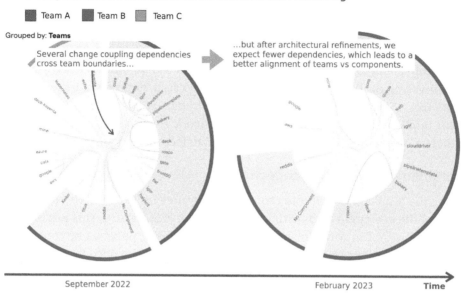

project teams has minimized communication overhead. (See *The Effect of Communication Overhead on Software Maintenance Project Staffing [DHAQ07]*.)

Measure the Truck Factor in Unhealthy Code

At this point, you've seen how modularity issues like coupling and inappropriate service boundaries matter. Another concern is that code smells, in general, can cause severe organizational problems. These problems get worse when the two interact: community smells influence the intensity of code smells. (See *Beyond technical aspects: How do community smells influence the intensity of code smells? [PTFO00]* for this exciting work.)

The most prominent community smells are the *organizational silo effect* and the *lone wolf* contributor. An organizational silo is simply an area of the development community that doesn't communicate with the rest of the project, while a lone wolf refers to a developer applying changes to the code without considering the opinions of their peers.

You have probably come across these community smells during your career. Often, we might not recognize the true socio-technical nature of the problem. Instead, we find ourselves condemning a piece of code as "impossible to understand" and avoiding touching it. If we have to, perhaps as a necessary step in resolving a bug, we keep our changes to a minimum to avoid breaking

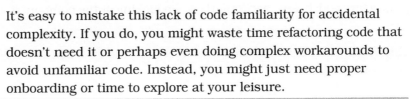

Joe asks:

Wouldn't Microservices with Feature Toggles Enable Loosely Coupled Teams Anyway?

No, that would be a shallow illusion at best. Feature toggles only work in code with good boundaries. Besides, a lack of cohesion causes enough pain in a monolith, yet all the issues multiply in severity when moving to microservices. I've seen it myself recently, so let me share another war story.

One large organization invested years into replacing a complex monolith with a microservice system. Each service was owned and operated by a dedicated team making heavy use of feature flags. While the teams could deploy their services independently, enabling a feature flag in production was a gamble. Often, services failed, and only disabling the feature again could restore operations. It turned out that the services more or less represented building blocks, not self-contained business capabilities.

Consequently, any interesting feature had to touch multiple services, and the opportunity for a communication mistake—such as misinterpreting the semantics of some exchanged data—dramatically increased as more teams were involved. It's all the drawbacks of a layered architecture combined with the expenses of operating a distributed system. That's a no-go.

anything in what looks only marginally more stable than a house of cards in front of an approaching tornado.

The consequences are that critical code smells go unrefactored. This implies that you need to consider the whole socio-technical axis to ensure your code is truly optimized for understanding. It's a complex problem, so let's look for supporting data by understanding the truck factor metric.

Don't Confuse a Lack of Familiarity with Complexity

Social factors like code familiarity influence how you perceive a codebase. In particular, code that you didn't write yourself will always be harder to understand. Not only do you have to come to grips with the code itself, but you also need to understand the problem domain.

It's easy to mistake this lack of code familiarity for accidental complexity. If you do, you might waste time refactoring code that doesn't need it or perhaps even doing complex workarounds to avoid unfamiliar code. Instead, you might just need proper onboarding or time to explore at your leisure.

Understand Knowledge Silos

Everyone who leaves a team takes a piece of the collective knowledge with them. The *truck factor* refers to the minimum number of people who can leave before the software becomes unmaintainable due to losing knowledge of how the system works.[4] The lower the truck factor, the higher the key person risks. This is because a low truck factor turns your system into a *knowledge silo*, meaning the intricacies of both code and domain reside in just one person's head.

The truck factor should be a prevalent concern in any IT project, but from experience, too few organizations are actively working to limit the impact. The main reason for this disregard is largely due to a lack of visibility for the risk. As shown in the next figure, code itself lacks social information.

The Tragedy of Software Design:

The people building the system are invisible in the code itself

When looking at a piece of code, we cannot tell anything about the organizational dynamics:

- Is this code a major coordination bottleneck for our 5 feature teams?

- Or is all of it written by a lone wolf so that we have a key person dependency?

The absence of social information in code is one of the grand tragedies of software design: we—the people who build the code—are invisible in the code itself. Consequently, many projects fail to mitigate the truck factor in time, as evident in *What is the Truck Factor of popular GitHub applications? [AVH15]*, which studied 133 popular GitHub projects. This study found that roughly two-thirds of projects have a truck factor of only one or two maintainers. That's low. There's also nothing to suggest that the truck factor is better in proprietary codebases, particularly when looking at the component or service level.

This raises the question: what's your organization's truck factor? Let's see how you calculate it.

---

4.   https://en.wikipedia.org/wiki/Bus_factor

Identify Main Developers to Calculate the Truck Factor

You determine the truck factor by linking people to their code contributions. In a way, this is similar to the task faced by a forensic psychologist preparing a geographical offender profile. You see, a prerequisite for any behavioral profile is linking a series of crimes to the same offender. Crime linking can be a challenging task, typically depending on additional evidence such as DNA, fingerprints, or witness reports. Fortunately, linking commits to people is a much simpler task; as shown in the next figure, the version-control system has all the info you need.

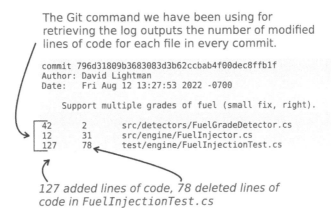

The Git command we have been using for retrieving the log outputs the number of modified lines of code for each file in every commit.

```
commit 796d31809b3683083d3b62ccbab4f00dec8ffb1f
Author: David Lightman
Date:   Fri Aug 12 13:27:53 2022 -0700

    Support multiple grades of fuel (small fix, right).

42      2       src/detectors/FuelGradeDetector.cs
12      31      src/engine/FuelInjector.cs
127     78      test/engine/FuelInjectionTest.cs
```

127 added lines of code, 78 deleted lines of code in FuelInjectionTest.cs

By aggregating the historically added lines of code for each file, you can now identify a main developer for each module. The main developer will be the programmer who has contributed most of the code. One advantage of taking historical contributions into account is the results become less sensitive to shallow changes; if someone else makes larger stylistic changes in code you authored, you still maintain knowledge of both the solution and the problem domain.

Joe asks:
What About Code Reviews? Aren't They Knowledge Sharing?

Indeed, they are. In *Bus factor in practice [JETK22]*, a research team investigated 13 projects developed at JetBrains. The study identified code reviews as the second most important mode of knowledge creation, second only to code commits. However, even if we can improve these algorithms by adding more data sources—and we should— we still need to keep in mind that no amount of metrics replace conversations and actions. Rather, metrics allow us to guide those actions by data so we focus on the right thing and use our time wisely.

With the data source covered, you're ready to test it out. For this case study, you'll return to the React codebase. According to its GitHub page, React has 1600 contributors. With those numbers, you'd expect the truck factor to be in the hundreds. But is it? Let's see.

You should already have a Git log from React. If not, then now is the time to create one as described in Create a Git Log for Code Maat, on page 23. Based on the Git log, you need to retrieve the added lines of code for each file and sum them up per author. The module's main developer or knowledge owner is the author with the most added lines. These steps are implemented in the main-dev analysis. (Feel free to check out the source if you prefer to see the algorithm as code.[5])

```
prompt> maat -l git_log.txt -c git2 -a main-dev
entity,                 main-dev,  added,  total-added,  ownership
.babelrc,               Sebastian, 25,     44,           0.57
.circleci/config.yml,   Andrew,    1174,   1858,         0.63
.codesandbox/ci.json,   Ives,      10,     25,           0.4
.editorconfig,          Paul,      14,     22,           0.64
```

As you can see, you even get an ownership value that reflects the relative contribution of the main author in terms of total added lines of code. A value of 1.0 would indicate that every single historical and current line was contributed by only that person.

Based on this data, you can finally calculate the truck factor. For that purpose, you're going to use the greedy heuristic from *What is the Truck Factor of popular GitHub applications? [AVH15]* where you consecutively simulate removing authors until more than 50 percent of the files in the codebase are abandoned. This task is straightforward using a spreadsheet application such as Excel. Just persist the analysis data to a file and instruct Excel to calculate a frequency table. You can now take your first look at the truck factor in React, illustrated in the top figure on page 231. (There are several free tutorials on how to calculate frequency distributions.[6])

Notice how quickly the contributions level off. This indicates that the project is sensitive to the truck factor. The bottom figure on page 231 shows how you determine the exact number.

So, despite React's total of 1600 contributors, the truck factor is as low as just two (2) developers. Scary.

---

5. https://tinyurl.com/main-dev-algorithm-code
6. https://www.extendoffice.com/documents/excel/5076-excel-chart-count-of-values.html

Visualizing the contributions of the top ten main developers in the React project.

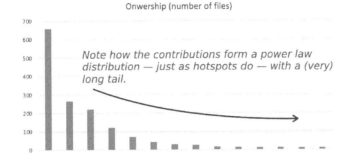

Onwership (number of files)

Note how the contributions form a power law distribution — just as hotspots do — with a (very) long tail.

Calculate the truck factor by identifying the number of main developers who have to leave for us to lose 50% of the files in the codebase.

Author	Onwership (number of files)
Brian	660
Andrew	267
Juan	221
Sebastian	122
Luna	71
salazarm	44
Josh	30
Justin	27
Esteban	17

There are 1650 files in total.

The top two contributors "own" 927 files, which is > 50% of the total so the truck factor is two (2) developers.

Evaluate the Key Person Risk When Adopting Open Source

It's estimated that 70 to 90 percent of the code in web and cloud applications is open-source code.[7] Not all those open-source dependencies are equally important. But when you adopt a framework or library that becomes an integral part of your application, in the sense that it's expensive to replace, then make sure to assess the truck factor of your dependency. A low number is an indication that you need to either a) be prepared to contribute yourself (bug fixes, documentation) or b) opt in to sponsor the project to make sure it's sustainable.

7. https://tinyurl.com/oss-usage-stats

Step Out of the Truck's Way

Since the low truck factor in React is the norm rather than an exception, chances are that you'll find a similar number in your own codebase. Of course, there's a big difference in how quickly a new developer can conquer an existing codebase should the truck hit. This means that you also have to consider the quality of the code when assessing the impact of the truck factor, which inevitably leads you to the concept of *legacy code.*

In his classic book, *Working Effectively with Legacy Code [Fea04],* Michael Feathers defines legacy code as code without tests. The main reason is that tests act as a safety net and an executable documentation of what the code is expected to do. Code without tests is hard to change. However, you should consider a slightly broader view of legacy code, which considers the social dimension: legacy code is code that a) lacks quality and b) you didn't write yourself.

Viewed in this context, the truck factor becomes something of a highway to legacy code—a legacy code-making machine. The implications are severe for any IT organization. Remember back in Know Why Half the Work Gets Done in Twice the Time, on page 86 when you saw how unhealthy code leads to excess time in development? A follow-up study shows that there's a significant onboarding cost: unless you're the main developer, you need 45 percent more time for small changes and 93 percent more time for large changes when you have low-quality code. (See *U Owns the Code That Changes and How Marginal Owners Resolve Issues Slower in Low-Quality Source Code [BTM23]* for the full research, which also shows that industry practices result in mostly dominant and marginal code owners.)

Hence, when you identify a hotspot, make sure to shine a light on organizational factors, too. You do this by visualizing the truck factor you calculated above and overlaying the information with indicators for complex hotspots. The figure on page 233 offers an example of how it could look in React.[8]

All summarized, code quality issues amplify organizational problems like the truck factor. When this happens in your codebase, a series of steps helps you remediate the situation:

- *Let community smells be a driver for refactoring*—Prioritize refactorings in hotspots with a low truck factor. This is important because the community smell will deepen the technical pains.

---

8.   https://tinyurl.com/react-truck-factor-view

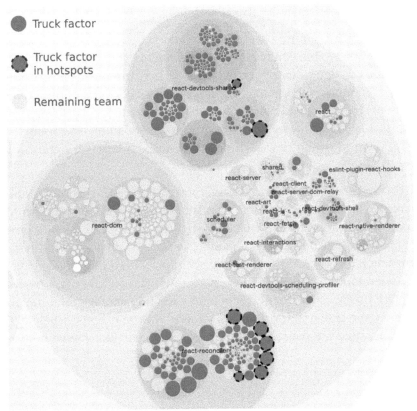

Legend:
- Truck factor
- Truck factor in hotspots
- Remaining team

Visualizing the truck factor: *If just two people leave, the project loses detailed knowledge of the red areas in the code. The problem is amplified by the complex hotspots, indicated with dashed borders.*

- *Pair on the refactoring*—Make sure to encourage any lone wolves to pair with another developer in the refactoring. That way, you distribute the knowledge of a critical piece of code in the process. It's a win-win situation since being the single developer who is a key person dependency is usually quite stressful (for example, being constantly texted on your rare day off).

- *Use mob cleaning*—*Mob cleaning* is a collaborative programming technique described by Ivan Houston.[9] Similar to mob programming, you team up and clean up a complex piece of code together. To make it effective, time-box the cleaning and stick to a set cadence like "each Tuesday, from 1:00 to 2:00 p.m." Not only will you increase the collective knowledge, but it's a fun activity, too.

9.   https://tinyurl.com/mob-cleaning-article

Uncover the People Side of Code

Successful software requires keeping code and people in balance so that one supports the other. This is a tricky problem, and as you saw in Part I, this is partly because code at scale lacks visibility. Unfortunately, the people side of code is even more opaque; looking at a piece of code, you cannot tell anything about these crucial socio-technical interactions. This information shortage is a key reason why software projects keep failing. Fortunately, you now have a set of brand-new techniques to shine a light on organizational factors.

You've covered a lot of ground in this chapter as you've learned how cohesion can make or break an organization and how the truck factor intermingles with code complexity. You now have most of the pieces you need to profile a development project, but there's one more aspect to consider: what happens once the truck has left? Are you simply stranded with a mass of code you no longer understand? To answer those questions, you should dig a bit deeper and explore the developer patterns behind each hotspot. So, take the opportunity to let the truck factor analysis sink in via the exercises below. Once you're ready, turn the page and prepare to meet code like you've never seen it before.

Exercises

As evidenced by the research you saw in this chapter, many popular open-source projects depend on a few key maintainers. There's no evidence that closed-source development is much different in this regard, which makes the truck factor a key metric. Here's your chance to explore it in other codebases.

Inspect the Truck Factor in Vue.js

- Repository: https://github.com/code-as-a-crime-scene/vue
- Language: TypeScript
- Domain: Vue is a framework for building user interfaces.
- Analysis snapshot: https://tinyurl.com/vue-js-truck-factor-view

A truck factor of just two developers, as you saw in React.js, sounds ridiculously low. Is React.js an outlier? Well, take a look at the competing Vue.js framework. There's a total of 314 contributors to Vue.js. What is the truck factor?

CHAPTER 15

Build a Knowledge Map of Your System

Over the past few chapters, you have gradually learned how organizational factors can cause severe problems for both the quality and delivery of software. You also discovered how the same organizational factors intensify code smells, a particularly problematic combination in the presence of a low truck factor. Now, you'll go deeper by exploring various author patterns and how they affect your codebase.

Once you've uncovered these more granular code contribution patterns, you'll be able to build a knowledge map over your codebase and use it to simplify communication and onboarding. As a bonus, you'll see how the information lets you predict defects, support planning, and assess the knowledge drain if a developer leaves your project.

By the end of this chapter, you'll have a radically different view of your system. Let's get started!

Know Your Knowledge Distribution

Back in Spot Conway's Law in Your Code, on page 205, you learned how to detect coordination bottlenecks by analyzing the intersection of people and code. Designing an organization that aligns with its software architecture is the gold standard for efficient teams. Unfortunately, it's easy to be deceived; the code ownership could look clear from a 10,000-foot view, yet well-defined team boundaries alone don't guarantee efficient communication. Let me share a story to clarify.

A while ago, I worked with a large organization. There were hundreds of developers organized in multiple divisions and teams. To make it work, each team was responsible for one subsystem. The subsystems all had well-documented interfaces. However, sometimes the API had to change to support a new feature. That's when things started to get expensive.

The team organization was closely aligned to the system architecture, as Conway's Law advises. Consequently, the communication worked well—at least on the surface. When one team needed to change an API, they knew which team to talk to. The problem was that these changes often rippled throughout the system; a change to one API meant another subsystem also had to change. To change that subsystem, our peers had to request a change to yet another API owned by a different team, and so on. As shown in the next figure, the organization had implicit dependencies between teams that didn't know about each other.

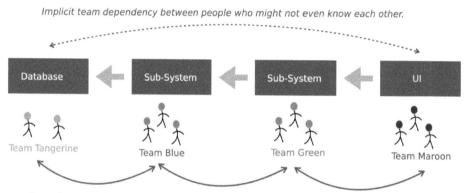

Implicit team dependency between people who might not even know each other.

Natural communication paths as encouraged by the organisation and software architecture. However, notice how the dependencies ripple over boundaries, from team to team.

In such situations, the collaboration across system boundaries suffers. If you have a system where a separate team owns each component, and these components depend upon each other, the resulting context is a tight people dependency.

You can uncover these dependencies via a change coupling analysis, but that still leaves you with only the software dependencies. You'd also need to know *who* to communicate with. While you may know the expertise of the team responsible for the interfaces you use, you rarely know what happens behind them. This is a problem when it comes to design, code reviews, and debugging. Ideally, you'd like to get input from everyone who's affected by a change. So, let's find out who they are.

Find the Author to Praise

Modern version-control systems all provide a blame command (I love that Subversion aliases the command as praise!). blame is useful if you know exactly which module you need to change. As you can see in the following figure, blame shows the author who last modified each line in a given file.

```
The author who made the last              The source code, annotated
change to each line of code
       ↓                                           ↓
cf60b1e3886 (Yagiz     2023-02-02 12:51:01 -0500    5) #include "v8-inspector.h"
39977db7c01 (Eugene    2018-05-21 16:59:04 -0700    6)
f2064dfc1fe (Refael    2019-02-25 17:27:19 -0500    7) #include <functional>
575e086b666 (gengji    2019-03-07 21:46:54 +0800    8) #include <memory>
39977db7c01 (Eugene    2018-05-21 16:59:04 -0700    9)
39977db7c01 (Eugene    2018-05-21 16:59:04 -0700   10) namespace node {
39977db7c01 (Eugene    2018-05-21 16:59:04 -0700   11) namespace inspector {
39977db7c01 (Eugene    2018-05-21 16:59:04 -0700   12) namespace {
39977db7c01 (Eugene    2018-05-21 16:59:04 -0700   13)
39977db7c01 (Eugene    2018-05-21 16:59:04 -0700   14) using v8_inspector::String
bfebfdb149c (Anna      2020-07-31 17:58:53 +0200   15) using v8_inspector::String
      ↑                        ↑
The revision where each    The date of the
line was last changed      last change
```

The information from blame is useful, but it doesn't take you far enough. If you don't know that part of the system, which is probably why you want to talk to someone else in the first place, then you don't know which file to inspect. And even when you do, the information from blame is low level. You'd need a summary, a high-level overview that isn't as sensitive to superficial formatting changes as blame is. Let's see how to get that info.

> \\//
> ⌣ ⌣   **Joe asks:**
> ⌣
>
> ## Can I Build Knowledge Maps Even if My Git History Is Incomplete?
>
> Yes, you can, but only if you keep an extra eye on the possible biases. A common reason is that the codebase was moved to Git, but its history wasn't. When that happens, the author who made the initial import gets the credit for all code, which is clearly misleading.
>
> In these situations, excluding the misleading import commit from your analysis is important. That way, the knowledge map will reflect the actual work areas of your team members. Further, a more advanced bias-reducing technique is to weight the known contributions to a file against its historical size. This technique won't solve the lack of history, but it will highlight the areas of the code where the knowledge maps aren't reliable enough. For example, you might have a file with 2000 lines of code, but the available history only explains 100 of those lines.

Expand Your Mental Maps with Social Data

Throughout the book, you have applied geographical offender profiling based on the idea that just as you can spot patterns in the movement of criminals, your version-control data lets you do the same with code. Another aspect of this for you to know is that the movement of offenders is constrained by a concept called *mental maps*.

A mental map is the subjective view of a specific geographic area. Mental maps deviate from how a real map would look. For example, geographical hindrances such as highways and rivers can constrain and skew the perception of an area. In the small town where I grew up, it took me years to venture across the heavily trafficked road that cut through the city. As a consequence, my mental map ended at that street. It was the edge of the world. Similarly, the mental maps of criminals shape where their crimes take place.

Programmers have mental maps, too. Over time, at least when you work with others, you tend to specialize and get to know some parts of the system better than others. These knowledge barriers shape your perception of the system by constraining your view of the system to the parts you know, as shown in the following figure. Let's see how you can tear down the barriers.

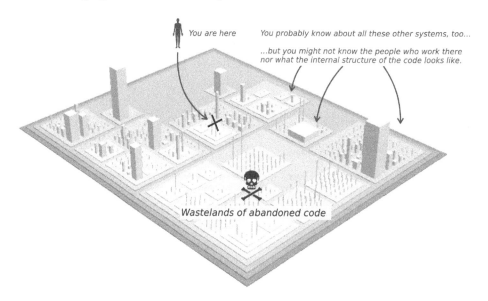

Explore Your Knowledge Map

Imagine for a moment that you had a map of the knowledge distribution in your organization. No, not some out-of-date Excel file stashed away in a dusty corner of your intranet. To be useful, the information has to be up-to-date and reflect how you actually work—in reality, in code.

The concept you'll explore is a *knowledge map*. A knowledge map lets you find the right people to discuss a piece of code, fix hotspots, and help out with debugging. You already know how to Identify Main Developers to Calculate the Truck Factor, on page 229, so let's start from there. The next figure visualizes the main authors in React.[1]

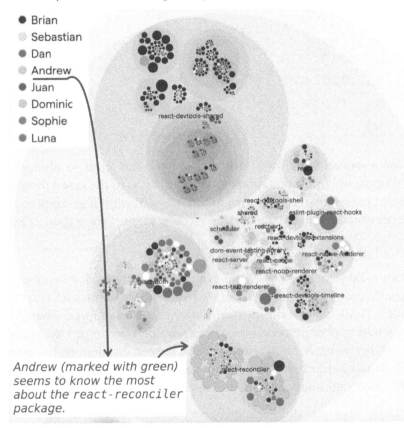

Example of a knowledge map: this is the social side of React.js

The preceding visualization of the knowledge map is created by assigning each developer a color. It's a simple technique for letting you think about knowledge distribution at the codebase level. For example, the map shows that components such as react-reconciler and react-refresh seem to be in the hands of one developer each—key person dependencies. In contrast, other components, such as the react-dom, exhibit a shared effort with contributions from

---

1. https://tinyurl.com/react-knowledge-map

multiple developers. The use cases, however, go deeper than merely detecting risks. Measuring the knowledge distribution simplifies communication, too, as explained in the next figure.

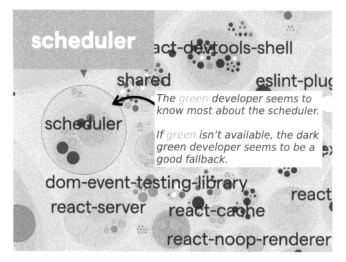

Imagine for a moment that you join this project and need to change the scheduler component. Your map immediately points you to the green developer as the correct person to discuss your proposed design with. If green is absent, the developer visualized using the dark green color seems to be a good fallback.

Scale Knowledge Maps to the Architectural Level

File-level knowledge metrics are useful in smaller codebases or when zooming in on a specific part. However, for larger systems, the file information is simply too granular. Think back to the story at the start of this chapter, where multiple teams had implicit dependencies; you wouldn't be helped by knowing which developer worked where. Rather, you'd need to identify the overall knowledge source behind each subsystem you depend on. That is, you'd need to scale file-level information to the architectural level.

This is exactly what you did back in Specify the Architecturally Significant Components, on page 142, when you analyzed architectural patterns. You can use the same techniques to scale knowledge maps. The first step is to specify an architectural transformation for React:

```
packages/react            => react
packages/react-art        => react-art
packages/react-cache      => react-cache
packages/react-client     => react-client
packages/react-debug-tools => react-debug-tools
...
```

The React codebase is well-structured, so you need to map each directory under packages to a component name. It's a mundane task that would benefit from some scripting. Anyway, once you have the components specified, save them to a react_arch_spec.txt file and request a main-dev analysis at the component level:

```
prompt> maat -l react_git_log.txt -c git2 -a main-dev \
           -g -g react_arch_spec.txt
entity,           main-dev, added, total-added, ownership
react,            Luna,     409,   1310,        0.31
react-art,        BIKI,     223,   266,         0.84
react-cache,      Andrew,   2,     2,           1.00
react-client,     salazarm, 375,   713,         0.53
react-debug-tools, Rick,    191,   514,         0.37
...
```

Wonderful! This looks much more useful as a high-level guide. If you're concerned about your dependency upon, for example, react-cache, then Andrew is the go-to person for your queries. Similarly, the BIKI contributor seems to know everything about the react-art component.

Armed with this information, you can always ensure the right people are involved. However, not all knowledge is equally deep. For example, contrast the ownership between react-cache and react-debug-tools. The former has a perfect 1.0, meaning all code is written by its main author, whereas the main developer in react-debug-tools only contributed 37 percent. This raises the question of who the other authors in that package are. Perhaps one of them could step in if the main developer should be away. To get this information, you need to explore a deeper analysis of developer patterns. Let's go there.

Dig Below the Surface with Developer Patterns

The main developer analysis is a good starting point, which in turn can drive more detailed investigations. A module with many contributors might still have one main developer who maintains overall consistency while other programmers contribute minor fixes to the code. Or, it could be a shared effort where many different programmers develop significant chunks of the total code.

To get those insights, you'll use an algorithm that summarizes the number of commits for each developer and presents them together with the total number of revisions for each module. First, look at the raw data, and then you'll take a step back to see where it comes from:

```
prompt> maat -l react_git_log.txt -c git2 -a entity-effort \
           -g react_arch_spec.txt
entity,           author,    author-revs, total-revs
...
```

```
react-reconciler, Andrew,     634,        1254
react-reconciler, Luna,       274,        1254
react-reconciler, Brian,       57,        1254
react-reconciler, Sebastian,   56,        1254
react-reconciler, salazarm,    44,        1254
react-reconciler, Josh ,       31,        1254
react-reconciler, Bowen,       29,        1254
react-reconciler, Joseph,      24,        1254
...
```

The results above are filtered on the react-reconciler module from React, the package containing the main hotspots you identified all the way back in Intersect Complexity and Effort, on page 28. The preceding output shows that there have been a total of 1254 commits touching any of the files in react-reconciler. Andrew has authored most of these commits, with Luna a clear second. This is useful info if you want to mitigate the consequences of a low truck factor, a topic you explored in the previous chapter and which you'll return to in a few pages. But before you go there, it's worth recognizing that even if this data is valuable, the raw text output soon becomes daunting; it's hard to get the overall picture. So, let's turn to a more brain-friendly approach.

Visualize Developer Effort with Fractal Figures

Take a look at the following figure. In contrast to the raw analysis results, the *fractal figures* visualization immediately provides a view of how the programming effort was shared.

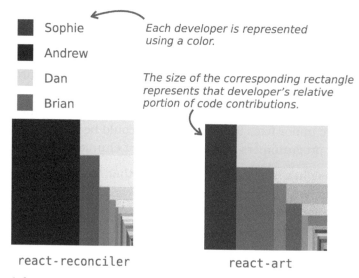

The fractal figures algorithm is simple: represent each programmer with a color and draw a rectangle whose area is proportional to the percentage of commits by that programmer. You can also see that the rectangles are rendered in alternating directions to increase the visual contrast between different parts. (You'll find more details in the original research paper *Fractal Figures: Visualizing Development Effort for CVS Entities [DLG05]*.)

If you want to try fractal figures on your system—and you really should—check out the implementation and documentation on GitHub.[2] All you need is a result file from a Code Maat entity-effort analysis.

The fractal figures also make it easy to spot the general contribution patterns. This is important since a fragmented development effort impacts the external quality of the code in question. Let's see what the different patterns tell you about the codebase.

Distinguish the Ownership Models

Three basic patterns keep showing up when you visualize development effort, and they can predict code quality. You can see the patterns in the following figure:

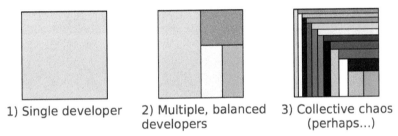

1) Single developer   2) Multiple, balanced developers   3) Collective chaos (perhaps...)

From a communication point of view, a single developer provides the simplest communication structure; there's just one person to talk to. It's also likely that the code within that module is consistent. The quality of the code depends, to a large extent, on the expertise of the single developer.

The second case with multiple, balanced developers is more interesting. Often, such code has one developer who contributed the most code. It turns out that the ownership proportion of that main developer is a good predictor of the quality of the code! The higher the ownership proportion of the main developer, the fewer defects in the code. (See *Don't Touch My Code! Examining the Effects of Ownership on Software Quality [BNMG11]*.)

An even stronger predictor of defects is the number of minor contributors, exemplified in case 3 above. When you change a module where you are the

---

2.   https://github.com/adamtornhill/FractalFigures

main developer, you sometimes need to change a related piece of code you haven't worked on before. But you don't know the background and thinking that went into the original code. In that role, as a minor contributor, you're more likely to introduce defects.

The fractal figures give you another investigative tool to uncover expensive development practices. Once you've identified one of the warning signs, such as many minor contributors, you react by performing code reviews, running a hotspot analysis, and talking to the contributing programmers to see whether they experience any problems.

Do More with Fractal Figures

An interesting variation on fractal figures is using their size dimension to express other code properties. For example, you can use the size of each figure to visualize complexity or the number of historical bugs in each module. Used that way, fractal figures allow you to present a lot of information in a compact and brain-friendly way, as shown in the following figure.

Use the size of each fractal figure to represent other dimensions, e.g. code complexity or number of historic defects.

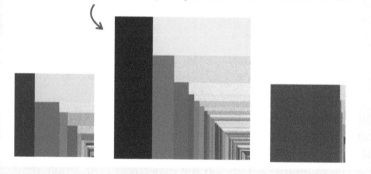

Use Fractal Figures to Mitigate Offboarding Risks

In the previous chapter, you learned about the truck factor. Losing a long-term contributor can be painful for the remaining team, particularly since it also comes with a quality risk. This was demonstrated in *The Influence of Organizational Structure on Software Quality [NMB08]*, which investigated various predictors of software defects. The research showed that the number of former contributors to a component predicts the number of post-release defects should new developers work on that code. Hence, it's important to always keep an eye on the knowledge distribution in your code so you can be aware of these additional risks.

Now, think back to the codebase you worked on for a moment. What if one of the core developers suddenly left—literally just walked out the door? What parts of the code would be left in the wild and risky to work on? What parts should the next developer focus on, and who would that be? In larger organizations, you rarely know the answers. Let's see how fractal figures can put you in a better position.

Investigate the Disposal Sites of Killers and Code

In addition to the spatial movements preceding a crime, forensic psychologists have also discovered patterns in the location of disposal sites used by serial killers. It sure is a macabre research subject, but the information gained is valuable in helping to catch the offender.

The deeds of a serial killer are bizarre. There's not much to understand there. But although the deeds are irrational, there is a certain logic to the places where serial killers choose to dispose of victims. One driving force is minimizing the risk of detection. That means the disposal sites are carefully chosen. Often, the geographical distribution of these locations overlaps with the offender's other non-criminal activities. (See *Principles of Geographical Offender Profiling [CY08a]*.) Consequently, the location of disposal sites contains additional information pointing to the offender.

Your programming activities are nowhere near as gruesome, but your codebases have disposal sites, too. Disposal sites of code that shouldn't be there are also hard to find, particularly inside organizations with strong key person dependencies and lone wolf contributors. Combine the knowledge analyses in this chapter with the hotspot techniques to identify code disposal sites. In particular, use the name of the design elements—just as you learned in Recognize Bad Names, on page 74—to discover issues in unfamiliar code.

Recruit a Replacement

In this case study, you're going to pretend that the key contributor behind Vue.js left. Vue.js is a JavaScript framework with a strong development community. It's a fairly small codebase, roughly 80,000 lines of code. If you did the exercise in the previous chapter (of course you did), then you know that the truck factor in Vue.js is low. Very low. As the next figure shows, most of the code was developed by its creator, Evan You.[3]

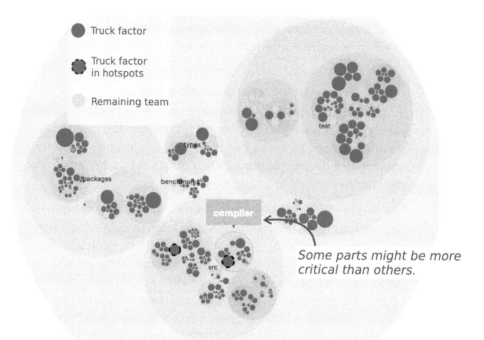

Visualizing the truck factor in Vue.js: If the project creator leaves, the project loses detailed knowledge of the red areas above.

Even if the project flourishes with developer activity, it's still hard to replace a core contributor. This is, of course, a hypothetical scenario to simulate an undesired situation—Evan is still active at the time of this writing—so again, you need to pretend a bit. When faced with the situation above, what would be the first step?

Looking at the preceding visualization, you might notice that it seems like the project would lose virtually all details of how the compiler works. That's probably a critical part. Let's apply our fractal figures to see how severe the situation is.

Start by cloning the Vue.js repository and generating a Git log in our agreed-upon format.[4] Just as you did for React, you start your analysis at the architectural level to focus on the larger picture. Use the following architectural transformations for Vue.js:

3. https://tinyurl.com/vue-js-code-familiarity
4. https://github.com/code-as-a-crime-scene/vue

```
benchmarks      => benchmarks
compiler-sfc  => compiler-sfc
packages        => packages
scripts         => scripts
src/compiler  => compiler
src/code        => core
src/platforms => platforms
src/shared      => shared
test => test
```

Notice how you break up the src folders into more granular components. The idea is that it gives you a more focused analysis, particularly for the component you consider critical, in this case, src/compiler. Persist the architectural transformations to a file, arch_spec_vue.txt, and proceed with calculating the entity-effort:

```
prompt> maat -l vuew_git_log.txt -c git2 -a entity-effort \
           -g arch_spec_vue.txt
entity,     author,     author-revs, total-revs
...
compiler,  Evan,        733,         951
compiler,  pikax,        64,         951
compiler,  cheng,        19,         951
compiler,  Jason,         9,         951
compiler,  Hanks,         7,         951
...
```

The analysis confirms what you already knew: Evan is the clear knowledge owner here. However, if this had been a real situation, you'd probably be relieved to see that Pikax has made significant contributions, too. That's great! Perhaps Pikax and Cheng might be comfortable in maintaining the compiler. That's good—now you know who to communicate with.

Starting from this overview of the critical component, you can then drill a bit deeper. Even if a couple of people have worked with the component, you still want to know that individual hotspots are maintainable. In this case, the concern would be the src/compiler/parser/index.ts file, which contains the code for converting HTML into an abstract syntax tree as part of the compilation process. It's a relatively complex piece of code, rich in conditional logic and bumpy roads.[5]

The analysis process itself is identical to what you just did, except you skip the architectural transformation and run on the raw Git log. That way, you identify the developer fragmentation at the file level. As shown in the figure on page 248, there are a couple of minor contributors who should be familiar with parts of the hotspot and could continue to maintain it.

---

5.   https://tinyurl.com/vue-js-compiler-hotspot-review

This is the portion of the hotspot where we lose knowledge due to the offboarding:

A way to mitigate the risk would be to have the developers represented as Green and Blue pair up and refactor the hotspot.

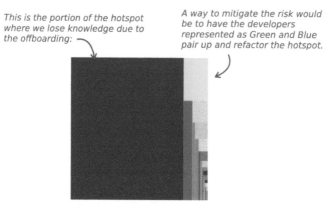

A fractal figure representing the contributions to the hotspot in the Vue.js compiler.

Survive the Truck

Up to this point, you've been looking at potential doomsday scenarios simply because that's where most projects end up when the truck hits. This was made evident in *On the abandonment and survival of open source projects: An empirical investigation [ACVS19]*, showing that only 41 percent of projects survive when the main developer abandons the code. However, given that several projects do survive, can you learn anything from their handover that increases the survival probabilities of your own product?

One prominent example is Git itself. Originally written by Linus Torvalds during a long weekend, Linus decided to hand over the project early. Since 2005, Junio Hamano has maintained the project.[6] The knowledge analysis in the figure on page 249 makes it clear that the handover was successful.[7] (And, of course, Git continues to evolve, bringing new and interesting features.)

So, what can you learn from the projects that continue to thrive, even after a former key person has left? As always, it's a combination of practices that lets you limit the impact of the truck factor:

- *Collaborate to limit key person dependencies*—When you work closely as a team, others also develop a deep understanding of design decisions, tradeoffs, and the experience that went into the current solution. This collective knowledge is invaluable and cannot be reverse-engineered from the code or replaced during this mythical activity our industry calls a "knowledge transfer."

---

6. https://tinyurl.com/linus-torvalds-linux-interview
7. https://tinyurl.com/git-linus-ownership

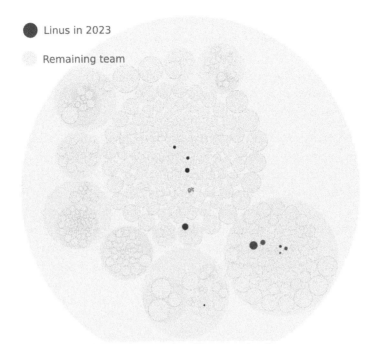

A successful handover: the files marked as gray are the only parts where Git's original creator, Linus, is still the main knowledge owner.

- *Keep your code healthy*—As you saw in Step Out of the Truck's Way, on page 232, code smells amplify the impact of the truck once it hits. If you have kept your code healthy, you're better positioned to become familiar with the now-abandoned code.

- *Establish strong guidelines and principles*: Good principles are liberating as they shape consistency. Capture them in (version-controlled) writing, and make sure to also include the rationale behind each principle.

- *Encourage a culture of collaboration*—Encourage your team to share ideas and work together on harder problems. Take the opportunity to lead by example and offer feedback—and ask for it yourself.

- *Plan time for learning*—If you're in a technical leadership position, then you can use the techniques from this chapter to keep an eye on the code familiarity and knowledge sharing within the team. Also, in case of an offboarding, use the knowledge analyses to identify risky areas of the code and make sure the replacement programmers get enough time to learn the domain.

High Developer Fragmentation Creates Immutable Designs

When identifying a complex hotspot in a legacy codebase, chances are its complexity trend reveals that the code has been problematic for years. This obviously raises the question: why hasn't anyone refactored it, and why did we continue allowing the code to deteriorate?

Well, it's a safe bet that the hotspot turns out to be a shared effort amongst tens of developers. Without a clear sense of ownership, no one feels the responsibility to act on the growing problem—a manifestation of diffusion of responsibility on page 202. Hence, the code will continue to grow within the bounds of the original design, independent of whether that design is still a good fit. We end up with an *immutable design*, where bug fixes and features are squeezed into a structure long past its expiration date (see the following figure).

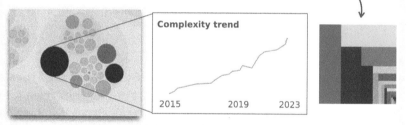

You'll frequently find that complex hotspots have been a growing problem for a long time, often years.

A fragmented development effort leads to unclear ownership and a diffusion of responsibility: no one feels responsible for taking on a risky refactoring.

Distinguish Use from Misuse

The knowledge analyses you explored in this chapter are useful to everyone on a project:

- Developers use them to identify peers who can help with code reviews, design discussions, and debugging tasks.

- New project members use the information both as a communication aid and for fast-track onboarding.

- Testers grab the map to find the developer who's most likely to know about a particular feature area.

- Finally, technical leaders use the data to evaluate how well the system structure fits the team structure, identify knowledge islands, and ensure they get the natural, informal communication channels they need to write great code.

Unlike hotspots, which you want to stay on top of every day, you'll probably use these knowledge analyses less frequently. Often, it's enough to keep an eye on the social side of your code on a weekly or bi-weekly cycle. Ideally, you'd make it part of other recurring activities, such as planning or retrospectives. And, of course, there's the occasional ad hoc usage. You see, when you need these analyses, you *really* need them: fractal figures can save the day when it comes to onboarding and offboarding.

Don't Misuse Contribution Data for Performance Evaluations

Based on experience, we also need to add a word of warning here. These social analyses are *not* a summary of individual productivity, nor were they developed to evaluate people. Used that way, the information does more harm than good. There are several reasons why using them that way is a bad idea. Let's focus on the one social psychologists call a *fundamental attribution error.*

The fundamental attribution error describes our tendency to overestimate personality factors when we explain other people's behavior. For example, when you see that I committed a bunch of buggy spaghetti last week, you know it's because I'm a bad programmer, irresponsible, and perhaps even a tad stupid. When you, on the other hand, deliver scrappy code (yes, I know—it's a hypothetical scenario), you know it's because you were close to a deadline, had to save the project, or just intended the code as a prototype. As you see, we attribute the same observable behavior to different factors depending on whether it concerns us or someone else.

There's also a group aspect to the fundamental attribution bias. When we judge the behavior of someone closer to us, such as a team member, we're more likely to understand the situational influence. That implies we can learn to avoid the bias. We just need to remind ourselves that the power of the situation is strong and often a better predictor of behavior than a person's personality.

My code   *"Their" code*

The fundamental attribution illustrated.

Finally, once we're being measured on something, the measurement itself becomes the target, not working software, not supporting our peers, but rather optimizing for our own "performance" (see Goodhart's law[8]). Eventually, we developers can learn to game any metric, and the quality of our code and work environment suffer in the process. Don't go there.

Take a Look at the Future

Now that you've learned how to mitigate truck factors and find potential replacements via fractal figures, you've completed this tour of the existing behavioral code analysis landscape. You're well-versed in the core techniques and ready to uncover the secrets of both code and organizations.

Software development is a constantly expanding domain with new techniques and concepts coming up regularly. In the final chapter, you'll see how the techniques you've learned will help you in a future consisting of increased automation, ever-shorter development cycles, and AIs that write code. But before you go to the next chapter, be sure to try the final exercises below.

Exercises

The knowledge analyses have two main use cases: optimizing people communication and handling onboarding and offboarding scenarios. The following exercises let you explore both use cases and combine them with hotspots.

Show the Impact: The Truck Hits Twice

- Repository: https://github.com/code-as-a-crime-scene/git
- Language: C
- Domain: Git is git, the dominant version-control system.
- Analysis snapshot: https://tinyurl.com/git-linus-ownership

You explored Git as a successful example of transferring a non-trivial codebase to a new maintainer, Junio Hamano. Perform an analysis of the impact should Junio decide to leave, too. Bonus points if you can identify specific Git features that would be impacted. (Hint: The Git codebase is a great example of aligning the code with the problem domain; the file names indicate which feature they implement.)

Prioritize the Offboarding Risk

- Repository: https://github.com/code-as-a-crime-scene/magda
- Language: Scala, JavaScript, TypeScript

---

8.   https://en.wikipedia.org/wiki/Goodhart%27s_law

- Domain: Magda is a data catalog system for organizations.
- Analysis snapshot: https://tinyurl.com/magda-hotspots-map

When a main contributor leaves, you'll likely face multiple upcoming gaps in your understanding of the system. In practice, you often get a transition period, for example, one month of notice before the person logs out for good. That's a period you can use to mitigate upcoming risks. One such task is to have the departing developer pair up with someone on the team to refactor critical hotspots.

As you see in the next figure, there's only one developer behind Magda's authorization API.

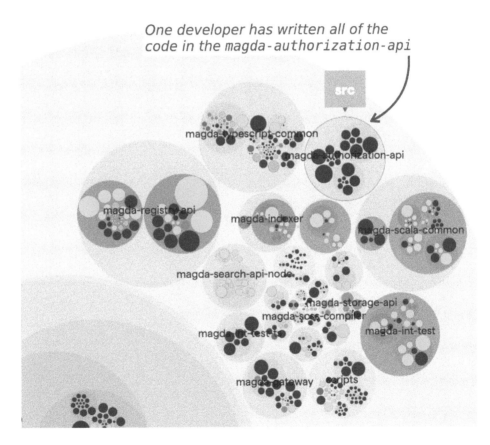

Let's pretend that person leaves. It's clear that you need to mitigate any barriers to understanding in the magda-authorization-api. Can you identify any hotspot you would prioritize as a refactoring target during the offboarding period?

CHAPTER 16

Move Toward the Future

You've almost finished this book, and it was great to share this journey with you. You've covered a lot of ground and mastered the core analysis techniques that apply to codebases of all sizes. That leaves you in a good position to step outside the boundaries of the book and look at possible next steps. Some of these analyses only exist as embryos and research prototypes at the moment, but that's enough to consider what the next generation of code analysis will look like. As part of that, you'll see how those tools need to go beyond version-control systems and track what happens between commits.

Speaking of things to come, this multifaceted software development profession is constantly evolving. Several trending technologies promise to change the way we program. Low-code platforms are on the rise (again), and novel AI applications are being used to write code. We have more powerful tools than ever, but there might also be existential concerns: will these techniques make us obsolete as programmers? And does behavioral code analysis still have a place in a world fueled by AI-assisted programming? These are questions we should consider since the answers will shape our careers over the coming decade. All right, I can't wait, so let's jump right into the final chapter.

Deepen Your Investigation

The techniques in this book are a starting point. There's much more information in our code repositories. So, let's look at some other approaches. What follows are strategies that give you even more information should the need arise. These ideas may also serve as an inspiration once you choose to explore the topic in more depth.

Investigate More Than Source Code

If you have other artifacts stored under version control, you can also include them in the analyses. Some examples include documents, requirement specifications, or manuals for your product. Perhaps you'll even look for temporal dependencies between your requirements and code.

The following figure is an example of a non-code analysis. It shows the hotspots in the book you're reading right now. (If you're looking to contribute to the errata, Chapter 13 seems like a chance to score big.)

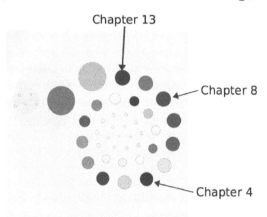

Of course, even if you're not writing books, it's helpful to highlight non-code content. A common artifact is *infrastructure as code*. In that case, behavioral code analysis has its place in revealing implicit dependencies, knowledge islands, and hotspots. As an example, the figure on page 257 shows an analysis of Terraform infrastructure code.

X-Ray the Internals of a Hotspot

Version-control systems record changes on a much more granular level than the file. This information is available to you through a diff between two revisions. The details that diff provides let you reason about how the interior of a class evolves.

One of the more interesting approaches in this area is Michael Feathers's[1] use of version-control data to ferret out violations of the *Single Responsibility Principle*. His technique uses the *added, changed, and deleted* lines of code to identify clusters of methods within a class. For example, you might find that some methods tend to change together within the same day. When you

---

1.   https://michaelfeathers.silvrback.com/using-repository-analysis-to-find-single-responsibility-violations

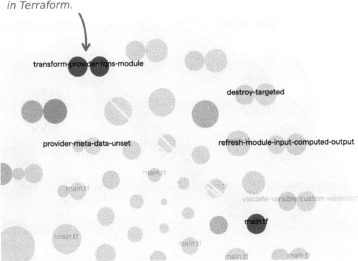

Analyzing infrastructure: hotspots and change coupling in Terraform.

spot a trend, it might mean you've detected a responsibility that you can express in a new class.

Michael's technique is basically a change coupling analysis between methods. The analysis is harder to implement because the tools need to be language-aware. The payoff is a tool that provides us with refactoring support based on what our code needs.

Another approach, which I covered in *Software Design X-Rays: Fix Technical Debt with Behavioral Code Analysis [Tor18]*, is to use the same information for calculating hotspots at the method and function level. Typically, the complex hotspots you identify also tend to be large files. Refactoring thousands of lines of code is often not a viable option. What if you instead could break down that hotspot into a prioritized list, indicating in which order to pay down the technical debt? The figure on page 258 illustrates the process by presenting an X-ray of the ReactFiberCommitWork hotspot from React, a file with 3000+ lines of code.[2]

Analyze Your Developer Networks

Social factors play an important role in how our code evolves. You've learned about communication and knowledge distribution. Let's take that a step further by analyzing developer networks.

---

2.   https://tinyurl.com/react-hotspot-xray

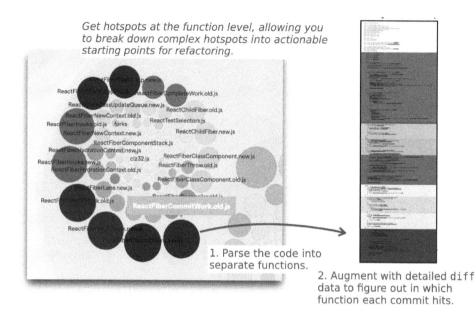

Get hotspots at the function level, allowing you to break down complex hotspots into actionable starting points for refactoring.

1. Parse the code into separate functions.

2. Augment with detailed `diff` data to figure out in which function each commit hits.

The following figure shows the relationship between different programmers based on their interactions in code. All programmers are represented by nodes colored with their team affiliation. Each time we touch the same piece of code as another developer, we get a link between us. The more often we work with the same code, the stronger the link. This information allows us to detect social dependencies across team boundaries.

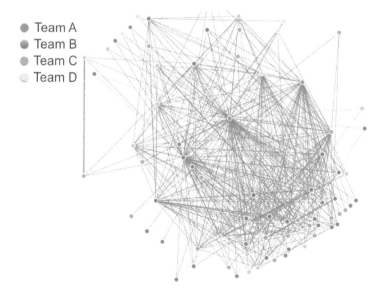

The network information is mined by Code Maat's communication analysis. An interesting approach is to analyze the data as a graph to extract complex relationships we cannot spot in the visualization alone. For example, a graph lets us find all the programmers that we depend on, together with all the programmers they depend on themselves.

Remember *Conway's Law*—our designs work best when we align them with our organization. A developer network lets you evaluate your design from that perspective.

Customize Your Analyses for Pair Programming

The socio-technical analyses from Part III rely on the author field in the commit info for building knowledge maps, analyzing parallel work, and so on. If you pair-program or work in mobs, the author field alone won't give you enough information. Take knowledge as an example: when pairing on a piece of code, you want to split the credits evenly between the authors. Instead, you'd need to record and identify the involved programmers through the commit message.

The most common format for multiple authors is to record them using a Co-authored-by field, as shown in the next figure.

Add other members of the pair or mob using the Co-authored-by field.

```
commit ee339ae88f6d0a4a84fabf169c29c268983f9a37
Author: Brian
Date:   Tue Feb 14 16:06:13 2023 -0500

    Developed the front-end framework & routes

    Co-authored-by: Brandon
    Co-authored-by: Joshuah
    Co-authored-by: Johnny

0       3       client/App.tsx
2       5       client/components/NavBar.tsx
```

The Co-authored-by convention is known as *trailers* in Git, and it's basically any key-value pair you put into the commit message. Make that a practice, and you'll have all the data you need. You'll just need to tailor your tools to pick that information instead of the author field in the log.

Watch the Next Steps

Remember the old saying that what happens in a commit stays in a commit? Well, probably not, since I just made it up. But it's nonetheless true, and that's a problem.

Today's tooling limits us to a commit as the smallest cohesive unit. If we knew what happened within a commit, we could take our analyses and predictions to a new level. Consider a temporal coupling analysis as an example. The analysis lets us identify modules that change together. But we cannot tell anything about the direction. Perhaps a change to module A is always followed by predictable modifications to B and C, never the other way around. That would be valuable information to have.

The next generation of tools has to go beyond version-control systems. We need tools that integrate with the rest of our development environment and that record our every interaction with the code. Once we get there, we can support the most important activities in programming: understanding and reading code. Let's look at how we do that.

Support Code Reading

Most analyses focus on the design aspect of software. But reading code is a harder problem to solve. The road to tackling this challenge will likely build on inspiration from other areas.

Think about how online sites tend to work. You check out a product and immediately get presented with similar products. What if we could do the same for code? You open a file and get presented with a "programmers who read this code also looked at the UserStatistics class and eventually ended up modifying the ApplicationManager module. Twice." Such reading recommendations are a natural next step to take.

The change coupling analysis you have mastered provides the foundation, but tomorrow's tooling must also capture reading patterns. That is, we would need to understand which files and functions are read before—or when—code is modified. Those functions are also likely to be logically linked to the changed code.

Integrate Dynamic Information

Another promising research area is integrating dynamic analysis results into our development environments. We could use that information to present warnings for particular pieces of our codebase. Let's look at an example.

You have learned that a high degree of parallel development leads to lower quality. What if we hooked the results of such an analysis into our code editors? When we started to modify a piece of code, we'd get a warning like, "Watch out—three different programmers have modified this code over the past day."

To work well, you'd also need a time aspect. If you had a problem with parallel development in the past, you reacted, and then you fixed the problem; the warning should disappear automatically over time.

We already have all the building blocks we need. The next step is to integrate them with the rest of our workflow. Perhaps some of these new tools will be written by you?

Enrich Hotspots with Performance Profiling

If you work on performance-critical applications, it's vital to have performance metrics easily at hand. That information would also be a perfect companion to a hotspot analysis; you identify a complex piece of code, but before refactoring it, you'd like to know the run-time characteristics. There's usually not much tradeoff between good design and performance—often, the first is a foundation for the second—but being on a hot path means you need to tread with extra care.

Stay Relevant: Programming in an AI World

AI seems to be on the brink of delivering the next productivity breakthrough and changing the face of programming as we know it. Some even go as far as to proclaim *The End of Programming [Wel23]*. So, let's grab our crystal ball and explore whether behavioral code analysis and programming, in general, still have a place in an AI future.

Face the Rise of the Machines

The industrial revolution took roughly 80 years (1760-1840). It radically transformed society, but given that it needed two generations, people had time to adapt. Now, the pace of AI development seems to push the boundaries of what's possible in a span of mere months. It's an amazing time for working in tech, but a fast pace also drives uncertainty about what the future holds.

In particular, there's a growing fear that AI will replace programmers. (Well, given some hotspots on page 169, you'd be forgiven for replacing "fear" with "hope.") So, are we programmers going the way of lamplighters and switchboard operators? No, it's unlikely, and here's why:

- *We keep raising the bar*—All tech revolutions so far have led to more code and more programmers, not fewer. With more power at our disposal, we keep raising the bar to take on increasingly complex problems. So, in the same way that standard libraries, packaged with each modern language, have replaced implementing linked lists and binary search trees by hand, AI will automate the boilerplate code of today. Not bad.

- *It will still be programming*—Today's AI, no matter how impressive, simply cannot be called intelligent by any stretch of the word. (See *A Thousand Brains: A New Theory of Intelligence [Haw21]* for a good discussion and a great read.) This means that we need to instruct the AI on *what* to build. Instructing a machine on what to do sounds very much like—yes, you guessed it—programming, doesn't it?

\\/ **Joe asks:**

What's the Tipping Point for AI?

Once you're comfortable getting on an airplane where a neural net has carried out all the code, verification, and security analyses, that might be the time to hang up the keyboard—for good.

The advances in machines that can write code have come far enough for current AI to be disruptive. AI *will* change how we code. It's happening right now. However, there's a flip side to it, so let's look at the challenges ahead.

Solve the AI Challenges

Using machine learning to write more code faster is an impressive solution to the wrong problem; remember that we spend most of our time trying to understand existing code, not writing it. So if we, as an industry, aren't careful, our promising AI-assisted coding might serve more as a legacy code generator than a solution.

Over the coming decades, we'll have a hybrid of code written by both humans and machines. Who has the overall mental model in that context, and how do we ensure our AI generates human-readable code? To face the challenge, we need a safety net to enforce healthy code with the qualities discussed in Chapter 6, Remediate Complicated Code, on page 63. This safety net could be an automated quality gate that the AI-generated code has to pass before making its way into our repositories.

Pay Attention to the AI-Human Hybrid

All paradigm shifts come with an adjustment phase. Consider how test automation went mainstream or the explosion in open-source software. Both developments have boosted our productivity, but to remain sustainable, we now need to address the weaknesses. You saw examples of this readjustment when you learned about technical debt in test automation code on page 161 in Chapter 11, Expose Hidden Bottlenecks: Delivery and Automation, on page 161, and the growing concerns for open-source maintainability on page 226.

We cannot foresee all future issues and risks with AI-assisted programming. However, the current hybrid phase where humans have to understand AI-written code does seem like one such candidate—even a very likely one.

So, to sum it up, we can expect to continue to write programs. Ideally, we'll be able to focus more on describing the problem and less on the details of its execution—pretty much like the shift from assembly languages to today's high-level programming models, only more radical. Over time, AI assistance will be integral to our work in the same way that we view a code editor or compiler today: no big fuzz.

Yet even in the short-term, AI will make software development more accessible by allowing people with little coding expertise to, well, code. Any task simple enough to be described precisely in a natural language can be auto-generated today. This brings us to a technology with a similar promise, so let's cover low-code approaches, too.

Watch Evolution in Reverse: Working with Low Code

Should AI fail to deliver on its full promise, then there are always *low-code* platforms. The computing industry has tried to simplify programming since the time mainframes roamed the earth. The low-code concept is a continuation of that drive, only now packaged within a new catchphrase. In the past, we would have known the low-code concept under different names: Visual Programming, Executable UML, Model-Driven Architecture, fourth-generation programming languages, and so on. Independent of its labeling, the core idea remains the same: instead of hiring programmers and having them work for months, let's just draw some boxes in a tool, connect them via various arrows, perhaps specify the occasional constraint, press a button, and—voilà–our solution appears. Magic.

And today's low code does empower people with little programming experience to create non-trivial software applications. As such, low code is a viable choice for evaluating a business idea and making complex domains more accessible. Want to explore computer vision or create an intelligent audio guide? Low code delivers. These benefits are clear and are already being marketed to you. The challenges start once we attempt to build general solutions on low-code platforms and expect them to replace programming. Let's explore the inherent complexity.

Analyze Low-Code Systems

Often, low-code programs are stored on disk using either a proprietary format or XML. Many organizations put those artifacts under version control. Since the core techniques like hotspots, change coupling, and knowledge maps are language agnostic, you can analyze the low-code content just like any other codebase.

Understand the Complexity Shift in Visual Programming

An example of ancient Swedish pictograms — the Vikings were here:

The periodical hype around low code is interesting since the approach is opposite to the evolution of natural languages. Several of today's writing systems evolved from pictograms. These ancient writing systems evolved for tasks like bookkeeping or inventory lists. Once people looked to capture more elaborate ideas in writing, the symbols in the language had to be augmented with phonographic hints for guiding interpretation and pronunciation. Over time, the format evolved into the textual representation used for most modern languages. This general tendency of natural languages should give us a hint: low code as a general-purpose programming approach would be a devolution rather than representing an evolution in how we code.

A more modern example of pictograms:

You can observe this if you watch a low-code demo. They tend to be impressive. However, the apparent simplicity is deceiving. Demos tend to solve simple and constrained tasks. Many real-world tasks are complex, and low code cannot simplify the problem domain. This is where it breaks down since any increase in the complexity of the problem space leads to an explosion in solution complexity. (For more detail on why this is the case, check out *Frequently forgotten fundamental facts about software engineering [Gla01]*, where Robert Glass argues that "for every 10-percent increase in problem complexity, there is a 100-percent increase in the software solution's complexity.")

This means that the effectiveness of low-code tools has an inverse correlation to the complexity of the problem domain. They are great as long as we stay within the boundaries of the supported functionality and customization options. The flip side is that low code simplifies these simple problems at the expense of making complex problems more complicated. (*The Influence of the Psychology of Programming on a Language Design [PM00]* is an old but still solid overview of the fundamental issues.)

It's unlikely that low code will replace traditional programming any time soon, much less likely than for AI. That said, it pays off to follow the low-code space. Being aware of the options means you can pick up a low-code platform when it's the right tool for the job. Used wisely, low code is great for quick prototypes and can even save thousands of programming hours in the domains the platforms are tailored for. Just be aware of the tradeoffs.

Write Evolvable Code

The specifics and tools of programming will change, but as long as people are instructing machines, we will have to deal with the resulting complexity. As we have seen throughout the book, most work happens once the initial system is built. This takes us full circle: for decades to come, optimizing code for understanding will remain a key requirement for succeeding with software development.

In this closing chapter, you also saw that the techniques in the book aren't the end: the field of behavioral code analysis keeps evolving, and there are several interesting directions ahead of us. In addition to integrating additional dynamic data sources, the future is also likely to be a place where modern AI enhances our analyses.

Ultimately, it's all about writing better software that can evolve under the pressure of new features, novel usages, and changed circumstances. Writing code of that quality will never be easy; software development is one of the hardest things we humans can put our brains to. We need all the support we can get, and I hope this modest collection of forensic techniques has inspired you to dive deeper into the subject.

I enjoyed writing this book and hope you enjoyed our journey through the fascinating field of evolving code. The scene is now yours. May the code be with you!

Solutions to the Exercises

Part I: Identify Code That's Hard to Understand

Chapter 3: Discover Hotspots: Create an Offender Profile of Code

Restrict the Hotspot Analysis to Parts of a Codebase

To restrict the analysis to the react-dom package, you tweak the arguments to Git and cloc. For Git, you do this by specifying a path. Move into your react repository and run the following:

```
prompt> git log --all --numstat --date=short  \
               --pretty=format:'--%h--%ad--%aN' --no-renames  \
               --after=2021-08-01 \
               -- packages/react-dom > react_dom_log.txt
```

The path separator, --, ensures that only the commits relating to react-dom get included.

For cloc, it's even simpler: specify the directory of interest, packages/react-dom/:

```
prompt> cloc packages/react-dom/ --unix --by-file \
        --csv --quiet --report-file=react_dom_complexity.csv
```

From here, follow the steps in Intersect Complexity and Effort, on page 28 to get a list of the local hotspots. The resulting analysis will point out two complex hotspots in the test code and one in the application code (ReactDOMServerFormat-Config.js).

Chapter 4: Hotspots Applied: Visualize Code from the People Side

Try the Language-Agnostic Analysis on Your Own

The main hotspot in Zulip is zerver/models.py. However, there's also a cluster of hotspots in the zerver/tests/ folder. In particular, zerver/tests/test_subs.py looks suspiciously complex. We haven't talked much about test code yet, but I'd recommend returning to test hotspots later when you have finished Chapter 11, Expose Hidden Bottlenecks: Delivery and Automation, on page 161.

Meet Vue.js—The Other Kid in Town

The hotspots in Vue.js are all roughly one-third the size of the corresponding hotspots in React. Of course, the size/complexity of a module is only one factor that determines maintainability. But it's an important one.

Spot Technical Debt in Kubernetes

The analysis identifies strong hotspots in proxy/iptables and apis/core/validation. Each package has a pair of hotspots: the application logic and its unit test.

The mere size of those tests—20,000-plus lines of code—is worrisome. Imagine hunting down a test failure in that amount of code. (You can always peek at Chapter 11, Expose Hidden Bottlenecks: Delivery and Automation, on page 161 for more insights.)

The hotspots with application code look more innocent at first glance, but that's only due to the size of the test cases. A hotspot like validation.go consists of more than 5,000 lines of code. Upon quick inspection, we see several coding constructs known to put a high cognitive load on the code reader. (See Chapter 6, Remediate Complicated Code, on page 63 for a discussion on problematic coding constructions.)

Chapter 5: Detect Deteriorating Structures

Investigate the Main Suspect in Kubernetes

validation.go in Kubernetes has a much less dramatic recent history than the React hotspot we analyzed together. The trend indicates a stable module where the changes seem small and focused. However, there was a bump in complexity around November 2021, when a couple hundred lines of code were added. Adding more code to an already complex hotspot might be questionable, and having these trends allows us to visualize and discuss the issue.

Use Trends as Canaries for Code Complexity

The complexity trend for AsyncSocketTest2.cpp should ring some alarm bells. The module grows moderately until late 2020, when it suddenly takes off on a wild ride with its complexity going through the roof. It plateaus ten months later, in October 2021. At this point, it's probably going to be expensive to refactor the code.

It's clear that if this was our code, then acting in the early phases of the complexity growth would have prevented a complex hotspot from forming. Regularly investigating your complexity trends helps you avoid similar issues in your own code.

For the bonus question, it's easy to dismiss test code as "just" tests. However, for the goal of optimizing for understanding, tests are at least as important as any application code. If your tests are hard to understand, they will hold back your overall efforts by causing frustration during development and debugging. Imagine making a simple change to the application code but then having to spend hours understanding why the tests fail. Always maintain the same level of quality in your tests as in your application code.

Chapter 6: Remediate Complicated Code

Hollywood's Calling

Applying the "Don't call us, we'll call you" principle implies that you encapsulate the whole query-and-do responsibility on the object itself. Let's look at the code once again:

```
if self._use_tensor_values_cache() or self._use_tensor_buffer():
    if self._use_temp_cache():
        # Create the temporary tf cache variable by concatenating all
        # statistics.
        graph_cache_var = self._cache_variable_for_graph(graph)
        if graph not in self._temp_cache_var:
            ...
```

The responsibility of checking and creating the cache should be moved to separate objects: use one class to represent cache support and represent the absence of a cache with another class according to the *Null object pattern.*[1] The Null object pattern is a much-underutilized refactoring that lets you eliminate special cases in your code.

---

1. https://en.wikipedia.org/wiki/Null_object_pattern

Simplify a Simple Button

There are two general issues: first, the presence of many function arguments suggests a problem with low cohesion. Second—and this reinforces the cohesion issue—repetitive code patterns look for the presence of the given arguments and then execute a copy-pasted block for initializing a frame object.

To refactor this code, you can use the following steps:

First, encapsulate the common concept so that it can serve as a chunk:

```
void advance_frame_for(DisplayObject *optionalDisplay) {
      if(optionalDisplay)
      {
             optionalDisplay->advanceFrame();
             if (!optionalDisplay->loadedFrom->needsActionScript3())
                    optionalDisplay->declareFrame();
             optionalDisplay->initFrame();
      }
}
```

This reduces the amount of repetition in the calling context:

```
...
advance_frame_for(dS);
advance_frame_for(hTS);
advance_frame_for(oS);
...
```

Second, now that you have separated the commonalities from the specific, you can perform deeper refactorings. The function depends on four DisplayObject arguments. What about encapsulating all four in a new class, MultiDisplay, responsible for broadcasting any method call to its collection of DisplayObjects? That would leave you with just one argument, and the application code wouldn't have to know about the details.

Chapter 7: Communicate the Business Impact of Technical Debt

Understand the Acceptable Risk

In terms of predictability, react-devtools-timeline carries much less risk. Sure, some Yellow code is in there, but react-reconciler is in worse shape. Given the amount of Red code in react-reconciler, you could conclude that there's an order of magnitude of greater uncertainty in terms of task completion.

Motivate a Larger Refactoring

You can try refactoring the config.go file based on the following reasoning:

1. *The file has code quality problems*—config.go contains several code smells, and it's the only Red Code in the package. Given what you know about Red Code, adding a new feature is high risk and likely to take longer than expected.

2. *The technical debt has a high interest rate*—Using the hotspot analysis, you can conclude that config.go is a development hotspot, meaning the identified technical debt comes with a high interest. You also see it's a growing problem in terms of its complexity trend: now is the time to act.

By combining a quality dimension, like Code Health, with the impact (hotspots), you can make the case for refactorings driven by data.

Spot the Symptoms of Technical Debt

In addition to excess unplanned work, the typical symptoms of technical debt hit three separate areas:

1. *Roadmap symptoms*—The lead times for delivering new features or fixing bugs tend to increase. Commitments and customer expectations get harder and harder to meet due to the increased uncertainty when working with bad code.

2. *Team impact*—Technical debt leads to unhappiness and frustration, a topic discussed in Learn How Bad Code Causes Unhappiness: The Scientific Link, on page 216. Technical debt also tends to encourage key personnel dependencies, meaning only one person "can" fix certain tasks.

3. *End user experience*—Having a growing number of open support tickets is a common symptom of technical debt. Since bug fixes to poor-quality code are tricky and high-risk, it becomes hard for the organization to respond to user needs. Over time, customer satisfaction drops along with the whole product maturity experience.

Part II: Build Supportive Software Architectures

Chapter 8: Use Code as a Cooperative Witness

Language Neutral Dependency Analyses

There are several dependencies which cross language boundaries. In fact, it's such a common use case for change coupling that CodeScene includes a special view for it. You see an example of how it can look in the following figure:[2]

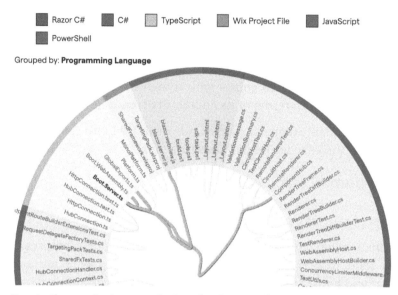

Grouped by: **Programming Language**

Navigating to the analysis snapshot and selecting the Programming Languages overlay reveals the dependencies, as shown in the preceding figure.

Spot DRY Violations in a Tesla App

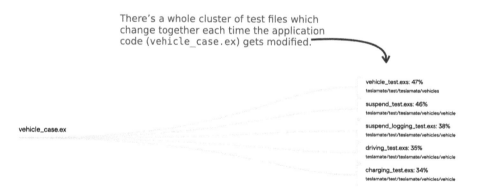

There's a whole cluster of test files which change together each time the application code (vehicle_case.ex) gets modified.

vehicle_case.ex

vehicle_test.exs: 47%
teslamate/test/teslamate/vehicles

suspend_test.exs: 46%
teslamate/test/teslamate/vehicles/vehicle

suspend_logging_test.exs: 38%
teslamate/test/teslamate/vehicles/vehicle

driving_test.exs: 35%
teslamate/test/teslamate/vehicles/vehicle

charging_test.exs: 34%
teslamate/test/teslamate/vehicles/vehicle

As the preceding change coupling visualization shows, a cluster of five unit tests is changing together with the application code. Partly, this represents a test structure where the behavior of a vehicle is partitioned into subdomains such as charging and driving. That's good. However, given the coupling, you should consider that some concepts might not be as encapsulated as they could be.

---

2. https://tinyurl.com/aspnet-change-language-filter

Looking at the solution to the next exercise reveals that there is indeed duplicated code inside the test cases. This duplication represents a violation of the DRY principle since the domain knowledge leaks across the test suite. Change coupling helps you detect suspicious patterns like this, but it's only by diving into the code that you can reveal *why* the modules co-evolve.

Design for a Single Source of Representation

The major issue in this change coupling relationship is the duplicated assertion block for checking that the vehicle reports its starting condition. With the current design, each time you expand or modify the startup report, you need to remember to also update all these copies of the assertions.

There are two general ways of encapsulating the condition and reducing the change coupling:

1. *Encapsulate the condition*—Introduce a custom assertion that encapsulates the duplicated assertion block. Rewrite the tests to use the common, custom assertion.

2. *Make the start condition a separate test*—Another option is to encapsulate the startup tests in their own test suite. That way, you have one place where the startup logic is covered, and subsequent tests don't need to test for it, only check the behavior in scope.

Your mileage might vary, but option 2 can give you cleaner tests with a better separation of responsibilities.

Chapter 9: Architectural Reviews: Support Redesigns with Data

Prioritize Refactoring by Combining Hotspots and SOC Analyses

The hotspot src/mongo/db/repl/oplog.cpp scores high on sum of coupling. Since it also contains several code health issues, this is a good refactoring candidate.

The second highest sum of coupling goes to src/mongo/db/commands/set_feature_compatibility_version_command.cpp. The code contains a complex method, _userCollectionsUassertsForDowngrade, with deep nested logic, so this is another refactoring candidate.

Run in Circles: Use Change Coupling for Design Improvements

Looking at the code for GlowWorld.java and ChunkManager.java reveals that they depend on each other: you've found a circular dependency. Not only does this make the code pretty hard to unit test, but it's also messy to think about.

A better solution would be the old and proven programming principle to an interface, not an implementation. There shouldn't be any need for the World to know about a ChunkManager.

Chapter 10: Use Beauty as a Guiding Principle

Explore Microservice Coupling: DRY or WET?

The main concern is the shared code, which seems to implicitly couple two services to each other:

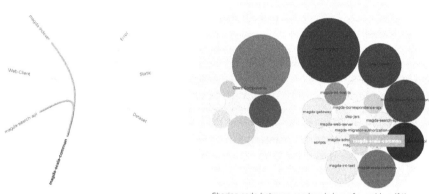

The shared code in magda-scala-common seems to implicitly couple to services that depend on it.

Sharing code between services is less of a problem if the shared library is stable. As an architectural hotspot analysis reveals, that doesn't seem to be the case here.

In the early days of microservices, the WET principle tended to dominate: avoid coupling at all costs, meaning duplicate code all the time. Of course, taking any principle to the extreme does more harm than good, and code duplication wasn't an exception. Just imagine if you have a security vulnerability and need to trace down all potential clones of that code across hundreds of services.

That said, WET might still apply. The tradeoff between DRY and WET depends on the nature of the dependency. The more stable the dependency, the safer it is to re-use shared code. There's a simple way of figuring out how stable a component is: run a hotspot analysis at the architectural level.

Decompose a Monolith

A change coupling relationship exists between the OrderController.cs and the CustomerController.cs. From a domain perspective, it's easy to see how this could happen since customers typically place orders. However, the strength of the dependency—change coupled in 32 percent of all commits—indicates that the modular separation might require more care.

Beautify Ugly Code

There are multiple ways to refactor control coupled code. The simplest one is to split the offending method into two, one for each responsibility. This approach can be handy if the control coupled method is called from separate classes. That's a sure sign the execution paths represent separate concerns.

Another approach is to introduce the strategy pattern. Instead of passing a boolean, let the method accept a method reference or function. That way, the client can specify the desired behavior (for example, pass a lambda function that knows how to notifyClients). Clients that don't have any need for notifications or post-processing could simply pass a no-op function or use the null object pattern. This solution has the added benefit of aligning your code with the open-closed principle.

Chapter 11: Expose Hidden Bottlenecks: Delivery and Automation

Act on Hotspots in the Test's Test

A change coupling analysis of JUnit5 reveals strong coupling between a whole suite of test cases.

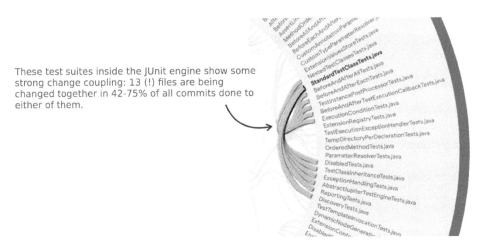

These test suites inside the JUnit engine show some strong change coupling: 13 (!) files are being changed together in 42-75% of all commits done to either of them.

Those tests likely duplicate knowledge, indicating a missing abstraction. The consequence is a change to the application code might result in failed tests in up to 13 different test suites. There is also, of course, the risk we might forget to make one of the necessary updates as the application behavior changes.

Uncover Expensive Change Patterns in Test Code

There are several examples in ASP.NET Core of clusters of test files that co-evolve, as shown in the figure on page 276.

Six test files co-evolve, all of which seem to be related to the templating mechanism (e.g. used to generate HTML).
In practice, this means that when you change the templating code, you might end up with six failing test cases.

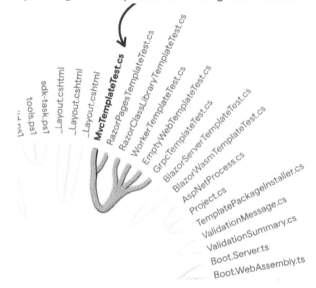

As a programmer, these co-evolving tests can be quite frustrating. You fix a bug, and now you have to make predictable changes across a whole cluster of files.

Refactor Test Code

This is an open-ended exercise with multiple possible refactorings. One approach you can try is to identify the different steps in each test and then encapsulate each one of them.

```
void serverHeaderCanBeCustomizedWhenUsingSsl() throws Exception {
  AbstractServletWebServerFactory factoryWithServerHeader = getFactory();
  factoryWithServerHeader.setServerHeader("MyServer");

  this.webServer = startSslServerAsDefinedBy(factoryWithServerHeader);

  ClientHttpResponse response = makeGetRequestFor(getLocalUrl("https", "/hello"));

  assertThat(serverNameIn(response).containsExactly("MyServer");
}

void serverHeaderIsDisabledByDefaultWhenUsingSsl() throws Exception {
  AbstractServletWebServerFactory anonymousServerFactory = getFactory();

  this.webServer = startSslServerAsDefinedBy(anonymousServerFactory);

  ClientHttpResponse response = makeGetRequestFor(getLocalUrl("https", "/hello"));

  assertThat(serverNameIn(response).isNullOrEmpty();
}
```

Both tests essentially follow the same pattern: use a factory to encapsulate the creation of a local server instance, make a request, and verify the result. The preceding code shows an example of how to make these steps more explicit. Note that the tests maintain some structural duplication—compressing the test code more would make it harder to understand—yet the differences pop out.

You can probably stop here for the initial refactoring, but there's still the concern that the webServer is bound to an instance variable rather than being local to the test itself. Limiting the scope of the webServer would be a refactoring for another day.

Part III: Meet the Social Side of Your Code

Chapter 12: Meet Norms, Groups, and False Serial Killers

Identify the Team's Modus Operandi

The term "Test" stands out in the preceding word cloud from Mongo DB's development activity. You can use this as a driver to initiate an investigation into the evolution of the tests, as you learned in Chapter 11, Expose Hidden Bottlenecks: Delivery and Automation, on page 161, to ensure the tests aren't becoming maintenance problems.

Drill into the Main Topic

Creating a Git log from Mongo DB and searching for the word "test" quickly reveals a common concern: the project seems to be using a golden copy strategy, and there are several bug fixes to that golden copy.

A golden copy strategy simply means executing specific scenarios and collecting the output. That output now serves as your gold standard, and future tests are written to check their output against the expected golden copy.

For what it's worth, a golden copy approach might work well as a safety net for larger applications. It is, however, a double-edged sword since failures in the tests tend to be hard to track down.

Chapter 13: Discover Organizational Metrics in Your Codebase

Find the Reason Behind the Decrease in Output

There are at least three reasons why the development output might decrease, even though the number of contributing authors remains static. Two of them indicate a problem, and the third reflects an organizational choice:

1. *Growing technical debt*—With more technical debt, changes take longer and require more rework. Basically, the organization gets less out of each developer, which is a common problem.

2. *High staff turnover*—Even though the number of people remains the same, there's no guarantee that the same people are still on the team. In organizations with high staff turnover, replacements must be recruited, trained, and onboarded continuously. This could explain the efficiency loss.

3. *Not full-time work*—The organization might also have other projects the developers work on. Perhaps there's a replacement system in the making, and what we see in this exercise is just the remaining maintenance work needed to keep the system operational.

Restrict the Analyses to Parts of a Mono-Repo

```
prompt> maat -c git2 -l git_roslyn_log.txt -a authors
entity,                             n-authors, n-revs
../NullableReferenceTypesTests.cs, 23,          144
../RecordTests.cs,                 21,           91
../InterpolationTests.cs,          20,           92
..CommandLineTests.cs,             19,           70
```

These results reveal that 23 authors have contributed code to the Roslyn hotspot, NullableReferenceTypesTests.cs.

Chapter 14: See How Technical Problems Cause Organizational Issues

Inspect the Truck Factor in Vue.js

The truck factor in Vue.js is just one (1) developer. This matches the research you learned about in the chapter: most popular open-source projects depend on just a few people.

Chapter 15: Build a Knowledge Map of Your System

Show the Impact: The Truck Hits Twice

Junio is the main author behind several important feature areas in Git:

- blame.c, which implements the git blame command.
- diff-lib.c and combine-diff.c, which form the core for comparing different file versions.

Prioritize the Offboarding Risk

The magda-authorization-api component contains one hotspot with several code health issues, Database.ts. The code has one major developer and only a few minor contributions by others. Refactoring the hotspot would mitigate the offboarding risk.

Get Started with Enclosure Visualizations

As you've seen throughout the book, you have multiple choices when it comes to visualizing source code. You've learned about tree maps, code as cities, bar charts, and much more. Each different visualization has its strengths. However, the enclosure diagram is the core visualization I keep returning to for behavioral code analyses. This appendix gives you a head start so you can start visualizing the results from your analyses without writing any code yourself.

Start by cloning the Python script that accompanies this book:

```
prompt> git clone git@github.com:adamtornhill/maat-scripts.git
```

At the time of this writing, the relevant scripts are on a python3 branch—if you're reading this later than 2023, please check the README for a potential update. Anyway, this means you have to switch branches via Git:

```
prompt> git checkout python3
```

Now, you just need two CSV files: one for complexity and another for hotspot information. Check back to Chapter 3, Discover Hotspots: Create an Offender Profile of Code, on page 21, in case you haven't run those analyses yet.

For now, let's assume your complexity data is in complexity.csv and your hotspot information is in revisions.csv. The next step is to combine them, as you did in Create Your Own Visualizations, on page 38. Note that you *have* to specify the absolute or relative paths to your analysis CSV files.

Start by navigating into the folder containing the csv_as_enclosure_json.py script, and then execute the script. Here's an example:

```
prompt> cd transform
prompt> python csv_as_enclosure_json.py \
        --structure ./analysis/complexity.csv \
        --weights ./analysis/revisions.csv > hotspots.json
```

This generates a new result file, hotspots.json. Now, you're finally ready to launch the actual visualization. The visualization is an .html file, so you can open it in any web browser. The .html file will load the JSON resource, hotspots.json, describing the hotspots. However, modern browsers introduce a security restriction on that. To make it work flawlessly, launch Python's web server module via the following command:

```
prompt> python -m http.server 8080
```

That's it—point your browser to http://localhost:8080/crime-scene-hotspots.html. You should now see a familiar picture. Congrats—you just generated a complete hotspot visualization!

Visualize via CodeScene

The CodeScene analysis platform represents the next generation of behavioral code analysis. It automated the hotspot visualization and many other behavioral code analyses, including more advanced team views and code quality perspectives. If you have your source code in a public Git repository, it's worth taking a look at Code-Scene's free Community Edition.

Bibliography

[ACVS19] G. Avelino, E. Constantinou, M. T. Valente, and A. Serebrenik. On the abandonment and survival of open source projects: An empirical investigation. *ACM/IEEE International Symposium on Empirical Software Engineering and Measurement*. 2019.

[AH92] G. Ainslie and N. Haslam. Hyperbolic discounting. *Choice over time*. 1992.

[ASS19] V. Antinyan, A. B. Sandberg, and M. Staron. A Pragmatic View on Code Complexity Management. *Computer*. 52:14–22, 2019.

[AVH15] G. Avelino, M. T. Valente, and A. Hora. What is the Truck Factor of popular GitHub applications?. *PeerJ PrePrints*. 2015.

[AWE21] A. Al-Boghdady, K. Wassif, and M. El-Ramly. The Presence, Trends, and Causes of Security Vulnerabilities in Operating Systems of IoT's Low-End Devices. *Sensors*. 21, 2021.

[Ber07] W. Bernasco. The usefulness of measuring spatial opportunity structures for tracking down offenders. *Psychology, Crime Law*. 13:155–171, 2007.

[BHS07] F. Buschmann, K. Henney, and D.C. Schmidt. *Pattern-Oriented Software Architecture Volume 4: A Pattern Language for Distributed Computing*. John Wiley & Sons, New York, NY, 2007.

[BK03] R.S. Baron and N.L. Kerr. *Group Process, Group Decision, Group Action*. Open University Press, Berkshire, United Kingdom, 2003.

[BMB19] T. Besker, A. Martini, and J. Bosch. Software developer productivity loss due to technical debt. *Journal of Systems and Software*. 41-61, 2019.

[BNMG11] C. Bird, N. Nagappan, B. Murphy, H. Gall, and P. Devanbu. Don't Touch My Code! Examining the Effects of Ownership on Software Quality. *Proceed-*

ings of the 19th ACM SIGSOFT symposium and the 13th European conference on foundations of software engineering. 4-14, 2011.

[BOW04]   R.M. Bell, T.J. Ostrand, and E.J. Weyuker. *Where the bugs are. Proceedings of the 2004 ACM SIGSOFT international symposium on software testing and analysis.* ACM Press, New York, NY, USA, 2004.

[BOW11]   R.M. Bell, T.J. Ostrand, and E.J. Weyuker. *Does Measuring Code Change Improve Fault Prediction?.* ACM Press, New York, NY, USA, 2011.

[Bro86]   Frederick Brooks. No Silver Bullet—Essence and Accident in Software Engineering. *Proceedings of the IFIP Tenth World Computing Conference.* 1986.

[Bro95]   Frederick P. Brooks Jr. *The Mythical Man-Month: Essays on Software Engineering.* Addison-Wesley, Boston, MA, Anniversary, 1995.

[BTM23]   M. Borg, A. Tornhill, and E. Mones. U Owns the Code That Changes and How Marginal Owners Resolve Issues Slower in Low-Quality Source Code. *Proceedings of the 27th International Conference on Evaluation and Assessment in Software Engineering.* 368–377, 2023.

[Cam18]   A. Campbell. Cognitive Complexity: A New Way of Measuring Understandability. *SonarSource S.A., Tech. Rep.* 2018.

[Con68]   M.E. Conway. How do committees invent?. *Datamation.* 4:28–31, 1968.

[CY04]   D. Canter and D. Youngs. *Mapping Murder: The Secrets of Geographical Profiling.* Virgin Books, London, United Kingdom, 2004.

[CY08]   D. Canter and D. Youngs. *Applications of Geographical Offender Profiling.* Ashgate, Farnham, Surrey, UK, 2008.

[CY08a]   D. Canter and D. Youngs. *Principles of Geographical Offender Profiling.* Ashgate, Farnham, Surrey, UK, 2008.

[DB13]   F. Detienne and F. Bott. *Software Design: Cognitive Aspects.* Springer, New York, NY, USA, 2013.

[DH13]   S. M. H. Dehaghani and N. Hajrahimi. Which factors affect software projects maintenance cost more?. *Acta Informatica Medica.* 21, 2013.

[DHAQ07]   M. Di Penta, M. Harman, G. Antoniol, and F. Qureshi. The Effect of Communication Overhead on Software Maintenance Project Staffing. *Software Maintenance, 2007. ICSM 2007. IEEE International Conference on.* 315–324, 2007.

[DL68]   J.M. Darley and B. Latané. Bystander intervention in emergencies: diffusion of responsibility. *Journal of Personality and Social Psychology.* 8:377–383, 1968.

[DLG05]   M. D'Ambros, M. Lanza, and H Gall. Fractal Figures: Visualizing Development Effort for CVS Entities. *Visualizing Software for Understanding and Analysis, 2005. VISSOFT 2005. 3rd IEEE International Workshop on.* 1–6, 2005.

[DLR09]   M. D'Ambros, M. Lanza, and R Robbes. On the Relationship Between Change Coupling and Software Defects. *Reverse Engineering, 2009. WCRE '09. 16th Working Conference on.* 135–144, 2009.

[Far22]   D. Farley. *Modern Software Engineering.* Addison-Wesley, Boston, MA, 2022.

[FBLK22]   B. Flyvbjerg, A. Budzier, J. S. Lee, M. Keil, D. Lunn, and D. W. Bester. The Empirical Reality of IT Project Cost Overruns: Discovering A Power-Law Distribution. *Journal of Management Information Systems.* 39:607–639, 2022.

[Fea04]   Michael Feathers. *Working Effectively with Legacy Code.* Prentice Hall, Englewood Cliffs, NJ, 2004.

[Fen94]   N. Fenton. Software measurement: A necessary scientific basis. *IEEE Transactions on software engineering.* 20:199–206, 1994.

[FHK18]   N. Forsgren, PhD, J. Humble, and G. Kim. *Accelerate: The Science of Lean Software and DevOps: Building and Scaling High Performing Technology Organizations.* IT Revolution Press, Portland, OR, 2018.

[Fow18]   Martin Fowler. *Refactoring: Improving the Design of Existing Code, 2nd Edition.* Addison-Wesley, Boston, MA, 2018.

[FRSD21]   N. Ford, M. Richards, P. Sadalage, and Z. Dehghani. *Software Architecture: The Hard Parts: Modern Trade-Off Analyses for Distributed Architectures.* O'Reilly & Associates, Inc., Sebastopol, CA, 2021.

[FW08]   S. M. Fulero and L. S. Wrightsman. *Forensic Psychology.* Cengage Learning, Boston, MA, 2008.

[GAL14]   E. Guzman, D. Azócar, and L. Li. *Sentiment analysis of commit comments in GitHub. MSR 2014 Proceedings of the 11th Working Conference on Mining Software Repositories.* ACM Press, New York, NY, USA, 2014.

[Gan03]   M. Gancarz. *Linux and the Unix Philosophy, 2nd Edition.* Elsevier Inc., Amsterdam, Netherlands, 2003.

[GF19]   D. Graziotin and F. Fagerholm. Happiness and the productivity of software engineers. *Rethinking Productivity in Software Engineering.* 2019.

[GFWA17]   D. Graziotin, F. Fagerholm, X. Wang, and P. Abrahamsson. On the unhappiness of software developers. *In Proceedings of the 21st international conference on evaluation and assessment in software engineering.* 324–333, 2017.

[GHJV95] Erich Gamma, Richard Helm, Ralph Johnson, and John Vlissides. *Design Patterns: Elements of Reusable Object-Oriented Software.* Addison-Wesley, Boston, MA, 1995.

[GKMS00] T. L. Graves, A. F. Karr, J. S. Marron, and H Siy. Predicting fault incidence using software change history. *Software Engineering, IEEE Transactions on.* 26[7], 2000.

[GKMS00a] T. L. Graves, A. F. Karr, J. S. Marron, and H Siy. Predicting fault incidence using software change history. *Software Engineering, IEEE Transactions on.* 26[7], 2000.

[Gla01] R. L. Glass. Frequently forgotten fundamental facts about software engineering. *IEEE software.* 2001.

[Gla06] Malcolm Gladwell. *Blink.* Little, Brown and Company, New York, NY, 2006.

[Gla92] Robert L. Glass. *Facts and Fallacies of Software Engineering.* Addison-Wesley Professional, Boston, MA, 1992.

[GMSS22] C. Gote, P. Mavrodiev, F. Schweitzer, and I. Scholtes. Big Data=Big Insights? Operationalising Brooks' Law in a Massive GitHub Data Set. *Conference: ICSE 2022.* 262–273, 2022.

[Har10] S. Harrison. *The Diary of Jack the Ripper: The Chilling Confessions of James Maybrick.* John Blake, London, UK, 2010.

[Haw21] J. Hawkins. *A Thousand Brains: A New Theory of Intelligence.* Basic Books, New York, NY, USA, 2021.

[HF10] Jez Humble and David Farley. *Continuous Delivery: Reliable Software Releases Through Build, Test, and Deployment Automation.* Addison-Wesley, Boston, MA, 2010.

[HGH08] A. Hindle, M.W. Godfrey, and R.C. Holt. *Reading Beside the Lines: Indentation as a Proxy for Complexity Metric. Program Comprehension, 2008. ICPC 2008. The 16th IEEE International Conference on.* IEEE Computer Society Press, Washington, DC, 2008.

[HSSH12] K. Hotta, Y. Sasaki, Y. Sano, Y. Higo, and S. Kusumoto. An Empirical Study on the Impact of Duplicate Code. *Advances in Software Engineering.* Special issue on Software Quality Assurance Methodologies and Techniques, 2012.

[JETK22] E. Jabrayilzade, M. Evtikhiev, E. Tüzün, and V. Kovalenko. Bus factor in practice. *In Proceedings of the 44th International Conference on Software Engineering.* 97-106, 2022.

[KBS18]   G. Kim, K. Behr, and G. Spafford. *The Phoenix Project: A Novel about IT, DevOps, and Helping Your Business Win*. IT Revolution Press, Portland, OR, 2018.

[KG85]   W. Kintsch and J. G. Greeno. Understanding and solving word arithmetic problems. *Psychological Review*. 92(1):109–129, 1985.

[KNS19]   N. Kaur, A. Negi, and H. Singh. Object oriented dynamic coupling and cohesion metrics: a review. *In Proceedings of 2nd International Conference on Communication, Computing and Networking*. 861-869, 2019.

[LC09]   J. L. Letouzey and T. Coq. The SQALE Models for assessing the quality of software source code. *DNV Paris, white paper*. 2009.

[Leh80]   M. M. Lehman. On Understanding Laws, Evolution, and Conservation in the Large-Program Life Cycle. *Journal of Systems and Software*. 1:213–221, 1980.

[LH89]   K. J. Lieberherr and I. M. Holland. Assuring good style for object-oriented programs. *IEEE Software*. 6:28-48, 1989.

[LP74]   E. F. Loftus and J. C. Palmer. Reconstruction of automobile destruction: An example of the interaction between language and memory. *Journal of verbal learning and verbal behavior*. 5:585-589, 1974.

[LR90]   J. H. Langlois and L. A. Roggman. Attractive faces are only average. *Psychological Science*. 1:115–121, 1990.

[MBB18]   A. Martini, T. Besker, and J. Bosch. Technical debt tracking: Current state of practice: A survey and multiple case study in 15 large organizations. *Science of Computer Programming*. 42–61, 2018.

[McC76]   T.J. McCabe. A Complexity Measure. *IEEE Transactions on Software Engineering*. 1976.

[MPS08]   R. Moser, W. Pedrycz, and G. Succi. A comparative analysis of the efficiency of change metrics and static code attributes for defect prediction. *Proceedings of the 30th international conference on software engineering*. 181-190, 2008.

[MW09]   A. Meneely and L. Williams. Secure open source collaboration: an empirical study of Linus' law. *Proceedings of the 16th ACM conference on computer and communications security*. 453–462, 2009.

[New21]   S. Newman. *Building Microservices, 2nd Edition*. O'Reilly & Associates, Inc., Sebastopol, CA, 2021.

[NMB08]   N. Nagappan, B. Murphy, and V. Basili. The Influence of Organizational Structure on Software Quality. *International Conference on Software Engineering, Proceedings.* 521–530, 2008.

[PAPB21]   N. Peitek, S. Apel, C. Parnin, A. Brechmann, and J. Siegmund. Program comprehension and code complexity metrics: An fmri study. *International Conference on Software Engineering.* 524-536, 2021.

[PM00]   J.F. Pane and B.A. Myers. The Influence of the Psychology of Programming on a Language Design. *Proceedings of the 12th Annual Meeting of the Psychology of Programmers Interest Group.* 193–205, 2000.

[PTFO00]   F. Palomba, D.A. Tamburri, A. Fontana, R. Oliveto, A. Zaidman, and A. Serebrenik. Beyond technical aspects: How do community smells influence the intensity of code smells?. *IEEE transactions on software engineering.* 108–129, 2000.

[RD13]   F. Rahman and P. Devanbu. How, and why, process metrics are better. *International Conference on Software Engineering.* 432–441, 2013.

[SAK98]   J. J. Sosik, B. J. Avolio, and S. S. Kahai. Inspiring group creativity: Comparing anonymous and identified electronic brainstorming. *Small group research.* 29:3–31, 1998.

[SEKH09]   C.M. Schweik, R.C. English, M. Kitsing, and S. Haire. Brooks' versus Linus' law: an empirical test of open source projects. *Proceedings of the 2008 international conference on digital government research.* 423–424, 2009.

[SF08]   V. Swami and A. Furnham. *The Psychology of Physical Attraction.* Routledge, New York, NY, USA, 2008.

[SP19]   M. Skelton and M. Pais. *Team Topologies: Organizing Business and Technology Teams for Fast Flow.* IT Revolution Press, Portland, OR, 2019.

[TB22]   A. Tornhill and M. Borg. Code Red: The Business Impact of Code Quality–A Quantitative Study of 39 Proprietary Production Codebases. *Proc. of International Conference on Technical Debt 2022.* 11–20, 2022.

[Tor18]   A. Tornhill. *Software Design X-Rays: Fix Technical Debt with Behavioral Code Analysis.* The Pragmatic Bookshelf, Dallas, TX, 2018.

[TT89]   B. Tversky and M. Tuchin. A reconciliation of the evidence on eyewitness testimony: Comments on McCloskey and Zaragoza. *Journal of Experimental Psychology: General.* [118]:86–91, 1989.

[VDC94]   J.S. Valacich, A.R. Dennis, and T. Connolly. Idea Generation in Computer-Based Groups: A New Ending to an Old Story. *Organizational Behavior and Human Decision Processes.* 57[3]:448–467, 1994.

[Wel23]   M. Welsh. The End of Programming. *Communications of the ACM.* 66[1]:34–35, 2023.

[WMGS07] K. Weaver, D.T. Miller, S.M. Garcia, and N. Schwarz. Inferring the popularity of an opinion from its familiarity: A repetitive voice can sound like a chorus. *Journal of Personality and Social Psychology.* [92]:821–833, 2007.

[WS01]   K. D. Welker and R. Singh. The software maintainability index revisited. *CrossTalk.* [14]:18–21, 2001.

[YC79]   E. Yourdon and L.R. Constantine. *Structured Design: Fundamentals of a Discipline of Computer Program and Systems Design.* Pearson Technology Group, London, UK, 1979.

[YS22]   R. Yadav and R. Singh. Ranking of Measures for the Assessment of Maintainability of Object-Oriented Software. *Journal of Optoelectronics Laser.* [41]:366–376, 2022.

[ZZC20]   Y. Zhou, Y. Zhu, and L. Chen. Software Defect-Proneness Prediction with Package Cohesion and Coupling Metrics Based on Complex Network Theory. *International Symposium on Dependable Software Engineering.* 186–201, 2020.

[ÅGGL16] D. Åkerlund, B. H. Golsteyn, H. Grönqvist, and L. Lindahl. Time discounting and criminal behavior. *Proceedings of the National Academy of Sciences.* 113:6160–6165, 2016.

Index

Thank you!

We hope you enjoyed this book and that you're already thinking about what you want to learn next. To help make that decision easier, we're offering you this gift.

Head on over to https://pragprog.com right now, and use the coupon code BUYANOTHER2024 to save 30% on your next ebook. Offer is void where prohibited or restricted. This offer does not apply to any edition of the *The Pragmatic Programmer* ebook.

And if you'd like to share your own expertise with the world, why not propose a writing idea to us? After all, many of our best authors started off as our readers, just like you. With up to a 50% royalty, world-class editorial services, and a name you trust, there's nothing to lose. Visit https://pragprog.com/become-an-author/ today to learn more and to get started.

We thank you for your continued support, and we hope to hear from you again soon!

The Pragmatic Bookshelf

Pragmatic Bookshelf

SAVE 30%!
Use coupon code
BUYANOTHER2024

Software Design X-Rays

Are you working on a codebase where cost overruns, death marches, and heroic fights with legacy code monsters are the norm? Battle these adversaries with novel ways to identify and prioritize technical debt, based on behavioral data from how developers work with code. And that's just for starters. Because good code involves social design, as well as technical design, you can find surprising dependencies between people and code to resolve coordination bottlenecks among teams. Best of all, the techniques build on behavioral data that you already have: your version-control system. Join the fight for better code!

Adam Tornhill
(274 pages) ISBN: 9781680502725. $45.95
https://pragprog.com/book/atevol

The Nature of Software Development

You need to get value from your software project. You need it "free, now, and perfect." We can't get you there, but we can help you get to "cheaper, sooner, and better." This book leads you from the desire for value down to the specific activities that help good Agile projects deliver better software sooner, and at a lower cost. Using simple sketches and a few words, the author invites you to follow his path of learning and understanding from a half century of software development and from his engagement with Agile methods from their very beginning.

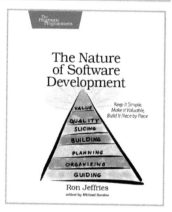

Ron Jeffries
(176 pages) ISBN: 9781941222379. $24
https://pragprog.com/book/rjnsd

Explore It!

Uncover surprises, risks, and potentially serious bugs with exploratory testing. Rather than designing all tests in advance, explorers design and execute small, rapid experiments, using what they learned from the last little experiment to inform the next. Learn essential skills of a senior explorer, including how to analyze software to discover key points of vulnerability, how to design experiments on the fly, how to hone your observation skills, and how to focus your efforts.

Elisabeth Hendrickson
(186 pages) ISBN: 9781937785024. $29
https://pragprog.com/book/ehxta

Debug It!

Professional programmers develop a knack of unerringly zeroing in on the root cause of a bug. They can do that because they've written a lot of buggy code and then gained experience fixing it. This book captures all this experience—use it, and you'll find you write fewer bugs, and the ones you do write will become easier to hunt down.

Paul Butcher
(232 pages) ISBN: 9781934356289. $34.95
https://pragprog.com/book/pbdp

Programming Ruby 3.3 (5th Edition)

Ruby is one of the most important programming languages in use for web development. It powers the Rails framework, which is the backing of some of the most important sites on the web. The Pickaxe Book, named for the tool on the cover, is the definitive reference on Ruby, a highly-regarded, fully object-oriented programming language. This updated edition is a comprehensive reference on the language itself, with a tutorial on the most important features of Ruby—including pattern matching and Ractors—and describes the language through Ruby 3.3.

Noel Rappin, with Dave Thomas
(716 pages) ISBN: 9781680509823. $65.95
https://pragprog.com/book/ruby5

Agile Web Development with Rails 7

Rails 7 completely redefines what it means to produce fantastic user experiences and provides a way to achieve all the benefits of single-page applications – at a fraction of the complexity. Rails 7 integrates the Hotwire frameworks of Stimulus and Turbo directly as the new defaults, together with that hot newness of import maps. The result is a toolkit so powerful that it allows a single individual to create modern applications upon which they can build a competitive business. The way it used to be.

Sam Ruby
(474 pages) ISBN: 9781680509298. $59.95
https://pragprog.com/book/rails7

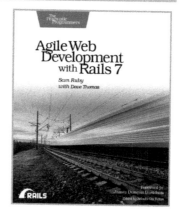

Text Processing with JavaScript

You might think of regular expressions as the holy grail of text processing, but are you sure you aren't just shoehorning them in where standard built-in solutions already exist and would work better? JavaScript itself provides programmers with excellent methods for text manipulation, and knowing how and when to use them will help you write more efficient and performant code. From extracting data from APIs to calculating word counts and everything in between, discover how to pick the right tool for the job and make the absolute most of it every single time.

Faraz K. Kelhini
(240 pages) ISBN: 9798888650332. $51.95
https://pragprog.com/book/fkjavascript

A Common-Sense Guide to Data Structures and Algorithms in Python, Volume 1

If you thought data structures and algorithms were all just theory, you're missing out on what they can do for your Python code. Learn to use Big O notation to make your code run faster by orders of magnitude. Choose from data structures such as hash tables, trees, and graphs to increase your code's efficiency exponentially. With simple language and clear diagrams, this book makes this complex topic accessible, no matter your background. Every chapter features practice exercises to give you the hands-on information you need to master data structures and algorithms for your day-to-day work.

Jay Wengrow
(502 pages) ISBN: 9798888650356. $57.95
https://pragprog.com/book/jwpython

The Pragmatic Bookshelf

The Pragmatic Bookshelf features books written by professional developers for professional developers. The titles continue the well-known Pragmatic Programmer style and continue to garner awards and rave reviews. As development gets more and more difficult, the Pragmatic Programmers will be there with more titles and products to help you stay on top of your game.

Visit Us Online

This Book's Home Page
https://pragprog.com/book/atcrime2
Source code from this book, errata, and other resources. Come give us feedback, too!

Keep Up-to-Date
https://pragprog.com
Join our announcement mailing list (low volume) or follow us on Twitter @pragprog for new titles, sales, coupons, hot tips, and more.

New and Noteworthy
https://pragprog.com/news
Check out the latest Pragmatic developments, new titles, and other offerings.

Save on the ebook

Save on the ebook versions of this title. Owning the paper version of this book entitles you to purchase the electronic versions at a terrific discount.

PDFs are great for carrying around on your laptop—they are hyperlinked, have color, and are fully searchable. Most titles are also available for the iPhone and iPod touch, Amazon Kindle, and other popular e-book readers.

Send a copy of your receipt to support@pragprog.com and we'll provide you with a discount coupon.

Contact Us

Online Orders:	*https://pragprog.com/catalog*
Customer Service:	*support@pragprog.com*
International Rights:	*translations@pragprog.com*
Academic Use:	*academic@pragprog.com*
Write for Us:	*http://write-for-us.pragprog.com*